08/08/03

For May,

With you I've
learned an incredible
deal about the world,
about myself and
about the meaning of sharing these
with someone else.
You mean so much to me.

love always,
Yvonne.
xoxo

On Equilibrium

Also by John Ralston Saul

NOVELS

The Birds of Prey
Baraka or The Lives, Fortunes, and Sacred Honor of Anthony Smith
The Next Best Thing
The Paradise Eater
De si bons Américains

ESSAYS

Voltaire's Bastards
The Doubter's Companion
The Unconscious Civilization
Reflections of a Siamese Twin

On Equilibrium

John Ralston Saul

PENGUIN

VIKING

VIKING
Published by the Penguin Group
Penguin Books Canada Ltd, 10 Alcorn Avenue, Toronto, Ontario, Canada M4V 3B2
Penguin Books Ltd, 80 Strand, London WC2R 0RL, England
Penguin Putnam Inc., 375 Hudson Street, New York, New York 10014, U.S.A.
Penguin Books Australia Ltd, Ringwood, Victoria, Australia
Penguin Books (NZ) Ltd, cnr Rosedale and Airborne Roads, Albany, Auckland
     1310, New Zealand

Penguin Books Ltd, Registered Offices: Harmondsworth, Middlesex, England

First published 2001

10 9 8 7 6 5 4 3 2

Copyright John Ralston Saul, 2001

Printed and bound in Canada on acid free paper ∞

Canadian Cataloguing in Publication Data
Saul, John Ralston, 1947–
    On equilibrium
ISBN 0-670-88882-6
1. Philosophical anthropology. I. Title.
BD450.S28 2001   128   C00-931630-2

Visit Penguin Canada's website at **www.penguin.ca.**

for
Michelle Lapautre, Mike Shaw, Olga Villalba
Michael Levine, Robin Straus, Ursula Bender
Anoukh Foerg, Roberto Santachiara, Diana Mackay

and
in memory of Bernard Paul
who brought the profound civilization of a humanist
to all of our conversations in Eygalières

Contents

COMMON SENSE

ETHICS

IMAGINATION

INTUITION

MEMORY

REASON

qualities are most effective in a society
when they are recognized as of equal, universal value
and so are integrated into our normal life

On Equilibrium

CHAPTER ONE

The Shape of Human Genius

Life, my little man, lacks rehearsals. That's why it so often fails. Now in the theatre...

René de Obaldia, *Exobiographie*[1]

The door-handle

Most mornings we turn a door-handle and walk out into a larger world. At first there is an interim stage of sidewalks or suburban highways, country roads or semi-abandoned stretches of urban tarmac. Sometimes we are walking, sometimes in cars, subways, buses, sometimes on bicycles, sometimes in boats.

We move across our world, at least across a tiny section of it. This is the society of which we are part.

Abruptly we are in offices, factories, lecture halls. We are delivering children to schools, entering shops or hospitals, working in fields or underground, working out in an exercise class or filling time in a community centre for the elderly. Many of us will drift about malls, trying to find ways to spend our money. It may or may not be much, but we feel a need to consume. Through these long corridors we will pass others dreaming of the consumption they can't afford, others simply not wanting to be alone.

All of this is the minutiae of our lives.

What does this reality imply? That we leave our homes each day for an incalculable number of reasons — from expressions of our blossoming into the fullness of life to feeling our way towards our death. Turning that door-handle can be a moment of adventure or joy. Of anticipation. Of purpose. Or a reminder of failure. Of emptiness. Of angry frustration. Of terrible anxiety. We may feel as if we are floating through a void, from home to a port of destination, as if we have no affect to offer this society, and it none for us. "The mass of men live lives of quiet desperation," Thoreau said in a not-romantic moment. This supposition has been common in the industrialized world. Everyone, from T.S. Eliot to herds of pop singers, has made the point. But it remains a supposition.

After all, the suggestion of generalized desperation doesn't square with the way many of us see ourselves, as loving or loved or driven by the forces which hold people together. The industry of love — a curious post-industrial phenomenon tying consumption to adoration — may have so confused what this relationship could mean, that love can no longer be seriously discussed. But that doesn't alter what people think to themselves.

That same industry has so far only marginally touched the other central relationship — our sense of friendship — which is deeply anchored in our ability to imagine the *other*. And from there it is but a small step to our sense of society as a gathering place beyond self-interest.

Whether there is despair or love or friendship — or indeed benevolence, ambition, tolerance, greed, sincerity, curiosity, a belief in truth or in new clothes — what is helpful is to be able to turn that door-handle with some sense as to what inner forces motivate us. To believe that forces exist and to be able to assume them — that is a beginning. The practical details of our days may then fade to a secondary focus.

We tend to think of this as a matter of knowing who we are. Or at least of making up our minds about who we are.

CONSIDERATION

These inner forces we believe we have, what are they? Talents? Characteristics? Virtues?

They seem to be a mixture of all three. The point is, they do act as an inner force. They do get us through the door. And they help us to function in a directed way.

The qualitative difference between humans and others is our ability to consider. By that I mean to consider not just our talents and characteristics, but also our lives and our societies, perhaps most obviously, our actions. To consider rather than be driven by inner forces. And to consider is not to reason, although consideration may sometimes have reason within it.

Our ability to consider means that to some extent we have the ability to shape events rather than be shaped. The operative word here is 'ability'. We may or may not use it. We may use it a little, periodically. Worst of all, we may convince ourselves that we are considering when we aren't.

To embrace this ability we need tools — qualities — which allow us to free ourselves from our own psychodrama, at least enough to consider real questions in a real context. These qualities are the tools of the human condition. We use them and that use makes us human. We use them and yet they have nothing to do with vulgar utilitarianism.

Convincing arguments can be made that this is the era of individualism; that a larger number of us than ever before have some control over our lives, as well as concrete rights and protections.

An equally convincing argument can be made that, whatever the rights, protections and prosperity of people, there is a widespread sense of personal powerlessness — a sort of gilded depression.

It does seem that, although we avidly consume, we do not respond at any serious level to the idea that consumption asserts our individualism. Nor are we thrilled by the demeaning assumption that we are driven by our self-interest. And how could we feel empowered by the constant assertions that great abstract inevitable forces are deciding the shape of our lives, that of our families and our society?

Any sense of power or powerlessness we have revolves around whether we believe we have the qualities with which we can have some effect on our destinies and on that of our society — not one great life-directing quality, but a whole range of them, all of equal importance, each with different roles. These permit us to change ourselves from passive beings to humans.

A moment ago I used the word *psychodrama*. Our days are made up of them. Line-ups, traffic jams; meetings about trivia which may destroy our careers or make our morning; personal relationships or professional or with myriad strangers on the street, in a restaurant; the proverbial seat in the crowded subway, the inevitable victim to be passed by on the other side, or not; the challenge of momentary tranquility, a confrontation with violence; a meeting with death; situations to be taken advantage of, with what effect for ourselves, for others, and on and on.

And while that endless personal army is marching past us every day, small and great public psychodramas swirl about us in ever-extending circles. The dramas of the public good. Sometimes we feel involved. Often we can pretend, if we wish, that we are not directly concerned — a war somewhere, interest rates. Often we cannot pretend. After all, some questions — to execute criminals or not — are attached to each of us as if by an umbilical cord. We belong to a society. We are citizens. When a lever is pulled or a switch flipped by our society in order to terminate someone, each of us pulls it.

Each of our hands reaches out, as if we were one, to move the switch. Upon consideration, each of us may wish to take that responsibility. Or not.

We cannot consider everything, every time. If we did we would never go out. We'd retreat to bed and pull the sheet over our heads in an Oblomov-like manner.

But that is part of our particularity. We can learn how to use our qualities. We can normalize the use of them so that much of the time we hardly need to stop in order to consider. Ethics, for example, can seem an exotic beast, dangerous, costly, for use by special people, by Heroes and Saints. Or it can be built into each of our lives and into our society, so that much of it is simply normal behaviour.

How do we normalize our qualities? The first step is to realize that we never use them one at a time. Ethics is always part of a context, for example, with memory and reason. As with each of them, the strength of ethics and its normalcy comes from its regular use, but also from its use in the context of the others.

In this way we can face what seem to be urgent questions with some equilibrium. We are then reminded that the urgency which seems to come with 'absolute truths' and ideology is really just bullying. And as with all bullying, if you refuse to panic and if you decline to respond quickly, it deflates and slinks away. So these questions may turn out to be urgent or not, real questions or not.

We also find that through these qualities, we can shape and direct our talents and characteristics — both ours and our societies'.

There is a fine point to be made here. We need the certainty of our inner forces to motivate us when we face the world; for that matter, when we face ourselves. The point is not whether we are entirely honest with ourselves about our forces. We all need a bit of self-delusion. It gets us over the difficult spots. It allows us to focus. But that is not the same thing as seeing the world as a place of certainties and therefore of opposing certainties.

●

Talents, characteristics, virtues

I would guess that most of us have two images of ourselves. One relates to our personality, the other to the fashion or style which reigns in our society. Our own idea of our personality — of our talents, characteristics and virtues — may be exact or delusionary or anywhere in between. The way others see us may be just as exact or inexact.

We may see ourselves as benevolent or seductive, as a woman who takes charge or a man who gets the better of others. Others may also recognize these talents or characteristics in us, but they will see them through the telescope of the dominant quality of our day.

The quality that our particular civilization has fixed on is reason. And so we will see others and they will see us as if through a rational lens. Just as everything, from government to family life and good works, was once justified through the grace of God, so today those same actions are justified through rationality. The phrasing used in both fashions is eerily similar.

Our inner view versus the outer view creates a curious conundrum. Of course we may well have these talents and characteristics. To some extent we do have them. We need them. They do give direction and force to our lives. The unpredictable way in which these things have been 'handed out' to us, the unexpected places in which they appear, produce a remarkable mixture of individuals; one which cuts wildly across all lines of class, geography, race, even education. This is precisely what creates the richness of any society. And being able to tap into all of this becomes the great test for a successful citizenry. That is part of the strength of any more or less democratic and egalitarian civilization. Because its legitimacy is based in the citizenry, it can give itself access to as great a percentage of these talents as its efforts can manage.

And so the disordered, messy, inefficient world of democracy can release a surprising percentage of society's genius. A meritocracy, on the other hand, is so busy concentrating on efficiently identifying who is the best and pushing him to the fore that it shuts down its confidence in the rest of us — those of us who are turning our door handles and willing to contribute, each in her own way and at her own level. The whole idea of a society of winners — a place known above all for its best — leads with surprising speed to a narrow pyramidal social structure. And then to division and widespread passivity. That in turn leads to false populism and mediocrity; to a world obsessed by bread and circuses, Heroes and the need for leadership.

●

THE PROBLEM OF COMPETING CERTAINTIES

But what drives a successful society or a successful life, by which I mean a good life? Is it our talents and characteristics? Is it our virtues?

If that were so, civilization would be little more than competing certainties. One talent against another. Talents allied against others. Even virtues opposed to each other. Benevolence against selfishness. Generosity against ambition. Tolerance against intolerance. Curiosity against indifference. And not just competing opposites. Perhaps benevolence against tolerance. Tolerance against curiosity.

There could then be no society. Only a utilitarian contract between specialist groups and a Manichean division of the whole, with each side claiming the truth on each particular issue. What holds them together? The answer over the last two centuries has been a gradual move towards a civilization of structure and form over one of content and consideration. The way we come at every question is structural, managerial.

Much of the last two decades has been taken up by precisely this view. The idea, for example, that we are driven by self-interest is the natural outcome of believing in competing certainties. And so the greedy are simply one version of self-interest, the benevolent another. Everything is self-interest. The only difference is what separates our idea of our own interest. The very idea of society seems to slip away, so that even those who struggle for the greater good — whatever their particular view of it might be — do so free of society and on their own group's tangential path. Society, they feel, slows them down in their quest for great solutions to the problems that interest them.

Take a very specific example. In 1997 the World Trade Organization ruled that the Europeans were wrong to ban American beef raised with hormones because there was no convincing scientific case that the hormones represented a health risk. Put aside what you might think about hormones and beef. The central question is elsewhere.

It begins with an absolute certainty: that social policy in a democracy must be based not on popular will — the legitimacy of the citizenry — but on proof; in this case scientific proof. In other words, that our choice must be based on science. But in fact the science in question is not exactly science because it is limited by an initial question formulated in the context of commercial interest. In other words, food should be considered first as a commercial object, second a scientific object and only third a matter of social, health, cultural or, indeed, of personal choice.

Hormones or no hormones. Health or sickness, sickness or health. The question on both sides is commercially constructed. Is the producer to be permitted to express the right of absolute ownership — that of maximized profit? Or is the producer to be punished by the cost of health needs? And in that context, what is the definition of a health need? No other more important, non-commercial question is admitted to.

This is curious. We know that the central question ought to be social. That is part of our shared knowledge — our common sense. Giambattista Vico, the great mid-eighteenth-century Neopolitan philosopher: "[Human] nature has this principal property: that of being social." "[T]his is the true civil nature of man...."² How then can we have fallen into such artificial choices between certainties — certainties which are disassociated from a balanced view of society? You might say that this is existentialism gone wrong — endless inevitable choices leading to action without context. But a choice without a context is not choice. How can we be judged on our actions when the options are presented without memory, without an ethical foundation, without the opportunity of imagining a broader uncertainty?

It is as if we believe that power creates all relationships. These we then treat as fundamentals. Many of these relationships are indeed the products of self-interest, of technology, of industrial structures, of various power structures. Others are the product of specific political policies. But all-consuming though they may seem to us when we venture out at the utilitarian level of our lives, these are often temporary, even incidental relationships. They may last a year or several generations, but they are on the service road of the human psyche. They are not central to it.

The problem seems to be that our talents and characteristics drive us more than we drive them. We may encourage and develop them or deny and frustrate them. Either way we are serving what exists within us — a form of personal reality or personal certainty.

There is nothing odd or strange about this; nothing wrong. As I've said, we need these certainties. They are our primary reality. And society needs these contributions from us. It is good to be a successful salesman or writer. The wings need to hold firm on the planes we build for others to fly in. We need to be sung to.

The limiting point which needs to be made is that, while our talents and characteristics may be particular to humans, that particularity is more quantitative than qualitative. All animals have inner forces, certainties, talents, characteristics, even virtues. Dogs communicate, have families, have friends, will be more or less courageous, loyal, intelligent, even honest. When you start the comparative list you realize how long it could be.

A SPECULATIVE ATOM

Our qualities are a different matter. I began this book by simply listing all six in alphabetical order. But then, naming them is the easy part.

Besides, a declarative list can create a false illusion of certainty. My aim here is not to produce a list of certainties and then to demonstrate truth. History, after all, is filled with lists:

Plato	Reason over what you might call Passion or Courage and Reason over what you might call Desire or Sensual Appetite;
The Stoics	Practical wisdom, Justice, Courage and Self-control, all seen through a rational eye;
Marcus Aurelius	Moderation, Wisdom, Justice, Fortitude;
Saint Augustine	Memory, Reason, Will;
Descartes	Understanding, Imagination, Sense, all three being instruments of Reason;
	Or Justice, Courage, Temperance, Piety;
Adam Smith	Prudence, Justice, Beneficence;
Tom Paine	Memory, Judgement, Imagination;
German Romanticism	Instinct and Memory;
Samuel Taylor Coleridge	Imagination.

There are hundreds more. And I've mentioned only the Western tradition. All the same, you can see a pattern emerging here. Imagination, Memory and Reason are clearly present in this pattern. There are various ways of saying Ethics, and various ways of saying Common Sense, but both of them are also present. There is even a hint of Intuition, for example, in the unspoken meanings of courage, wisdom, justice and, of course, instinct.

But you can also see a confusion in these lists; a confusion between what is a talent, what a characteristic and what a virtue; and then a second confusion between these three and our actual qualities. Many of these lists are based on an order of priorities or powers. Note that Plato saw each quality as belonging to a different political class: Reason for the *guardians*, the élite; courage for the soldiers; sensual appetite for the farmers and artisans. He was a true, conscious corporatist. Humans were not only to be divided up into corporations, they were to be assigned one philosophical quality appropriate to their role in that corporation. The Stoics on the other hand saw each quality as belonging to every person.

But, again, the difficult point here is the confusion between these talents, characteristics, virtues and qualities. Which element belongs to which category?

A talent or a characteristic is not a quality in and of itself. It is not shared. It belongs to you. You may find ways to share it, but it is yours. Thanks to these inner forces you may leave something behind — an object, a memory, an idea, an image, an emotion, a structure — but, in and of themselves, these talents and characteristics die with you. A virtue, on the other hand, is more complicated. It is difficult to tie down. Most often it is the outcome of how we use our qualities; or how we use our qualities to shape our talents and characteristics.

What then of our qualities? They exist whether we as individuals do or do not. They exist whether we admit their existence or not. We may deny them. We will only succeed in denying our personal reality. We may define them as we wish. That will only superficially alter their reality.

We often think of definition as a cornerstone of reason — as our protection against superstition, prejudice and ignorance. A definition is therefore intended to clarify things, to free us for action. But what we have seen in our society is that a definition can just as easily become a means of control, a profoundly reactionary force.

'Well, what is your definition of ethics? Ah, well, if that's your definition…'

And so, rather scholastic conventions can lock us into assumptions of inevitability and give comfort to received wisdom. A definition then becomes a crutch for certainty and ideology.

The essential point about a quality is that it is not ours as individuals. It is not an *intellectual property*. It is shared, laterally and over time. This has been clear throughout the history of Western civilization.

Socrates recounts this through a metaphor tied to our creation.[3] At first, we lived alone in a way which made survival impossible. Then we created *polis* — call it societies. Zeus instructed Hermes to hand out all the neccessary crafts, skills, talents and characteristics to various people, spreading them around here and there throughout society — a bit of this talent here, a bit of that talent there. Some farmers, some philosophers, some athletes, some mathematicians, some skilled in financial manipulation. This was the corporatist model. The aim was to help humans make sense of their *polis*. But it didn't work, and the societies began falling apart. We still lacked the art of living together.

Fearing our extinction, Zeus sent Hermes back to give us *aidos* (reverence) and *dike* (right). These are the components of *political virtue*. They make society possible. Here Right could be taken to mean free speech, debate, justice, decision-making, public truth, law, social order. Reverence could mean a sense of community, a shared knowledge of restraint and belonging — the obligations and limitations incumbent on life with others. Our qualities are intrinsic to these general concepts.

What followed in Socrates' story was the core of the conversation between the two gods, and as it turned out, the core of the difference between humanists and corporatists over all time.

Hermes listened to his instructions and then reminded the senior god that he had handed out the skills on a specialist basis. He then turned to Zeus and asked: "Is this the way I should distribute Right and Reverence, or shall I give them to everyone?"

Zeus: "To all! Let all have a share; for societies cannot exist if only a few share...."

What then do we all share?

I would speculate that the list of our qualities is Common Sense, Ethics, Imagination, Intuition, Memory and Reason. I put them in alphabetical order because they strike me as being of equal importance. What is Common Sense? Intuition? Reason? Each of the six has a chapter in what follows. This may seem a rather indirect way of getting at them, but then these are not definitions.

I would say that each of these qualities takes its meaning from the others — from the tension in which they exist with each other. Think of them as a strange atom, in which each quality is both a proton and a neutron. Curiously enough, the most common isotope of carbon — carbon 12 — has six protons and six neutrons. Or think of our six qualities as atoms on a force field. They are, to appropriate a phrase of the scientist Richard Feynman, "particles that move around in perpetual motion, attracting each other when they are a little distance apart, but repelling upon being squeezed into one another."[4] You might call this a dynamic equilibrium in which the balance comes from the flow. "Equilibrium is what makes life possible," is how the chemist John Polanyi puts it.

If you try to define these qualities each by themselves, you will end up back in the Manichean world of ethics versus unethical behaviour, reason versus the irrational. A nonsense world of stand-alone qualities and black-and-white certainties. Isolated in this way, ethics will become unethical, reason irrational. That would be a manifestation of the fear we all carry within us. It is there. If we give in to it, we begin seeking not specific forces, but an all-encompassing truth. And so we choose a single quality as our godhead, and then gather all the rest of our existence beneath its umbrella. This is ideology.

Our protection against this is our ability to seek equilibrium. To try to balance our qualities. We won't succeed. But the process itself does make our life and our society possible. In this process our genius as humans is released — our humanism — and if we can continue that effort, we can continue to act in a more or less balanced manner.

Ideology

We know the good but do not practise it.

Euripides, *Hippolytus*

The process of seeking equilibrium is the essence of civilization. This sounds simple enough. Why is it then that social structures seem so often to discourage us from acting in this way? Is it precisely because the need is ongoing? Without resolution? Because non-resolution is a complex way to live? Is it a fear of uncertainty? Or an impatience with uncertainty?

Let me ask the question in a grander way. Why does Western civilization have so much trouble embracing its own genius? Its own humanism?

Perhaps the answer is simple: We are uncomfortable with our genius being tied to attempting an equilibrium we will never achieve. Periodically we seem to stare at this uncertainty in amazement, as if overwhelmed by such an unsatisfactory requirement. And then we turn back to the utilitarian manifestations of our thousands of talents and characteristics — organizing and measuring and executing — as if these talents were more real and we more mediocre than our qualities promise; as if we were incapable of embracing what we are.

Why is this? Any number of answers are possible. For a start, life is something that goes by, and when it's over there isn't any more.

Time is therefore the essential human condition and fear of its passing the essential human emotion. Or worse still, fear of our ceasing to exist.

The constant challenge of trying to balance our qualities does seem a difficult, time-consuming business. The Koran summarizes this nicely — "Impatience is the very stuff man is made of."[5] Writer after writer comes back to this challenge. We'd rather have the illusion of certainty. We don't want to hear, as Rohinton Mistry puts it, that we "Cannot draw lines and compartments and refuse to budge beyond them." The great Japanese novelist Sōseki Natsume created a hero who was a highly domesticated cat. With a sharp tongue he commented on his owners and others.

> Consider human eyes. They are embedded in pairs within a
> flat surface, yet their owners cannot simultaneously see to
> both their left and right.... Being thus incapable of seeing
> in the round even the daily happenings of life in his own
> society, it is perhaps not surprising that man should get so
> excited about certain one-sided aspects of his limited view
> of reality....

And so we slip into ideologies. Strangely enough, there are often several at a time. Overarching truths and tiny truths. Certainties at all levels. At least, it could be said, this is a multiple view of how our inner forces drive us on. But as the cat pointed out, each of these views is linear, incapable of seeing in the round.

And if we do move across our society with this linear confidence, the very uncertainty involved in balancing our qualities in order to use them then becomes a subversive act. During his Nobel acceptance speech, Günter Grass said that "Often all it takes is a literary allusion to the idea that truth exists only in the plural...to make the defenders of one or another truth sense danger, mortal danger."[6] And so to fight back in the name of truth. Absolute truth.

After all, an ideology is the easiest of mechanisms for leading the way. Why? Because it makes the larger world small. And seemingly certain. Faced by such self-indulgent certainty, a strong-willed person may simply withdraw — 'If that's the way you want it, I'm leaving.' This is a long-established reaction; an echo of Rimbaud's, "La vrai vie, c'est ailleurs. Real life is elsewhere." But it isn't. It's right here.

Desire as uncertainty

When he banished doubt, he also banished desire.

Tolstoy[7]

Most mornings we turn a door-handle and walk out into a larger world, armed as best we can with the certainty of our inner forces. Is it true what Tolstoy said — that if we banish doubt, we banish desire?

Desire in its narrowest sense can survive certainty. In its narrowest sense it may even need certainty.

But in its larger sense — the desire for life, for a life with others, the desire for relationships, the desire to create, to be part of the society to which we belong — in that sense, perhaps certainty does banish desire. Perhaps Thoreau was both right and wrong. Perhaps our quiet desperation does exist, but comes from a feeling that, in order to survive, we must banish doubt.

This is not simply the result of mortal fear. I would say that it has to do with a certain idea of progress — a certainty that our ideas have unfolded in a linear manner over the decades, just as technology or medical skills have.

But most of our history is not linear. Ideas have tumbled out upon us in a disordered way. Even the medical line is not as straight as we pretend. If it were straight, how could we have conquered malaria by the 1960s only to have it come rushing back at us, stronger than ever, two decades later?

Think of the ideas which surround us. Much of what is true today — absolutely true — will seem ridiculous in a few months, and be quickly forgotten. On the other hand, certain ideas introduced two and a half millennia ago are as fresh as if born today.

We have a clear experience stretching over thousands of years. Much has changed. Much hasn't. Much is better. Much is worse. Two thoughts come to mind. One, self-evident, from Paul Valéry to the young André Gide. "Il faut se donner un but impossible. We must give ourselves an impossible goal." The other from the Estonian poet Jaan Kaplinski. "Truth is that which breathes, and allows others to breathe."[8]

What does he mean? Perhaps that the push and pull of tensions between our qualities produces a form of truth. Nothing linear or absolute. At its most "modest" this tension represents a "search for error and not for truth".[9] At its best a form of consciousness. That "when we walk we know that we are walking, when we stand we know that we are standing." It is that consciousness that permits a form of progress.

Each of the six chapters which follows is devoted to one of our qualities, how we use it, how it can be used, how we find meaning in each of them because each is a reflection of the others.

As I leap towards Common Sense, I feel a hand on my shoulder reaching out to restrain me — 'What about love? What about compassion?'

Perhaps compassion is one result of our search for equilibrium; our use of more than one quality at once, and so of an uncertain, non-ideological approach. Being conscious of how well or poorly we ourselves walk enables us to see the *other* walking in his way. Ideology, being in the possession of truth, has no need of compassion, which would be an expression of weakness. As for love, it comes in many forms. One is desire in its broadest sense. This desire is released by what I have elsewhere called our acceptance of permanent psychic discomfort. Call it instead our active embracing of permanent psychic uncertainty.

Think of each of us at our door, turning the door-handle and using our inner forces to help us know who we are. If we embrace our six qualities and the push and pull of tension which holds them together, they can help us shape our lives, by opening ourselves up to the whole idea of who we are.

CHAPTER TWO

COMMON SENSE

SHARED KNOWLEDGE

What is common sense if not shared knowledge?

It is not understanding. Many may find this a difficult idea to accept — that we can know something we don't understand. Not only can we know it, we can use the knowledge. We must simply be careful not to slip into superstition.

Curiously enough, that problem is more theoretical than real. We talk a great deal about analysis and expertise, but most of what we do we don't understand. We are able to do these things because we do know and because we share this knowledge with others. Shared knowledge or common sense lies at the core of any successful society.

In fact the importance of our ability to use it continues to grow as that of structure and technology grows. Why? Because these structures interfere with our ability to use our common sense. They are linear, interested in control, essentially simplistic. Common sense is essentially complex, lateral and disinterested.

It demands a very unusual form of intellectual concentration during which the implications of reality are digested. This is not analytic. It is tied to our sense of society — our sense that society exists.

Common sense has never been easy either to explain or to exercise. While reason may be the easiest of our qualities to deform, common sense has always been the easiest quality to turn into nonsense; the easiest to capture for ideological purposes. Why? Because a pretension of simplicity and truth can readily be presented as self-evident, meaning that we can but agree. This is false common sense, a manipulative mechanism to ensure the passivity of others.

It is quite different to think of common sense as an expression of shared knowledge, something which links us to the *other* and acts as the foundation of societies of all sorts — a foundation of undefined commonality which allows us to engage in conversation. You might call this the ongoing debate of human relationships, small or big.

Watkin Tench, a young officer of the Royal Marines, arrived with the first convict ships in Australia. It was 1788. Only months later he was declaring in his diary that "the first step in every community which wishes to preserve honesty should be to set the people above want."[1] He was living in a hungry, uncomfortable encampment of jailers and prisoners. They were failing miserably in their attempts to grow crops. And yet he and others with him were thinking about the shape of a future society and the necessary standards of the commonweal.

Of course, you could simply categorize Tench as a child of the Enlightenment. But that would hardly explain the Icelandic Althing — their parliament established outdoors in AD 930. These nascent citizens were poor and uneducated. You could equally draw parallels between the Althing and the Athenian *agora*, except there is nothing which suggests that the Icelanders knew about Athens. Or you could think of other isolated colonial backwaters. In the 1830s and 1840s, Canada's population was largely made up of illiterate and poor farmers. They worked for the democratic movement which was opposed by most of the small élite. Thanks to the farmers' energies and support, the movement succeeded in 1848. There is a revealing detail here. They were obsessed by the need for public education, a very expensive service.

And their obsession was not primarily to train their children to make money. Their desire was to equip them to participate as citizens in their society. Self-interest and wealth would follow behind.

Similar examples can be found in almost every era in almost every place where humans have gathered. The explanations vary, many are contradictory. Together they constitute a shared knowledge of the necessary existence of society as a primary human force. Perhaps shared knowledge is the relationship which carries us above self-interest.

All of this suggests an innate human quality and that's something which makes many people nervous. Rightly so. If you open the door to innate human knowledge, are you not opening it also to superstition and even to the idea of non-human forces of inevitability? If one thing can be innate, why not the other? Why not innate, inevitable natural economic forces with invisible hands popping out of the clouds to discourage us each time we are tempted to think about what direction we wish to take? Why not inevitable forces of technology — man-made machines — telling us to dismantle our social structures?

Superstition is indeed an innate force within us. But we have qualities to help us control it. The shared knowledge of common sense is one of them. You can't banish superstition. You deal with it. There is a surprising calm in common sense, a stubborn calm which resists the negative aspects of panic.

Take what are presented as natural economic forces. They can only exist to the extent that humans exist and therefore are not natural. The market in software would be surprisingly quiet if put in the hooves of sheep. Cattle have a minimal interest in e-mail. Economic forces must take their appropriate place as dependents of humans; more precisely, as dependent upon human characteristics in order to be shaped appropriately to our circumstances. And those human characteristics are themselves inferior to and shaped by human qualities. What history tells us is that economics — commercial activity, production, trade — usually falls in importance about halfway down the list of human activities, far off the radar screen of our desire for society. So the complexity of shared knowledge reminds us that, if one globalization model claims to be the voice of inevitable forces, a dozen other models will appear which don't. If humans deal with their superstitions and ideologies in an unpanicked manner, then the sensible not-inevitable models will predominate in the long run.

All of this is tied to common sense as shared knowledge. We have no trouble accepting its existence in other species. A single example: the Monarch butterfly. It is large, seemingly delicate, bright orange and black, with a brain the size of a pinpoint. It winters in Mexico, summers in northern Canada and reproduces in the United States on the way between the other two. It takes three generations to make the round trip, over thousands of kilometres. That means there are no Monarchs witness to the whole process. And yet they fly precisely the same thousands of kilometres, year after year, summering precisely where they always summer and wintering on a few precisely chosen, high, wooded hills in central Mexico. These hills are isolated one from the other. On each hill the Monarchs gather, tightly packed, onto the branches of the great trees, millions of them, creating the patterns of monstrous tigers in the half-light of the forest canopy.

What I am describing is not instinct. There is no element of the intuitional choice. There is no conscious choice of risk-taking. They are not making up their minds to follow this nomadic life. Nor is this the product of understanding. It is, if anything, shared knowledge. Innate shared knowledge. And it is one of the most complicated of realities.

Why should it be such a stretch to accept that what an idiotic butterfly can do in a non-analytic and essentially inexplicable way, a human ought to be capable of doing?

Think of Watkin Tench. His social optimism stands as a denial of those enormous non-human inevitable truths which are so often presented to us today as the self-evident nature of common sense. Most of them turn around general assumptions of utilitarianism, self-interest and uncontrollable forces. This false common sense so often imposed upon our debates is essentially pessimistic about human nature and human intelligence. It is the wink-wink-nudge-nudge cynic's version of how the world works.

Tench is a witness to the reality of common sense as a human quality. He reminds us that every day most people are seeking how to take human relations beyond isolation and beyond self-interest.

So it seems that there are two versions of common sense and they are in permanent conflict: the quality of shared knowledge within society versus the superstition of truths which are declared to be visible, evident and inevitable. Shared knowledge by its very nature is a consideration of the whole. It is essentially inclusive and human. As for the self-evident and inevitable false sort, it is centred on disembodied forces and thus denies the very society in which shared knowledge could have effect.

Because this latter sort now dominates our use of the term, we have difficulty focusing on the power of common sense to help us act in a balanced and creative manner. So long as we accept the idea of self-evident and therefore inevitable truths — for example, that we are driven by self-interest or that technology leads society — our passivity will prepare us for ideological manipulation.

Look at the interpretation of individualism common today: our successful assertion of our identity is to be measured by our ability to distance ourselves from commitment to society. There is no denying that it is a tempting idea — that each one of us could fulfil ourselves by walking away from the others. This tantalizing thought has always been with us one way or another. Even Kant, who described common sense as a social characteristic, could be found contradicting himself:

> A man abandoned by himself on a desert island would
> adorn neither his hut nor his person.... Man is not
> contented with an object if he cannot feel satisfaction in it
> in common with others.[2]

He seems to be suggesting that society is a pleasure, not a need. He has forgotten the optimism which accompanies common sense and the deep resonance it finds through memory. The castaway — Robinson Crusoe — is not fully abandoned because he remembers the society to which he belongs. He wants to go on sharing his knowledge of society. Like Crusoe, if abandoned, we may well adorn ourselves and our hut more than we did at home.

The romantic illusion that we could all walk away from the reality of society is fed by the reality that some do. A small percentage of any population will, as they always have done, abandon it. One, three, five per cent. They walk out into the desert, physically or figuratively. They reject the shared knowledge. Or rather, they opt not to share the knowledge and its implications. This is a healthy phenomenon. We need a percentage who stand on the outside. But if all of us, one by one, walked away, the whole would collapse. Society does not exist in the abstract. Our shared knowledge exists as a continuation of citizens and their recognition of the *other*.

Watkin Tench belonged to the ninety-five per cent. He and his few hundred were "abandoned" in every way understandable to Europeans. Yet the shared knowledge remained with them. And with that they adorned their hut — they built a society which was both an extension of the known and an adaptation of something new.

So they had no difficulty retaining their shared knowledge. The real challenge was quite different. It was something they shared with the other European colonial experiments around the world — how do you adapt in the profound unspoken sense to a new place?

Shared knowledge seems to have two aspects. One is the relationship between humans. The other is the relationship of those humans to a place. There is then a third aspect, which is how you join together in some way those shared knowledges which may have very different assumptions.

In Australia, as in Mexico or Canada or the United States, there was another shared knowledge already in place — another common sense — of another civilization. One which was a profound statement of that place. There and throughout the Americas and parts of Africa, the need to mesh these different forms of shared knowledge is still being struggled with. In Latin America they have been struggling with it for five hundred years. When I say that common sense is the most complex of our qualities and sometimes the most difficult tool to use, this profound adjustment is a prime example.

Not plain

And so this sense is something we hold in common. It is shared, which does not make it ordinary. There is no such thing as "plain common sense". Bishop Berkeley's early-nineteenth-century invocation to simplicity and the self-evident may even have laid the foundations for the manipulation of common sense by the false populists. That manipulation began only a few years after him. It is still with us.[3]

This "plain" argument has a tendency to treat common sense as a counterweight to cynicism or scepticism or even courtierism. Thus a class — which apparently includes most of us in our role as the common man — listens to the smart talk of the élites, declares it too smart by half, and sees right through to the essential truth or untruth. How? Well, WE are down-to-earth and therefore wedded to realism. WE are capable of truisms, while THEY flit about in their abstractions. According to today's *Bishop Berkeley/woodsman* wisdom, we common people see through the obscurantism of modern expertise and the forest of modern structures and understand essential truths and untruths.

These romantic Lincolnesque versions of wisdom are of course sitting ducks for propagandists and PR experts. What's more, they feed the false-populist dogma. Indeed they feed anti-democratic illusions of direct democracy, as in, 'we know what we want, let's make a decision.'

Even G.E. Moore's applied defence of common sense early in the twentieth century can be seen as inadvertently devaluing its importance. Why would he try to attach it to truth or "truisms" — "everyone of which (in my own opinion) I *know*, with certainty, to be true"? His hedgings with brackets and subclauses only make it worse, as if common sense were a simile for boring. In fact, understated though he was, he was still talking about certainty, thus accomplishing the almost impossible feat of turning common sense into an absolutist ideology. By piling what he said were self-evident truths one upon the other, all he created were tautological soufflés.

Common sense as a quality does not lie in self-evident truths or plain self-evidence or the citizen's *backwoods'* sharp eye seeing through the sophisticate's double-talk. These approaches merely undermine the importance of 'shared knowledge' as a characteristic of all societies and therefore of healthy, responsible individualism.

Einstein, in his ironic, direct manner, said that "the whole of science is nothing more than a refinement of everyday thinking." Beneath the apparent glibness is a very different approach. Here, shared knowledge is not a lower, simple tool; not a crutch for theoretically simple people. Instead, the genius of the whole civilization becomes the foundation for such things as specialist breakthroughs. There is no essential separation of the two.

This is about as self-explanatory as common sense gets. Einstein is warning us of its essential complexity, its resistance to being encapsulated.

But what then will protect us against it being used as a cover for prejudice or a source of false *gravitas* for nonsense? After all, we are witnesses today to what is presented as common sense being used by false prophets to advance social prejudice and by economic ideologues to advance nonsense and injustice. The very idea of plain common sense has become a crutch for pretensions of self-evidence and inevitability.

The partial answer is that we must try to see common sense in the context of our other qualities. In those mirrors, it will take on its real shape. And so there is instinct, which does have an element about it of the common man's sharp eye. There is our sweep of memory, which reminds us of what shared knowledge has meant and can mean. There is reason, which provides a counterweight of conscious analysis. Imagination, which allows us to give shapes to what we are not certain we know. Ethics, which can protect us from destructive conclusions.

These are the corrective effects which we gain by examining a quality through the light of another, as opposed to the isolating reflections produced by self-analysis.

Society

In spite of all of this, common sense is increasingly invoked by false populists in a simplistic, absolute manner. And it seems increasingly difficult to use it in the normal complex ways which imply shared knowledge.

One reason is that common sense is intimately tied to society — societies at all levels — and the very existence of these societies has been under ever-greater attack over the last twenty years.

Indeed the central theme of the dominant ideologies of our day has been that society doesn't exist. Has never really existed. That is the subtext of trumpeting self-interest and the fall of national borders — not a breaking of negative barriers but a removal of the central powers of the social contract. The idea of shared knowledge then loses its meaning.

What we hear most often is that societies as we know them can no longer exist, and this because of radical changes in external conditions. For example, because of new technology, future meaningful communications will take place via technological mechanisms. Society is therefore no longer necessary or desirable as an intermediary. Not only corporations, but citizens will be in direct contact with each other and make direct decisions. Society as we know it therefore no longer has a function.

There is also the basic economic argument: because of new international interest-centred and specialist-based groups, linked by new technology, the need for disinterested geographically based groupings — societies — is at an end. The nation-state is therefore declared dead or dying. The people who say this sort of thing tend to be the same who at the time of the fall of the Berlin Wall declared the victory of democracy over all other systems. What they seem to have forgotten in their second declaration is that democracy only exists as a reality inside the nation-state. That is not an accident. Democracy is an expression of calm, long-term relationships between people. It is an expression of shared knowledge. So if the nation-state is dead or dying, so is democracy.

There is a subsidiary fashion, now being constituted, which claims that democracy has simply moved down to the level of city-states, given that in the older democracies most people now live an urban life. Territory as such is treated in this argument as irrelevant unless filled with people. What then is it for? To be the plaything of urban interests? Parks and country houses? Commodities and waste sites? This is just a modern version of nineteenth-century hinterland commodity-exploitation politics. In our cities, we are told, we will be in much closer contact with our governments. There will be a social contract inside our city-states. But this supposition is built around a defensive, loser's formula: real power is moving to large international corporations, which are becoming the new state, except that they have no nation and no disinterest and no citizenry. They roam the globe as their interests dictate. The citizens — living, as most do, in a real place — then have no choice but to take refuge behind the walls of their city-states to defend themselves against these overwhelming forces.

This is a formula for urban decline and poverty — at best for limited services — since a municipally based citizenry will not be able to get at the tax base that lies within the control of the corporations.

Of course there are new international relationships, many of them containing the promise of a new shared knowledge. But the idea that our central relationships — the heart of our common sense — should have urban walls put around them would be a major step backwards.

Let me go back for a moment to the pretension that society has never existed, is now dead or is dying. History is a continual expression of the individual's desire to live in society. Individualism itself is the expression of our life with others. We see this in our social habits, in the way we organize ourselves, the way we live together, in our relationships. These 'expressions' may require optimism, but that doesn't make them romantic. Optimism is an essential tool in social progress. To be sensible is not to be pessimistic.

KNOWING OVER UNDERSTANDING

This idea of sharing knowledge with others is the key to actually using common sense. But how can you share knowledge if you don't share understanding? The Scottish philosopher Thomas Reid, defending common sense in the 1760s, wrote that it was about "the reach of common understanding".[4] And whatever I claim about the correcting effects of other qualities, surely to rely on knowing alone is to endorse prejudice and superstition. In short, how can you know what you don't understand?

Well, that is a very intellectual question. The reality we live is quite different. If we limited knowledge to what we understood we'd all have been dead long ago, for a start from lack of reproduction — that is, no sex — from hunger and from not reacting quickly to situations which would immediately or eventually be fatal to us. Reid more sensibly pointed out that "when a man is conscious of pain, he is certain of its existence." That doesn't mean he understands it.

Until two hundred years ago, we didn't understand most of what we knew. You could argue that with every year we have understood more. But the percentage of examined, argued and satisfactorily identified pillars of understanding, able to act as the structure of our knowledge, still only represents a tiny part of what allows us to go on existing. Indeed, most of our recent understandings are limited to small groups of specialists who cannot and/or are unwilling to explain themselves to the rest of us. In many cases, we have neither the training nor the interest to understand. It is enough to know. In fact, with the explosion of technology over the last quarter-century, the percentage of what we understand versus what we know has probably slipped back to where it was a century ago.

There is another more surprising aspect. As the quantity of understanding has grown, we have made an appalling discovery. Understanding does not necessarily help us to use our knowledge in a sensible or shared way. Let's say in a commonsensical way.

The exact opposite seems to happen. Our rational possibilities of understanding, in the absence of strong corrective effects from other qualities, tend to split off into ever-narrower specialist streams, carried on at a great pace by the momentum of their own internal logic. Yes. Logic. Self-justifying, self-fulfilling, self-interested logic.

To put it bluntly, understanding often seems to rush on like a blinkered runaway horse. It rushes on and on with a curious combination of determination and panic, indifferent to the consequences. This sort of disembodied understanding — in which the process of seeking a particular truth is justification in and of itself — actually flees the perceived limitations of shared knowledge.

As this fracturing is destructive for society, you might imagine that the various élites would make a point of removing their blinkers. Not discouraging the fractured search, but counter-balancing it with a sense of lateral connections. Political, financial and specialist power seems purposely to do the opposite, and so stands in the way of the sensible use of understood knowledge. Why? Because a 'sensible use' undermines the powers of fractured specialization. Or, quite simply, a sensible use of understood knowledge might not offer the best short-term financial return. And politics is now so dependent on the specialists and the large businesses that few politicians would push seriously for an integrated approach.

Reid said it would be "absurd to conceive that there can be any opposition between reason and common sense", because common sense existed "to judge of things self evident". In the latter half of the eighteenth century, when so many mysteries were beginning to surrender up their meaning to mankind, this statement must have seemed to make perfect sense. The twentieth century, on the other hand, was witness to a growing and often disastrous opposition between reason and common sense, in general to the disadvantage of the latter.

Such differences weren't new. The twentieth century simply made the most of them. In the past they had always been the product of the same desire to give one quality more importance than the other. Or even to make one dependent upon the other. It was precisely this tricky relationship, with ethics added in as a third contender, that both Solon and Socrates had struggled with in the first decades of Western civilization's existence. They had a real justification for struggling. They had had to invent these very concepts.

And yet Solon found his way very neatly. A century and a half before Socrates, he was brought to power because the Athenian city-state was crippled by the unmanageable debt levels of the farming class. The beneficiaries were a small, aristocratic business class. The farmers represented an important part of the citizenry and their status as debtors removed them from their role as citizens. So the Athenian citizen-based society was crippled.

Solon's solution was pure common sense. He cancelled the debts, thus reactivating the citizenry. It was a revolution because it clearly demonstrated the precedence of citizen rights over contractual rights. At the same time it was a prudent revolution. Solon *broke the chains —*

those were his words and he was Athens's leading poet — but he did so in a way which did not bankrupt the business class.

All of this was done without any expert understanding of the specific economic implications of such an action. What Solon knew was that the destruction of the powers of the citizenry effectively shattered their shared knowledge. Put another way, contractual obligations had destroyed the ability of the citizenry to use their collective unconscious. This is not the way Jung used the term when he introduced it, but you could argue that shared knowledge is a manifestation of our collective unconscious. And in that sense you could argue that democracy has little to do with counting votes and a great deal to do with using its legitimacy. And that legitimacy is lodged in its citizenry and in their expression of their shared knowledge through their collective unconscious.

To understand our situation today, think of a Solon of the twenty-first century. She would find herself advised in such a debt-ridden situation by a flurry of experts who 'understand' the precise effects of such an action. They would tell her that it was impossible to cancel the debts. Through analysis and calculation they would demonstrate conclusively why. Any clear, strategic action today could be factually demonstrated to be catastrophic. In general, expert analysis tends to reduce political initiative — that is, public strategy — to introverted and narrow tactics. In other words, our determination to place contractual rights first forces us to try to see citizens' rights primarily through that small, utilitarian keyhole. The result is false sophistication: the complexity of our methodology obscures the naïveté of our assumptions. They are far more naive than those of a poet-statesman and his fellow citizens two and a half millennia ago.

Take the Third World debt situation as an example. It is common sense that breaking the chains, at any time since 1980, might have changed the catastrophic lack of options in Africa. And no Westerners or Western banks would have been bankrupted by writing off those debts. Tortured bit by tortured bit, we have cancelled some of these debts, but always too little too late and in such a way that the total number continues to grow and the requirements for interest payments to outweigh any charity we offer in return. And so, for reasons of economic 'understanding' we enforce the shattering of citizens' rights in favour of contractual obligations. We use understanding to destroy knowledge — both ours and theirs.

In other words, the intellectual process of understanding, if taken out of the context of other human qualities, tends to eliminate the very real importance of the incalculable — the non-understandable factors.

In the case of Athens, the power of the incalculable was double. First, Solon released the energy and creativity of a large part of the citizenry. This impetus gave a kick-start to their society, including its economy. Second, he imposed a salutary slimming upon a rather lazy business class which was living off interest and other people's labour. He got them back out into the real market — manufacturing, selling and trading.

In other words, a comparison between our Third World debt crisis and that of Athens suggests that understanding can produce a serious form of stultification, which has nothing to do with prudence. On the other hand, with a shared knowledge of how his society functioned, Solon was able to use prudence in a radical manner and so unblock society. His revolutionary prudence was in good part a product of common sense.

●

A QUALITY OF LANGUAGE

That Solon was Athens's leading poet is relevant here. Language is often the key to common sense in those moments when it is clarified that there is shared knowledge.

Think of the response of the constituted élite of the American

Revolution to Tom Paine's essay *Common Sense*. It first appeared in January 1776 in Philadelphia and, in an astonishing roll of successive editions, flooded across North America and Europe.[5] Everyone who could read, read it. Many others had it read to them. George Washington seems to have been converted to the breakaway cause by it. Individual after individual made up his mind for or against American independence because of Paine's book.

Yet what it brought to the public debate was not understanding. Rather it was a statement of what many people felt they knew already. Paine's genius was that of every great public intellectual. He provided language for their shared knowledge; language which did not exist within their old formulations.

Faced with this explosion of shared knowledge throughout the colonies, the Continental Congress was "stunned...into nervous silence". But Paine had literally changed the perceived reality of America by providing a language in which it could express itself. You might call it a knowledge of public currency. With Paine's language, this public knowledge had leapt ahead of the deliberations — the understanding — of the Continental Congress, which had been created precisely to work out what actions were possible. Suddenly, much of the population knew its own intentions. All that lacked was a form — a legal form. It would be thirteen years before those legal mechanisms of understanding caught up with the American people. It took that long to create the Constitution of 1789.

That common sense had leapt ahead of reason was not an accident. It is far more likely to provoke an intellectual revolution than the slower analytic deliberations of rationality. How can common sense leap so fast? It has the prudence of shared experience already built in. Predigested, if you like.

Voltaire joked about the gradual reduction over modern time of common sense to "a state midway between stupidity and intelligence. 'This man has no common sense,' is a great insult. 'This man has common sense' is also an insult; it means that he is not exactly stupid...."

Earlier, he said, "Among the Romans, *sensus communis* meant not only common sense, but also humanity, sensibility."

Our society has gone a step further — redefining common sense as not up to scientific standards, and then not up to the self-perpetuating standards of the social sciences, all of this as if language didn't matter, except as a mechanism for motivating the common man. But as Paine demonstrated, that true power of language is always potentially present.

●

THE ARGUMENT AGAINST

The standard argument against taking this quality seriously goes as follows: to say that knowledge exists innately in a shared form is to propose an emotional herd instinct as a quality. Hegel was vitriolic about this. "It is not a pleasant experience to see ignorance, and a crudity without form or taste, which cannot focus its thought on a single abstract proposition.... The anti-human, the merely animal, consists in staying within the sphere of feeling...."[6] These seething words tell us that it is Hegel himself who is drowning in emotion; terrified by anything which moves beyond safe, dehumanized analysis.

The Romans were calmly accurate about shared knowledge. It is a *sensibility*. It is part of *humanity*; that is, of society. "If you haven't got it," Harry Truman used to say, "the best thing to do is not get out of bed in the morning."

So it is useful, but not utilitarian. There is a danger in confusing these two, which is related to the danger of taking common sense on its own, without context. Without the correcting reflections of the other qualities, you quickly end up mired in the lowest forms of utilitarianism. Education turns from learning to training. Justice is reduced to the law and its letter. Health policy is reduced to isolated attacks on sickness.

This slippage begins with the tempting idea that what matters is just getting on with things — 'Let's just get it done!'

Before you know it, you are deep within pure self-interest and corporatism. This leads to an obsession with the mechanics of action — *the trains will run on time* syndrome. By then you're ready to become a slave to any ideology which, by mysterious or mythological means, has a clear view of what must be done. There are a number of Western governments, democratically elected at various levels, which fall precisely into this category.

One of the ways of confronting this false common sense is to look at early fascism — before it could afford its military spectacles and false grandeur. If you peel away the seedy, demented, low-level ambitions from these early descriptions, what remains is a utilitarian core, essentially corporatist. Suddenly you notice how eerily similar Mussolini's approach was to what has become our everyday politics. For a start, his party remained an anti-party, anti-government movement through decades of holding power. No matter how big and structured the Fascist Party became, it always declared itself to be the voice of anti-party and anti-government politics. Mussolini's was the first of the modern anti-government governments.

It was a method copied almost phrase for phrase in the creation of the false-populist model which developed from the 1970s on and led to a series of powerful governments all over the democratic world. The obvious contradictions would eventually catch up with each practitioner, but by then the model would have skipped on to another country. What began with Reagan and Thatcher proved so politically easy to use that — even in the most *political* and *party* and *governmental* of political party governments — we continue to hear the call for anti-government government.

As in the 1920s and 1930s, this whole approach draws on a partially unconscious alliance between big business and people who see themselves as populists. The combination is always surprising as these two are natural opponents, if not enemies. Yet there they are, arm in

arm. Why? Because the voice of the democratically structured common good, instead of evoking real choice and real internal public
debate, has slowly fallen into the error of worshipping and defending
the smooth inevitable truths of expert public management, as if this
were the core of public policy.

You can see that the very idea of anti-government government
represents a destructive approach for a democracy in that it sets the
people against themselves. And yet somehow it escapes the normal
'shared-knowledge detector' of common sense. The explanation is
that common sense has been denied as a reality and so has been recuperated as an ideology — a virtual parody of itself. The false populists
have merely exploited a situation. The fault lies with the obsessive
linear managerialism of our élites. It is they who have found themselves incapable of using common sense, with all of its internal
contradictions and openness to admitting that the truth is not understood. And so they have taken to demeaning it.

Mussolini's local version of the anti-party party was an action-
oriented collection of what we would now call stakeholders. These *fasci*,
or *fasci di combattimento*, were "organizations which would get things
done pragmatically and resolve problems by acting decisively, and would
not be inhibited from action by any ideological preconceptions".[7] Note
the classic anti-ideology claim of the ideologue. The point is that this
concept   this very phrase — would fit comfortably into most of the
'common-sense action' strategies used by Western governments today.

I am not hurling epithets of 'fascist' at the neo-conservative movement or at our linear élites. Rather, I am suggesting that what now
passes for common sense is a low-level inversion of the real thing. It
is common sense taken in isolation and turned in upon itself so that
it becomes nonsense. I would argue that the real opposite of common
sense is egocentrism; that is, obsessive self-interest; that is, the refusal
to recognize the reality of society.

Common sense as nonsense is easy to identify. It trips over itself.
A single example: the anti-party parties and the anti-government

governments are almost without exception fixated on power and therefore on party and government. Or, they are against public-good programs, but desire the enforcement of public morality. Note that it is morality, not ethics, they are fixated upon. The enforcement of morals requires two things. First, a definition of them, which must favour one school of morality over another. And, since morality at this level is profoundly personal, they must then repress the other schools. Second, the enforcement of private or group morals, as if these were the common good, requires the use of a great deal more state power than does the administration of today's public services. Which brings us back to anti-government governments being more reliant on the power of government than their opponents are.

Or, again, there is the peculiar ennoblement of utilitarianism as a sensible approach. And worse still of pragmatism, a manipulative manifestation of utility which belongs on approximately the same level as efficiency.

Efficiency and pragmatism are needed. They are mechanical skills in human form. But their utility only functions at that mechanical level. They are perfectly incapable of leading or shaping society. This is where false common sense meets false reason, since they are identified with both qualities but in reality are neither.

Bereft of context and perspective, common sense does sink quickly to the lowest common denominator. You might say that in the name of efficiency and methodology, it drags us down into the mud and the reeds where our view is obscured as we attempt to push our way through, getting things done. Talent, leadership, professionalism are then reduced to building little walkways from rock to rock, just above the mud, but well down in the reeds.

Curiously enough, the more practical we become, the more the bedrock seems to evade us and the mud to become more bottomless. What passes for common sense becomes a panicked, determined obsessiveness. Anyone who looks up or around is marked as irresponsible or romantic.

NORMALIZING KNOWING

There is no need to treat common sense as a parody of itself. Better to embrace its natural complexity. Primo Levi, looking back on his time in the Nazi death camps from which he was one of the few to emerge, worried about trying to understand what it had meant.

> Perhaps we cannot, what is more we must not, understand what happened, because to understand is almost to justify. "[U]nderstanding" a proposal on human behaviour means to "contain" it, contain its author, put ourselves in his place, identify with him. Now, no normal human being will ever be able to identify with Hitler, Himmler.... This dismays us, and at the same time gives us a sense of relief, because perhaps it is desirable that their words...cannot be comprehensible to us....[8]

Perhaps that was what made so many who had survived the camps nervous about a film like *Schindler's List*, which seemed to reduce inhuman behaviour to the requirements of a classic Hollywood screenplay, with bad guys, good guys, victims, heroes and all the standard emotions. It gave the sense that something had been understood and so we, the viewers, could participate emotionally. Levi's argument would probably be that there was no possible understanding and that participation was a form of normalization. "If understanding is impossible, knowing is imperative."

He also believed, rightly I think, that these incomprehensible forces are never dead. How then can you retain your ability to prevent their re-emergence? They come back in new clothes, almost unrecognizable. Ethics easily loses its context for action. Memory becomes confused. Rational analysis is slow, awkward and so defensive as to be virtually powerless. "At that point," Levi says, "wise counsel no longer serves, and one must find the strength to resist." The stubbornness in common sense — so often resented by those who want to get things done and on time — is the element which gives us the strength to resist. We know and therefore we refuse to acquiesce. There is a knowledge that something is wrong. In and of itself, that becomes a judgement.

To know is to judge. To judge without understanding makes your standard, rational intellectual nervous. As I pointed out earlier, we make judgements thousands of times a day without considering whether we understand. These judgements are the result of our consolidated knowledge — ours and others, that of society. This sort of judgement works precisely because it is not linear. It is a maze of interwoven elements. To obsessively proceed through analysis would be to sink, as the Buddha put it, into a "wilderness of opinions".[9]

What I am suggesting is the essentially non-linear, non-didactic nature of common sense. You might say that it is the witness of society's existence.

The normalization of such a non-didactic quality is limited in part by our tendency to approach it through the political mindset. But human qualities are as much or more about dealing with daily life, with personal relationships, indeed with our dreams, our most unlikely expectations.

Philip Glass, the great American composer, was asked when it was that he came to his calling:

— By fifteen I was interested in modern music.
— Where had you ever heard any of it?
— I hadn't! I didn't even know what it was! I just knew that
   I was interested in it.[10]

Now what is that? He says he didn't know what it was — that is, he couldn't understand it — but he knew it was what he wanted. This

is the sort of knowledge we cannot deal with in any standard intellectual manner.

Leonardo da Vinci was very clear in an Aristotelian way about this.
We see something as a whole, he said. We register it as a whole. We
then send "this *impression* to the common sense, and there it is
judged". And so the artist's work is a judgement from the whole. "The
eye, that is called the window of the soul, is the principal way whence
the common sense may most copiously and magnificently consider
the infinite works of nature."

Many would dismiss this as mere 'art', not reality; the assumption
being that reality is a tough, down-to-earth business which demands
structure, method and management. In this view, civilization is a
process and 'art' is a marginal after-dinner diversion for the middle
classes when they come home from managing reality.

The curious thing is that no one can name a single manager or
administrator of the Renaissance. Yet there were lots of them. And
everyone can name Leonardo. Is that unfair? Well who can name one,
let alone two, of the last ten CEOs of General Motors? Of BMW? Of
the Midland Bank? Yet we can all name Picasso. And not because the
artists are celebrities. In general they are far less in the public eye than
a well paid CEO.

It seems that memory does work. It retains what is central and fil-
ters out what is tertiary or marginal. Leonardo remains because he is
an expression of our shared knowledge. The manager does not. He
has a role but remains marginal to society's sense of itself, even to the
manager's own sense of himself. That is the personal drama which
explains the aggressive disquiet in our enormous managerial class.
And it is accentuated by the growing assumption that 'to understand'
does mean 'to know'. That is the meaning of our corporations of
expertise. It is because the expert understands that we are expected to
accept her knowledge.

How disturbing, confusing it is to be so powerful minute by
minute and yet to be marginal to everyone's perception of our

ongoing reality; even one's own perception. This frustrating confusion is shared by our economic leaders. In both cases it partially explains the aggressivity with which they present their activities as inevitable truths. Seen more positively, these marginal people with power need Leonardo and Picasso and their expressions of everyone's shared knowledge. And so to be involved in some way with the arts is to have access to that pool of knowledge which is both shared and eternal.

What we remember reinforces the importance of a human quality which revolves around knowing. It demonstrates that to install understanding as the predominant filter for civilization is outrageous. Our reality constantly reminds us that we accept without difficulty the role of shared knowledge, whether in the arts, in public life or elsewhere.

PRUDENCE

We have always had a problematic relationship with truth. Shared knowledge does not assume it. For Giambattista Vico common sense was a statement of what is probable or likely. It is not, he argued, "the Cartesian *bon sens* with its rational capacity to separate true from false".[11] Nor, you could add, is it an ideological form which declares what is true.

The jury is an evocation of common sense at its best. The court itself appears at first to be centred on a lengthy rational process dominated by a variety of experts: judges, lawyers, police, witnesses and, not surprisingly, an increasing number of increasingly expert, and increasingly narrowly expert, *expert witnesses*. Yet when the definitive moment comes, the jury is devoted to making a judgement not on what is true, but on what is most likely.

The instruction from the judge to the jury or the recommendation to the panel of judges is that a decision of guilt requires the elimination of doubt. As the cliché goes: better a freed criminal than an imprisoned innocent.

What does this really mean? Not that those deciding must declare truth, but that they must believe without doubt in guilt or find the accused innocent. Because "those deciding" — the authorities, an array of experts, those with information, facts and argument — cannot eliminate doubt. Only doubt itself can eliminate doubt. Which is why the act of judgement is turned over to a jury or a panel of judges.

What do they offer?

Shared knowledge. This is clearly set out by Aeschylus in *Oresteia*. He has Athene declare that anger must be assuaged not through vengeance, but through the exercise of law. This comes with a provision. "[N]or should I let the law, like an axe, fall mechanically on a murderer.... Let me select a jury of the wisest...."[12]

By the wisest, she means the audience. And all citizens in Athens were expected to go to the theatre to improve their civic education. So by audience she means the citizenry as a whole. And when the jury makes its recommendation, Athene responds:

> In this court you have a fortress...
> A sleepless, armed, unconquerable guard
> Over the peace of men and their families.

Today we have juries of citizens and juries of judges. What do these two have in common? First, they have shared knowledge. Second, they have doubt. The panel of judges must work their way through a particularly difficult dance. They have to checkmate each other's authority, expertise and use of facts in order to eliminate all of these, in order to get access to their own doubt as individuals. At that point they resemble a jury.

And if jury or judges can agree to set aside their doubts, then their shared knowledge will become not a truth but a judgement. This act of common sense will have little to do with imagination or intuition or reason. Instead, it will require the acceptance by all of perpetual complexity.

All of which explains why justice is decided by non-experts or experts who free themselves from their expertise. The assumption with a group of judges or a jury is that the individuals have among them a variety of strengths and weaknesses when it comes to human qualities. The expectation is that this mix will produce a dynamic equilibrium just long enough to produce a just decision.

You could say that justice is a constant assertion that we can know things of which we are not certain; and that certainty is not a fact. What about the growing use of expert witnesses in courts? Well, that is precisely what you would expect in a falsely rational or corporatist society. But not all systems are falling into the trap of calculable truth. Australian courts have rejected the use of experts "to testify about the behaviour of an alleged victim of child abuse".[13]

> Jurors are not ignorant of the behaviour and reaction of children.... They have been children themselves. Most have experienced, and all have observed, family relationships.

Chief Justice Beverley McLachlin of Canada takes this further by using the word *fact* in an unusual way. She talks of "the fact that delay in a child telling of a sexual abuse may not necessarily be an indication of the child's untruthfulness." Other judges point out that you must not judge the attitude or even the responses of every witness on a Western middle-class model. If you do, the credibility of young aboriginals on the stand may suffer if they whisper, need to be drawn into answering and often reply with a *yes* or a *no*. It is common sense that this does not mean they are not credible witnesses. Similar warnings might be made about the testimony of an immigrant from a society where police and courts are the enemy, or an illiterate witness from the margins of society, or a well-educated lawyer who is practised at manipulating language.

Where does our ability to judge what is likely come from? Vico believed it could in part be taught: "[C]ommon sense must be developed as much as possible among adolescents." But he didn't believe, as Aristotle sometimes did, that it was merely the product of training or experience. Vico argued that there were "uniform ideas originating among entire peoples unknown to each other...." This was "the common sense of the human race".

Our experience over the last quarter-century — for example, in repeated environmental crises — suggests that Vico was right. Highly professional, indeed experienced understanding has been used repeatedly to justify increasingly destructive behaviour. The tendency is to break reality down into a multitude of factors and then to make decisions on the basis of one or two of these factors at a time, without asking basic questions about the whole.

In contrast, much of the sensible, consolidated thinking about what is healthy, long-term activity has come from adolescents with no experience. Far more accurately than those who claim an understanding of truth, they seem able to identify what is probable. Their common sense appears to be an expression of shared societal knowledge. Aristotle at one point talked of common sense as rooted in the collective experience of a group, a city, a nation, a human race. "The exact opposite," as Alain Pons put it when summarizing Vico, "of Descartes' *tabula rasa*."

Whether it is inherited, learnt or experienced as part of life in a society, the practical effect of common sense is best described as prudence. To take care is neither conservative nor radical. It is a form of consciousness — conscious that we are part of *something* which precedes us and, if we are prudent, will follow in as good or a better state. We are both reliant upon it and indebted to it.

But where does this prudence come from? You cannot sort out the matter according to political allegiances. A conservative such as Xenophon saw prudence as "the result of training".[14] Michael Oakeshott, a twentieth-century conservative, seemed to agree with

Hobbes that prudence "…is the power to anticipate experience by means of the recollection of what has gone before". Thus it comes with memory. A liberal like Edmund Burke believed in a combination of memory and experience. He talked of "natural moderation and of wise hands" which can handle difficult crises. A more radical figure, like Thomas Jefferson, also believed in both. He admired George Washington for his character; that is, his apparently natural prudence.

Beyond politics, many would assume that prudent behaviour meant in a sense conservative behaviour. But that would be to misunderstand the meaning of common sense. The very essence of good military strategy — which often means radical behaviour — has always been built around prudence. Two and a half millennia ago Sun Tzu set out the basic rules. His incisive summary was further summarized by Mao Tse-tung into a sixteen-character jingle which provided the general instructions for defeating Chiang Kai-shek:

1. When the enemy advances, we retreat!
2. When the enemy halts, we harass!
3. When the enemy seeks to avoid battle, we attack!
4. When the enemy retreats, we pursue!

The Viet Minh and the Viet Cong in turn took this perfect evocation of common sense as their method for defeating two of the most rationally organized armies in history — first the French and then the American.

"The enlightened leader is prudent," Sun Tzu said, "and the good general is warned against rash action. Thus the state is kept secure and the army preserved." You will notice the calm which surrounds most references to common sense. "[W]hat a leader has to do," Harry Truman said, "is to stop the panic." He doesn't mean that the people are not to be trusted and must be lied to in order to keep them calm. To the contrary. He was always direct and saw this as a function of common sense or, more precisely, prudence.

The point is not whether difficult, even radical things can be done, but whether they are approached with a certain humility. If field marshals such as Haig and Foch and Ludendorff were criminally incompetent in the First World War, it was because their theoretically rational certainty made them believe they could accomplish the military equivalent of Descartes's intellectual *tabula rasa*. They forgot or didn't know Euripides' warning that "to know much is not to be wise."[15] They had forgotten the nature of shared knowledge, of prudence. They were not clever enough by half to deal with the complexities of common sense. The reality of the *other* seemed to escape them. After all, their enemy also existed, also had thoughts, plans, was capable of action and reaction. But each of them believed he had fully analyzed and uncovered the truth. What the other was thinking or doing or, indeed, what the circumstances of other realities might impose, was beyond his horizon.

Much of our inability today to accept common sense as a human quality could be put down to this loss of humility before the existence of the *other*. For Kant, common sense was a form of communications dependent on our ability to accept that the *other* would also think. And what was true for Immanuel Kant and for any military commander is true for all of us. An incapacity to imagine the *other* implied a lack of common sense. It is a form of ideology.

To put it bluntly, it's a form of insanity. "The only general symptom of insanity," Kant wrote, "is the loss of common sense and the logical stubbornness in insisting on one's own sense."[16] The term he uses for "one's own sense" is *sensus privatus*. Insanity is the loss of our sense of the *other*. Interestingly enough, this explanation of a technical medical state, written well before most modern breakthroughs in psychiatric understanding, stands up remarkably well.

Using common sense

If we organize our society so that we can't use our common sense, then we become dysfunctional. I would call this a sort of institutionalized self-humiliation. Responsible individualism, healthy human relationships, representative democracy, an inclusive approach towards civilization — all of these are impossible if we are unable, first, to invoke our common sense of what is probable, second, to do so with others as part of our shared knowledge, and third, to act accordingly.

What happens when we can't use it? Think of our attitude towards change. Any opposition to progress, as narrowly defined by the particular received wisdom of the day, is claimed to be panicked opposition to progress itself. Ludditism. Logic of this sort has been with us since the first conflicts of the industrial revolution in the early nineteenth century.

Accusations of Ludditism have become the all-purpose, pro-progress response. This is revelatory because the well-trained, hard-working, conscientious craftsmen who became the Luddites, in response to their sudden exclusion by the owners of a few new machines, more or less had it right. And they had it right two centuries ago. They didn't call for an end to machines or progress. If you transform their language into ours, they were simply proposing a more inclusive, balanced, employment-conscious, profit-sharing, societally aware approach towards progress. It was a commonsensical, prudent, sophisticated approach towards change, an approach which accepted complexity and took the *other* into consideration. In other words, their approach went beyond a few machines belonging to a few factory owners who saw progress as the equivalent of a gold rush and their ownership of those machines as something which trumped the public good.

It was this refusal of the owners and of their supporters inside public institutions to pay attention to complexity that led directly to the social fracturing of the nineteenth century. The results were unbearable social and work conditions, poorhouses, unprecedented urban slums, the continuation of labour defined solely by commerce, almost constant violence between the authorities and the urban citizenry, the repeated use of military forces against civilians, civil wars, the Commune, *coups d'état*; oh yes, and the rise of communism, with fascism hard on its heels. So you might say that the few extra dollars made by the owners, thanks to the arrest of the Luddites, did not quite pay off for society — not if you are doing any kind of integrated cost accounting.

It took us a hundred and fifty years to recover as a civilization from the damage done by simplistic, non-commonsensical attitudes towards progress. And no sooner were we free of that damage, more or less in the 1970s, than a new wave of machinery came along and a new narrow élite saw the glittering of quick gold and began to shout that ownership of technology trumped the public good, whatever the human consequences. We must, they cried and continue to cry, inevitably rush again down the same old road of simplistic progress.

As in the early nineteenth century, they accuse their opponents of Ludditism, which means they are rejecting a more careful, prudent, complex, indeed intelligent approach towards progress. Frightened by the complexities of a citizen-based society, they cling to the simple formulae of technological and economic inevitability. Their wildly flung accusations of Ludditism are the equivalent of security blankets. What common sense and memory tell us is this: if the dissidents are a new breed of Luddites, well then, we should pay very close attention to what they have to say.

Historical comparisons are best used loosely, in search of indications, not truths. Today's Luddites are to be found in the steady rise of the endemically poor and homeless, but also in much of the new part-time labour market. Part-time, for some of the rising new-technology middle classes, may mean freedom from the constraints of employment. It may even mean the ability to design their private lives. For most people, however, it means the need for more than one job, four jobs to a couple, plus pre-university students working for basic wages at ever-younger ages.

What is fascinating, from an historical point of view, is that some large companies, such as American Ford, cooperating with the United Auto Workers' Union, now recognize the destructive social and economic effects on their employees and their families of what we officially call progress. In 2000, they announced the creation of a community program which would involve building thirty centres across the United States. These Family Service and Learning Centers will offer retraining, some child care, after-school programs, computer classes, summer camps, art studios, book clubs and so on. This was precisely the approach called for by the Luddites and proposed by Robert Owen in *The Model Factory*, during the first industrial revolution. He successfully put it into effect in his own business.

As in the early nineteenth century, this inclusive approach has been provoked by the rapid growth of an exclusive economy. The problem is that you could convert all of the larger, stable corporations to Ford's initiative and still leave the modern Luddites out in the cold. Why? Because, even if employed, they are probably caught up in the unsecured part-time labour market. That was why Owen's common-sense approach eventually led to all-inclusive public programming and universal public education in most Western democracies. These programs were neither exclusive to those employed by particular companies nor dependent on the socially responsible commitment or irresponsible whims of a board of directors or a manager, themselves responding to the fluctuations of the market.

DEBATE

There is something else implicit in these accusations of Ludditism. Any resistance to the inevitability of what is presented as progress is to be interpreted as an admission of fear and ignorance. This means that expertise and analysis are to be treated as a simile for debate.

But that just isn't so. The primary mechanism of public debate is common sense. The secondary may be reason, but ethics and memory, imagination and even intuition play a role.

This is a reminder of how our qualities are shaped by acting as each other's mirror. What does common sense learn in the mirror of reason? That what seems probable is not a self-evident truth. What could be more static than truth, except perhaps the idea of a collection of truths which provide a foundation for everything else? If we admit to self-evident truths, then debate would be reduced from questioning to mere comparative expert analysis.

It would lead, as it has, to the cutting up of the whole into isolated self-referential compartments, each compartment delivering narrow, self-justifying inevitabilities. You'll note the curious similarity between self-referential and self-reverential. Rousseau said "those sages who insist on speaking in their own language to the vulgar, instead of in the vulgar language, will not be understood."[17] But he missed the point. The choice is not between an introverted expert dialect and vulgarized simplicity. Communication at its best has clarity. It is neither simple nor vulgar.

Our sages are not speaking to be understood. Introverted expert dialect is what Vico called a decline into "barbarous thought". This form of debate does not assume or desire shared knowledge. Nor is it interested in discussing the probable. Instead "people get used to thinking only of their particular interest…and so they live, like ferocious beasts, in the middle of a crowd but in an absolute solitude of spirit and desire."

And so any demeaning of common sense leads to the degradation of debate and therefore weakens the legitimacy of the citizenry. What is lost is the idea of shared knowledge, the healthy uncertainty of probability and the celebration of complexity, all three of which make up the common-sense elements of debate.

In the absence of these three, the way is open for false populism to co-opt common sense and turn it into a force for anti-intellectualism. It becomes a denial of itself — of our capacity to live with complicated, unresolved opinions. And so our mechanism of debate is turned into a rhetorical trick against debate.

Again, this simply doesn't reflect reality. Shared knowledge and probability both imply complexity, but in a language which can be shared. Common sense thus expands debate by putting complexity of thought and clarity of language together.

The key element here is that shared knowledge, clear language matched with complexity, and complexity itself, all mean that we are both capable of and willing to live with unresolved questions. It is because they are unresolved that they are useful to us.

That is one of the curious naïvetés in old-fashioned Freudian analysis — that there must be closure on issues before the patient can move on. There is never closure on any issue. We move on because we are able to debate issues, not because we have left them behind.

To believe that something is resolved is to freeze ourselves into a static limbo where we are passive by conviction and dangerously exposed to the whim of anyone with ambitions. We pretend we believe something we don't believe because we feel anxious about our inability to resolve it and our inability to admit that we haven't resolved it. We panic. We surrender up our intellectual mobility in order to satisfy our fears and artificially to calm our panic.

Common sense requires a great deal more from us. Let's call it a state of calm in the face of welcome uncertainty, or indeed of unwelcome uncertainty. That calm releases us to use our intelligence. That's why common sense is the mechanism of debate and therefore so central to citizenship and responsible individualism.

THE ECONOMICS OF COMMON SENSE

Take the question of trade. Of course we're all for it. What about free trade? Well, let's put aside this bizarre misuse of the concept of freedom in order to look at the underlying idea. We're talking about commerce, not freedom. Commerce is a good thing. That's motherhood. But a sensible person would probably phrase her approach in a more realistic, down-to-earth way.

'The more commerce the better — local, national, international — but, as at the local and national levels, so at the international level, the more commerce the better, so long as it is within the desired political and social context.' That's just common sense — down-to-earth and inclusive common sense. No sensible, intelligent person would imagine that our desire to buy and sell as effectively as possible should eliminate other considerations.

And of course trade and economics do not stand alone. Without us, they don't exist. And being subsidiary activities, if allowed to lead the way, they will deform every aspect of our society.

What are our other considerations? What order of importance would we rank them in?

The top of the list is not very difficult to pull together — not if you live in a democracy. Citizenship comes first, along with freedom of speech, responsible individualism and of course the social well-being Watkin Tench spoke of in Australia's first days. This was the ranking we slowly pulled together in the second half of the nineteenth century, once it had become perfectly clear that unregulated markets led to unconscionable poverty and suffering, and did nothing to encourage free speech, active citizenship and responsible individualism.

The top of the list thus consists of the inclusive, democratic elements which have made us such successful societies and which, incidentally, have provided the stable and flexible context for a long-term healthy market. You could call this the democratic culture.

The idea, therefore, that the very real citizen rights upon which we have built our society should be trumped by tariffs, or the absence of tariffs, or the theoretical right of a private corporation to do whatever it wants, simply doesn't make any common sense. Economics has to fit into its proper place. And in an advanced civilization that is usually about halfway down a list headed by complex, unresolvable political and social considerations or questions. If political leaders tell us that things have changed and that unfortunately this is no longer the case, what they are really saying is that they don't have the commonsensical energy to maintain the public good above private interests. We have been through periods like that before, periods when self-interest reigns. At the time they seem endless, but our memory reminds us that they come and go.

The history of sensible policies also tells us that economics is a domain particularly given to mysticism, romanticism and to sudden optimistic enthusiasms followed by equally sudden depressions. Fashion and economics are often interchangeable terms.

Is this an exaggeration? One major illustration will do. The new truth of the 1980s was the merger and acquisition of large corporations via leveraged buyouts. This was the new economics, intimately tied to the great truth of deregulation. This was modern. It was financial engineering. It was described as the inevitable outcome of a larger marketplace in a borderless economy speeded up by new technology. One of its most brilliant engineers was awarded a Nobel prize in economics for his work.

A recent study looked at twenty-five cases in the second half of the 1980s in which corporations took on more than $1 billion worth of debt each as part of a leveraged buyout. Almost half defaulted on their loans. More than half filed for bankruptcy or sold off large parts of their assets to escape collapse.[18] So, as it turned out, the true modern breakthrough in economic engineering wasn't true at all. It was just a clever Third Empire, nineteenth-century scam of the type Zola described in his novel *Money*. As for fashion, it moved on.

Look at the merger question from another angle. Over a quarter-century, the conformist clamour from romantic economists and microeconomists has been for national and international deregulation in order to release the competitive energies of the marketplace. By the end of the nineties these had been largely released. The almost immediate result was a wave of emotional competition, followed by a still-rising tidal wave of bankruptcies, mergers and acquisitions, leading to a rapid return of national monopolies and oligopolies and now international oligopolies. That is, to a lessening of competition, to a return of the late-nineteenth-century problems associated with monopolies and oligopolies. A decline in public services, rising and spreading poverty, a concentration of ever-greater wealth in fewer hands. Oh yes, and a familiar nineteenth-century combination — economic growth accompanied by a lack of funds for public services.

A sensible society is therefore very careful when it comes to market fashions parading as intellectual truths. And it never lets such a perpetually virginal domain as economics get control of the public agenda. Not that there is anything wrong with having juvenile enthusiasms in the marketplace. These strong emotions are necessary. They drive capitalism onward. But when it comes to society's well-being, they are best kept in a subsidiary position.

What about the very real, ongoing technological revolution, which is leading to new industrial patterns, which are leading — or so the fashion declares — inevitably to more deregulation? That's what philosophers call the fallacy of the undistributed middle. Wojtyla is the Pope. He is Polish. Therefore all popes are Polish. You could far more easily argue that the global nature of new-communications technology has greatly facilitated increased regulation, transnational tax collection and enforceable monitoring of all levels.

Take a more institutionalized example, this time involving the worst delusions of managerialism married to the worst romanticism of the market.

There is nothing wrong with creating an international body to help regulate global trade. It is even an excellent initiative, since it is a form of global regulation.

However, it does not follow that all items exchanged across borders are merely or entirely or even primarily trade goods. Nor does it follow that a regulatory body which deals only with the economic aspect should have the primary say over the shape of those items. If economics is to be the defining core of international exchange, then its power of definition will be capable of moving in reverse from the point where these exchanges intersect internationally, back down the track of their production to the actual communities from which they emerge. That is a case of severe naïveté. Suddenly an abstract theory of international economic exchange is telling a town how to live or die. Yet many of these items are not in their totality trade goods. We know that at their source they may be part of social patterns central to the well-being of one society or another. If all elements are considered, they may not even be primarily commercial products.

Take the example of apparently inert agricultural produce such as meat and grain. I can already sense urban fingers itching to turn the page. But wait. This is more an urban matter than anything else.

Think of two immense geographical areas: the Argentinian *pampas* and the Canadian prairies. Add to this rolling image an administrative device called marketing boards. These are the result of cooperative approaches towards agriculture. They are designed to remove the instability proper to commodities. After all, for thousands of years commodities, although essential to our lives, have struggled with boom-and-bust cycles. Great civilizations have always created some sort of marketing-control system in order to moderate the cycles — in order to downgrade the romantic economic aspect of commodities and upgrade the very real social aspects. After all, we're talking about basic food, not this year's shape for evening shoes. Only the most transitory of civilizations lets commodities run as they wish.

Current economic fashion — as embodied in international trade agreements — has it that marketing boards are artificial impediments to free trade in agriculture. The fashion *mavens* of trade feel that the World Trade Organization should ban them.

How do the *pampas* and the prairies fit in? Well, we know that the *pampas* developed into a politically unstable area. Why? In the nineteenth century the Argentinian government didn't hand out land for family farms or ranches to the urban poor or to immigrants. Instead it permitted the creation of vast private domains — *estancias*. The result was an oligarchy and a class of tenant-farmers without local power or commitment. These tenants shifted from *estancia* to *estancia*, in search of better living and work conditions. In the absence of possible landownership, most new immigrants drifted to city life. So political instability on the *pampas* was the result of having no solid family-farm, landowning class to build local societies.

On the Canadian prairies, the government handed out land to immigrants with the specific intent of creating a community-based region. The farmers were owner-operators. Isolation and difficult conditions made them band together. The result was a cooperative approach, citizen activism, marketing boards, and out of all that came most of the ideas which would shape twentieth-century Canada.

Today, industrial agricultural methods focused on the new international market structures are marginalizing these prairie communities. Families are becoming dependent on, or even selling out to, a new oligarchy of immense chemical corporations which are building up *estancias* upon which to use their own products. What role is there for cooperative approaches and marketing boards in such a situation? As the farmers sell out, their families drift off the land, or become dependent on the companies. The voices which might debate this industrial approach to farming are gradually stilled. And so, in the growing absence of citizens, communities and ideas dry up.

What is presented as the inevitable outcome of new economics is in reality a step backwards into the failed model of the nineteenth-century Argentinian *pampas*. One question comes to mind: what is the difference between the Buenos Aires élite living off their *estancias* and the large chemical companies? Both are absentee landlords. Both undermine local communities. Both undermine the citizenship central to democracy.

In other words, to choose as the point of supreme policy judgement that disembodied instant when one product intersects elsewhere with another, is to reverse the order of considerations so that a relatively low level of economics — trade goods — is promoted as if it were civilization's first item of importance. Citizenship, freedom of speech, responsible individualism and social well-being are arbitrarily shoved down to the bottom of the list. This is Humpty Dumpty at his most brilliant demagoguery, inverting reality to make nonsense appear to be common sense. This fits exactly the model I described earlier as false common sense, because it is built on inevitabilities and demands passivity from the citizen.

Of course, there is nothing inevitable at work here. Trade technicians have been permitted to run ahead of international negotiations in other areas, such as justice and social justice, and so have managed to establish an order of importance at the global level which they are denied at home. Can you blame them for defending their success?

Is this an argument against the existence of the World Trade Organization? Absolutely not. It could have a useful role — properly utilitarian — at an appropriately subsidiary level in world affairs. Am I suggesting a solution to our current dilemma? More an observation of reality and its complexity. We are obsessively attempting to regulate society through trade. If we don't ease off our obsessive, linear approach, we will invite increasing dissatisfaction, because we are betraying our basic democratic conditions. And that dissatisfaction may well suddenly fling us hard in the opposite direction, right into the arms of negative nationalism and closed markets. There are signs of that dissatisfaction on all sides. The troubles at the 1999 World

Trade Organization meeting in Seattle was one. The repetition of events at the 2001 G8 meeting in Genoa was another. At the other extreme, the rise of the hard right in several European countries is yet another. There are dozens more.

Nothing is forever. If you swing too hard one way, forces will appear to swing you equally hard the other way. All of these forces are present, somewhere deep within our civilization. The solution? Prudence. Dynamic equilibrium. An acceptance of complexity. And a return to the sensible ordering of conditions proper to democratic societies.

THE POLITICS OF COMMON SENSE

Without serious consideration given to common sense, we have difficulty dealing with many of our most basic questions. Homelessness and a persistent increase in poverty among a growing percentage of our populations have accompanied a remarkable increase in financial wealth at the opposite end of the society.

This problem will never be absolutely resolved. However, there is the question of how many poor and how extreme the differences. After all, those suffering are those on the edge of normal life. They have been shoved or have fallen off that edge for a whole range of reasons. A successful society, as a strict minimum, sets out to minimize the number cast over into free fall.

This can be done with little effort and little money. Often all that is needed for people to keep themselves upon the plateau or to climb back up over the ledge is a few solid, long-term basics such as affordable housing. Instead, the false common sense of utilitarianism has tended to put more money into homeless shelters, emergency services, food banks and drop-in centres. Why? Because managerial

societies are desperate to measure crises and responses. Decent housing at the margins is not a measurable solution. Treating those who
have fallen over the edge as charitable cases is perfectly calculable.
Treating the excluded as excluded fits quite naturally into corporatist
societies which do not believe in inclusion or in citizenship as the
basis of society's legitimacy.

Look at it another way. We know that for decades there has been a
continual rise in broken families and in the number of single-parent
families. Put the complexity of causes aside. Look instead at their reality. We know that the market has gradually adjusted to the
two-income family by increasing the cost of living so that what a family could once support on one income now requires two. The broken
or single family is therefore caught in an impossible corner.

A sensible approach would therefore be not to punish the failure
to meet these conditions; and certainly not to push these people into
a humiliating world of charity — public or private — which will scar
them for life with a sense of exclusion. Instead, it would make sense to
ensure, for example, that the one remaining all-inclusive public structure in most of our democracies — public schools — would be
strengthened and rounded out to ensure that meals, after-hour programs and smaller classes picked up on what is missing in many
families. Instead, increasing numbers of democracies are trying to
apply private-sector models to public education. They attempt to
shave off the non-utilitarian elements and to charge for them, as well
as for use of the facilities after-hours. The result is a gradual return to
mid-nineteenth-century moralism in which those children without
must either be left behind or be humiliated by entering a category
deserving of charity. Whether public or private, charity indicates a
return to societies divided by class. This is ethics denied in favour of
moralism; citizens' rights converted into clientism.

Take an example at the international level. Images of a famine
somewhere out there in the world are brought to our attention. We
vibrate with momentary horror and guilt. There is instant consensus —

or an intense campaign produces consensus. Action must be taken. Lives must be saved.

The reality, however, is that the structure of expert analysis has converted famine into a process. What does that mean? Well, unless there is an established right, our public structures require a proof of 'need' before they feel empowered to act. They require body counts. They can't respond to unsubstantiated warnings. Substantiation may indeed unleash money. But can we wait for a ghoulish audit? "If there aren't enough bodies, there isn't a famine."[19] The whole idea of forethought — a characteristic of shared knowledge — is excluded from this process as unprofessional. Michael Glanz describes famine as a spike which rises above the norm. Through heroic activity governments can push the spike back down, by flying in food, troops, cash. None of which addresses the ongoing causes.

It isn't that those responding are unwilling to address the issue of civil wars and landownership. But before they did so, they would have to address key structural problems. For a start, most international aid agencies have one department for dealing with development issues and another for emergency issues such as famine. As if one did not lead to the other.

If we really did believe in systems — as opposed to simply dividing up power — we would at least have developed an early-warning system for famines. That would set off a process of anticipation. But such movement on the horizon is considered not sufficiently calculable. Not sufficiently disembodied and utilitarian. Anticipation would suggest an active use of shared knowledge in order to identify what is probable, with action based on probabilities not substantiation. To put it in health-care terms, this would mean building policy around health not sickness.

The same could be said about our response to global warming. For every problematic statistic a theoretically rational reply can be made with a reassuring statistic. The North Pole melts and there's an immediate chorus chanting that it has happened before. Specialists

say polar ice has reduced by forty per cent in recent years and continues to shrink by four per cent a year.[20] Someone funded to argue the
opposite pumps out a reply from an 'independent' source.

In an era of utilitarian facts, each side argues its numbers, like
little boys caught up in an analytic sandbox struggle. I could add
something I have personally seen — the Inuit in Nunavut in the High
Arctic are starting to use artificial ice on their unheated hockey are-
nas. The natural winter season is now too short.

A sensible question on hearing all of this would be not: 'what is
the truth?' but 'what are the probabilities?' As with war, the stakes are
high for the loser. What if it turns out that the Cassandras are right?
There might be no turning back by then. Why choose the most optimistic probability and plough on with the blustering self-assurance of
false masculinity? "Retreat is not flight," Sancho Panza said, "nor staying wisdom, when danger outweighs hope."[21] Why not use the sort of
prudence which indicates that we are conscious and responsible
enough to limit our risks?

Or take the question of fish stocks. We know that species after
species is in decline. They are sinking to levels which make commercial fishing impossible. Everywhere there are fewer and fewer
fishermen on a shrinking number of boats. But still the stocks do not
regenerate. There are great all-encompassing theories, but they don't
really help us.

There are, however, elements which can be separated out as part of
the complicated puzzle. For example, although there are a shrinking
number of boats, each of them is increasingly large. They are increasingly indiscriminate by nature. The industrial nature of their approach
means that, while fishing for a particular species of a particular size,
they actually damage smaller fish of the same species, other species of
different sizes and even the physical environment.

After several years of a virtual cod ban inside various territorial
waters, we are suddenly informed that the same factory ships now
vacuum the same waters in search of halibut. Many of the new cod are

caught by accident. At that point, they are dead, but not counted as a catch. Add to this pattern the fact that fifty per cent of the fish consumed in Europe is now imported. With little left in its own waters, the European Union now pays US$100 million a year to fourteen developing countries in return for vacuuming up their fish.[22]

The deregulationists say, 'well look at what a mess government management has already made. How much worse could the market do?' But the mess has been made by disembodied expertise; an expertise shared by the public and private sectors. It produces economic models unrelated to reality and subdivided strategies unable to look at the whole situation. The result is fractured, short-term, clumsy strategies.

We know that the factory ships have an unquenchable hunger. They appear modern and efficient. Why then are they so clumsy? Because they are actually the product of late-nineteenth-century industrial production management theory. The Ford assembly-line model.

Factory ships are not even in the business of catching fish per se. A high percentage of the catch goes into low-value fish by-products, such as fertilizer. The economic logic is clear: the indiscriminate vacuuming up of fish types for a blunt-ended market uninterested in quality product is far cheaper and more *efficient* than, for example, catching a halibut for some people who want to eat a halibut. And if the fish stocks are eliminated, well, too bad. The fertilizer market will find another ingredient and the fish eaters will support a larger fish-farm industry. That massive fish-farming produces a whole series of other complex consequences would be described as a separate issue for analysis by a separate group of people.

Common sense might suggest that we get our fertilizer elsewhere, because the fish stocks, taken in their own terms, are far more valuable. The cash value of the product is being dangerously devalued by a highly abstract, but old-fashioned, industrial means of production.

It might turn out that if you removed the factory-ship model and the fertilizer by-product component, and converted from nets to lines as the highly effective Icelandic industry has, you would actually have protected fish stocks and increased employment in both the fisheries and agriculture. But to do that would require accepting the complexity of common sense as well as life without a series of independently linear resolved questions. And perhaps accepting the advice of the great Haida poet Ghandl: "These will be of use to the last people in the world."[23]

You could describe our obsessive overfishing as a sort of institutionalized panic — a terror before the idea of simply looking at all we know, putting it into an integrated consideration and then acting upon the resulting probabilities. You could call our current state a lack of leadership. But that would be a passive response. A way to do nothing. That would be the Tristan and Isolde syndrome. We have taken a love potion and we can but love each other, whatever the catastrophic consequences, until the potion wears off. Then we'll see.

This syndrome is not simply pure romanticism. It is an extremely low-level type of ideology. It replaces restraint, which is what common sense provides in a non-moralizing way. The effort needed to be intelligent in an integrated manner is certainly not easy. "But this yoke," Montesquieu said, "seems hard to carry: you would prefer to be subjected to a prince and obey his laws, less demanding than your own standards."[24]

Panic is brought on by a denial of shared knowledge. It feeds on the absence of belief in a larger good. And results in an urgent conviction of the absolute necessity of apparently utilitarian, narrow, short-term actions. That means the absolute necessity of selfishness and of self-interest — let's call it selfishness — as the essential human characteristic.

What common sense provides is a clear sense that nothing is inevitable; that we belong to a society. Panic of this sort is therefore unnecessary. We are too intelligent for that.

What prevents us from acting as if we were that intelligent is our unwillingness to insist upon integrated thought — that is, to act as if we shared knowledge with others in our society.

CHAPTER THREE

Ethics

Public evil enters the house of each man, the gates of his
courtyard cannot keep it out, it leaps over the high wall;
let him flee to a corner of his bedchamber, it will certainly
find him out.

Solon

A practical habit

No other quality is almost unanimously recognized as being of great importance and yet equally thought to be inapplicable in the real world. This is the conundrum of ethics.

Received wisdom has it that only an idealist or a romantic could think otherwise. We are expected to grow up and get a job, as if there were an implied precedence of employment over ethics. A strange undercurrent of self-loathing accompanies this line: in order to succeed, a certain conformity is required when faced by ethical choices. This is called loyalty. In fact it is a structured denial of the central role of ethics.

But ethics is not romantic. It is perhaps the least romantic of all human qualities. It has a steely edge which makes its existential nature impossible to ignore.

That steely edge is there precisely because ethics is down-to-earth and practical, a matter of daily habit. Of course the heroic sort exists — the ethics of crisis. It and the great heroes it produces exist as a reminder of the ultimate cost of honest consciousness.

But the citizen's ethics has to wake up every morning. There is an element of drudgery to it. This is something which must be present everywhere in tiny details. There is a need for constant effort, constant evaluation. Ethics is like a muscle which must be exercised daily in order to be used in a normal manner.

Why should we make this effort? Because ethics is central to the way we see ourselves and our society. Responsible individualism is, to a great extent, an expression of ethics.

Because it is one of our most practical qualities, its use can be made much easier or much harder by the social structures we put in place. A corporatist society is organized precisely in order to marginalize ethics. On the other hand, straightforward structural reforms could restore its relevance.

But that isn't what we're doing. Instead, we avoid ethics by structuring it out of the way. We refer to it with dismissive paternalism. This requires an enormous, continual effort because it means not registering what almost every seminal thinker has said.

How do you avoid Adam Smith? "The wise and virtuous man is at all times willing that his own private interest should be sacrificed to the public interest. . . ."[1] Smith was in a direct line from Socrates who, in a conversation with his friend Crito, mocked the tendency to see ethics as theory not practice:

> — "You'll agree," Socrates said, "that when you need to keep
> a shield or a lyre safe and not to use them, justice is a
> useful thing, but when you need to use them, it is sol-
> diery or musicianship that's useful?"

— "Necessarily."

— "And so...justice is useless when they are in use but useful when they aren't?"

— "It looks that way."

— "In that case, justice isn't worth much, since it is only useful for useless things."

Socrates' irony was a reference back to the well-established usefulness of ethics as laid out a century earlier by Solon, with his evocation of "public evil entering the house of each man" when ethics is marginalized. If Solon's point is the essential and practical nature of ethics, what does that mean for us? Perhaps just that a democracy is dependent on the ability of its public institutions at least to match what are considered to be ethical standards for an individual citizen.

In other words, "public evil" is not an abstract theory. It is 22,000 registered lobbyists in Washington. Registered or not, there are equivalent numbers in each democratic capital. And each of those lives is a personal ethical choice. But the success of the lobbyists has a limiting effect on each of us and on our ability to make ethical choices.

Solon's image emphasizes the practicality of ethics: choice is a personal challenge or crisis, but ethics itself is a public matter. And it is only sustainable for citizens if it is taken to be a public matter and is supported by our public structures.

Ethics has been twisting and turning in the trap of all-purpose reason for the last two centuries. It has been measured, factualized, scholasticized, defined, reduced to absolute truths, computed, managed, relativized and rendered incomprehensible as an intellectual question. The result has been to structure it into marginality. Ethics will eventually find its way back out into the mainstream by balancing reason against other qualities such as common sense, instinct and memory.

What is ethics? It is heroic in extraordinary circumstances. But these are rare and ethics is not. It is therefore intended to represent normal behaviour in normal times.

That is the key to the conundrum. And it is probably the key to the fragile link between personal engagement and real change.

●

THE GOOD LIFE

What is the good life?

This sounds remarkably like the opening of a beer commercial or a holiday brochure. Yet, from Athens to our day this question has been the standard summary of ethics.

It has been asked in many different ways, often phrased as an existential choice — What should I do? What shall I do? How should I live? In each of these questions the 'good' of the good life is unstated but understood. The full question is: How should I live, given the context of the larger good? The larger good assumes the existence of the *other*, of the family, of the community. Of the public good.

Ideologues and cynics aside, most of us are perfectly capable of asking ourselves the ethical questions. Once asked they demand not so much replies as continual, sustained questioning. To ask is to admit that we have both a need and an obligation to ask, to go on asking and, along the way, to act in accordance. To ask and not go on is to admit personal failure as an ethical being. And not to act is to embrace self-loathing. Better not to ask in the first place.

We know that, while the philosophical and the legal foundations of our civilization permit and should even encourage us, the functioning reality of our society, particularly contractual law, will not sustain us in such a debate. It will discourage, mock, marginalize and if necessary punish. And we all have or may soon have families, careers, mortgages and a rightful desire to enjoy that personal good life.

Still, there are tens of thousands of young, in the first quarter or half of their lives, who are engaging themselves at an ever-increasing rate in public debates over public causes, from the environment to poverty. Others in society, who are more interested in control than in questioning, tend to dismiss these engaged citizens with a flick of the hand. And indeed they are not the majority in their own generation. It sometimes seems that the majority feel particularly alienated from society and depressed about their future.

But any dismissive interpretation of today's questioning and of how change might come about misses both the slow burn of disagreement building now for a quarter of a century and the new structures created by those engaged in the debate to sustain their questioning. All of this activity resembles a revival of the central ethical question of Western civilization — What is the good life?

THE GOOD DEATH

What might the good life be? Ask first what is the good death?

In a normal, good life, we will die in bed when our moment — as yet unidentified — comes. We will neither be in pain nor require drugs which cloud our thoughts. We will have family and friends around us. We will say meaningful things which will indicate that we know the meaning of our life. And then we will die. How isn't terribly clear, since this scene includes no element to kill us.

In reality, we'll probably come to an end with the sudden explosion of our heart. Or after a long, painful cancerous decline, our mind fogged by drugs. Or after the gradual degradation of age, which often includes a loss of mind.

Of course medicine has pushed back death. But death cannot be treated as the great enemy of progress since it, perhaps alone, is inevitable. The end is merely delayed. This is reality not as process,

but as life itself. It is in the context of seeing reality as life itself that
ethics can become a normal part of our everyday existence.

The trick to the good life is to be conscious of the good death
before it comes upon us. Not to prepare our actual exit. The disorder
of reality will deal with that. Rather to imagine ourselves in a non-
linear way. To integrate the idea and the reality of the end into life itself.

THE PERFECT DEATH

What then is the good death? As you might expect, Socrates offers us
the neatest and clearest example. He lives a long life according to his
ethical measure, thus provoking his own trial, gives an ethically sound
defence centred on democratic responsibility, convinced that it will
provoke his condemnation, which it does, and then has the time to
both consider and explain his taking of his own life as a final defence
of the ethical position of that life. He dies, his virtue intact. Those
who condemn him go down in history, as he said they would, for
having ordered an unjust death.

The clarity of Socrates' situation is remarkable. Not clear enough,
of course, to prevent generations of Platonists from inverting the
meaning of his death in order to mount an attack on democracy and
its citizenry. This wilful misinterpretation aside, his exit is wonder-
fully seductive. It is calm, clear, convincing. Friends are present, wise
words are said, the ethical unfolding of life is tied up in a neat pack-
age. And then he slips away, slowly becoming stone-cold from the feet
up. It is our fantasy of the normal death, with the addition of social
and prophetic implications, to say nothing of heroic proportions.
Again, most of us will likely drop dead on a subway platform, in the
middle of an orgasm or straining on a toilet seat early in the morning.
The real tragedy of death may be just how often it is comic.

But there is something fundamental in the conscious clarity of

Socrates' departure. It matches the idea set by every great civilization. The Buddhist formula is identical to the Greek. Sulak Sivaraksa: "[T]he cause of suffering is ignorance, by extinguishing ignorance, suffering is extinguished."[2] Adam Smith: "Self-command is not only itself a great virtue, but from it all the other virtues seem to derive their principal lustre."

These of course are abstract propositions. Socrates' was the thing itself.

THE EXISTENTIAL DEATH

Most deaths which include such a complete normalization of ethics have more of the disorder of reality about them, particularly when that reality is so dramatic. Jean Moulin is known as the man who organized the French Resistance during the Second World War. He was betrayed in Lyons on June 21, 1943, was slowly, horribly tortured, and died without revealing any names, thus saving the movement and many other lives. His was a classic martyr's death in the great religious tradition. He died for his beliefs and his honour and had the opportunity to consider both as his body was slowly destroyed by other humans.

But that is not the key ethical story. Three years earlier, on June 17, 1940, the first German soldiers reached Chartres, the cathedral town which was also the capital of the surrounding *département* or region. The *préfet* was Jean Moulin, and as such, he had all the delegated power of the central government.

Moulin was forty-one, a star of the public service. He believed in the Republic. His politics were moderate left. He was considered ambitious, a realist, a good administrator. He was reasonably well known in the inner circles of Parisian political life, but unknown to the public. He was variously described as delicate, discreet, an amateur painter, a fanatic skier, a wonderful dancer, a womanizer.

He had remained at his post in the prefectoral palace in Chartres, waiting for the German army to arrive. It was his job to maintain order and to ensure the well-being of the population. By a linear rational process, this initial sense of responsibility would lead other *préfets* in other regions to slip into a state of long-term collaboration with the Nazis.

Did Moulin know what he himself would do? How could he? He didn't yet know what would happen.

On that first day of Occupation he was summoned to his office by two young Nazi officers. He greeted them in his navy-blue prefectural uniform, hoping to place the dignity of his official role between them and his existence as an individual. The officers asked him to countersign a statement confirming that during the local battle French colonial troops (Africans from the Senegal) had massacred French women and children — nine in all. As he was the local French authority, they needed his signature, they said, in order to ensure justice was done. At one level they were showing respect for his position. At another they were drawing him into formal approval of their policies. He refused. You could say that he instinctively refused and only subsequently employed a rational argument. He pointed out why their story was unlikely.

Before this refusal he was a member of the élite, a man respected by his community, a man tested only in the way civilizations habitually test their élites — softly, delicately. Suddenly he was alone, functioning in a vacuum.

The two officers set upon him with their whips and fists. Why they were so eager for his signature isn't clear, except perhaps to establish a gesture of collaboration. They beat him at great length. He continued to refuse to sign and demanded proof.

They took him off in a car to a hangar some ten kilometres away to see the dead women. He pointed out that their clothes and bodies had been ripped apart in a way which indicated a bombing raid, not a massacre. The officers set about a second round of violence, then threw him into a tiny dark cellar, the floor of which was filled by the swollen cadaver of a woman whose legs had been blown off. They left him there for a while, took him out, beat him up again, and so on. After seven hours of this he was thrown into a dark room. It was the middle of the night. They left, threatening that he would sign the next day, June 18.

Moulin thought about his situation. He concluded that he would probably give in the next day. Apart from that, we know nothing about his inner reflections. We can imagine, given his rational training, that he went through his options. The Senegalese soldiers he was theoretically protecting by refusing to sign had probably already been executed. In any case, they would be. The absence of his signature wouldn't keep them alive. His refusal was therefore not aimed at saving other people's lives. Second, the anarchy of the day was the result of war. That war would pass by quickly. Some sort of order would return. He was a star of the French public service. He had already done more than could be asked. His talents would be necessary in whatever rebuilding process took place. For example, in his absence, would others work against racism?

This is the classic utilitarian argument. We see ourselves as useful; our death a loss to others. Our compromise today will save us to do better tomorrow.

And there is an element of truth in all of this. Compromise is a necessary characteristic of civilization. It is one of our most important talents. Compromise keeps people talking to each other and living together, whether couples or nations or continents. Our days are filled with the healthy and practical experience of it.

But there is a very real difference between this talent and the marginalization of ethics in the name of smooth process. We can be forgiven, in this civilization of structure, for thinking that there is no clear line to cross between the two; process so dominates our lives as to obscure those moments of choice. In fact the difference between necessary compromise and ethical choice is a great deal clearer than our managerial methodology, our daily routine and our self-interest suggest.

Because we so often fudge that line, hundreds of thousands of adults, who believe themselves to be good people, have collaborated over foreclosures, expulsions, deportations, inappropriate dams, humanitarian inaction, dubious scientific advancements, dubious payouts, information of myriad sorts held back or rearranged and so on. Kurt Waldheim, defending his own wartime activities in 1988, was heard to say: "It is not guilt if you are trying to survive." And in each of these cases we try to tell ourselves that one day, when we are in charge, things will be different. Unfortunately, when someone who has made those sorts of compromises reaches the summit, he usually discovers himself to be too compromised, too dependent, too tired, to do as he intended. Periodically there is an exception to the rule — a Gorbachev. But most improvements are brought to societies by those who have all along acted and spoken in a reasonably consistent manner. In Socrates' words: "All knowledge that is divorced from justice must be called cunning."

The conclusion reached by Jean Moulin was that he must remain loyal to his own ethical sense. In the darkness, he found a piece of broken glass on the floor and slit his throat. Quite simply: die rather than give in. As he put it a few months later: "The decision taken, the execution of the necessary gesture was simple."[3] He fainted from the pain, only to come to in the morning, weak from the loss of the blood which soaked his uniform. It is remarkably difficult to cut your own throat or wrists. The main arteries are protected by muscle. The smaller veins will clot themselves. In the meantime, the Nazi officers had apparently been given orders to back off. Their doctors treated him.

The point of the story is that Moulin didn't really know what he would do until he did it. I have no idea what I myself might have done. Nor do any of us. Moulin demonstrated abruptly that the good life and the good death could be one and the same.

It's worth repeating that all of these events took place in a vacuum. Had he died, no one would have known how or why. He would have been just one more accident of war.

This discovery of himself in 1940 meant that, when he was captured by Klaus Barbie on June 21, 1943, in Lyons, he knew what would happen and what he would do. This time his torturers were professionals with a specific goal. Had he weakened, the leadership of the Resistance would have been decimated. Although he was tortured in private, it was nevertheless a public act. This, in the grand tradition of public mythology, was his moment of heroic martyrdom — the act that would secure him a place in the imaginations of millions of others, of those not yet born. It would bring his ashes two decades later to the Pantheon, where they would be laid to rest during an astonishing public ceremony, caressed by the sounds of André Malraux's greatest funeral oration. But the failed suicide of 1940 was far more important. It had the existential purity of a man facing only himself, as he confounded the tidal wave of public events with his own ethical bridge.

Since Athens, philosophers have spoken of the importance of exercising the ethical muscle, so that when the ultimate test or tests come we will be ready. "[T]hose who do not train the body cannot perform the functions proper to the body," Xenophon wrote, "so those who do not train the soul cannot perform the functions of the soul."[4] Almost two millennia later, Thomas Jefferson gave identical advice to a young man. Ethics are muscles which "... will gain strength by exercise".[5] You could say that 1940 had been Moulin's ultimate exercise. But you could also say that, in a moment of great confusion and threat, he had instinctively discovered what he himself believed his own virtue to be.

There are insights and dangers attached to this story. The insight was best put by Camus, writing in the last days of the Second World War about those who had resisted versus those who had not. Instead of the good life, he wrote of the ordered life. "When can we say that a man has put his life in order? Well, he has to be in agreement with his life and to have aligned his conduct to that which he believes true. The rebel who, in the disorder of passion, dies for an idea which he has adopted, is in reality a man of order — an orderly man — because he has aligned his conduct to a principle which appears obvious to him."[6]

Camus is talking about the disorder we can permit ourselves when the core is in order. If we are clear, for example, about "our capacity to say no", well, we can relax about the rest.

What does that mean? Again Camus is perfectly clear. "You could never make us believe that an orderly man is that privileged fellow with his three meals a day for a whole life and his fortune carefully invested and who runs home the moment there is a noise in the street. He's just a man of fear and of savings."

The stories of Socrates' and Moulin's choices are seductive in their clarity, and yet the first story seems to come from a world open to choice and the second from a world far away — a world of massive violence and massive disorder in which more people than we can imagine are given extreme opportunities to measure themselves against ethical standards. Not a cool abstract measurement. They found themselves, as Vico put it, in a charged atmosphere "...dominated by the moment and the choice, both being extremely uncertain".[7]

I say these worlds seem far away, yet Yugoslavia is in Europe. And the world is filled with places of violence and disorder where ethical choices are being made or not made every day. In some places the disorder and violence are institutionalized by dictatorships, so that the world can pretend there is calm. Thus, Aung San Suu Kyi exists for years under house arrest in Rangoon — a diamond-like object embodying ethics — ringed by people who would be only too happy to remove her presence by any means. And the Nigerian writer Ken Saro-Wiwa, step by step over the years, as he opposed the military dictatorship and the role of Shell inside his country, found himself focusing ever more precisely on what he believed his ethical obligation was. After trying everything to discourage him, the generals had Saro-Wiwa hanged.

His son, Ken Wiwa, struggling with the reality of an executed father, points out that "there is a fine line between martyrdom and suicide, and this is one of the most troubling aspects about martyrs."[8] In one of his letters, Saro-Wiwa wrote, "You know what is going to happen to me. I know too and have known all along."

I wrote earlier of the hard, unromantic edge of ethics. This is neither Socrates' cool nor Moulin's holding on through torture. Saro-Wiwa's was a sharp focus on a destiny which lay years away. A clear, hard focus.

Socrates, Moulin, Suu Kyi, Saro-Wiwa. These four lives and three deaths are very different from our own sense of the options available to us. In our world, the very idea of making a personal, public, ethical choice is treated as unprofessional. It is often ridiculed. 'If she had a job...if she had a career...if she had a family...a mortgage...if she understood what we understand about the real situation...we were in the midst of negotiations...there was going to be a breakthrough, but by speaking out she has...cheap grandstanding!'

At their best, stories such as those of Suu Kyi and Saro-Wiwa are treated as founding mythologies against which we might measure ourselves, if ever extraordinary circumstances presented themselves. At worst, Socrates and Moulin and Saro-Wiwa are classified as Heroic. In the real sense of the word they are. The philosopher Richard Rorty says, rightly, "We should not regret our inability to perform a feat which no one has any idea how to perform." Having performed one, it is there as an example. Given a chance, most of us would probably do our best. Few of us will be tested as they were, though we will all be tested.

You will notice the natural tendency of societies veering away from ethics — away from responsible individualism — to lament the lack of Heroes and Leaders, as if the role of the Hero is to allow us to become followers. Every day the heroic act is banalized to refer to sports stars, actors, business leaders and Guiness-Book-of-Records–style adventurers.

Our corporatist society functions in a contradictory manner. *As if* we were in a situation of permanent war and crisis and require Heroic Leadership. At the same time, because we are meant to be motivated by self-interest, we have the right to interminable distractions. The Heroes in such a situation have to do with power and entertainment. And we are to measure ourselves as rather juvenile followers.

Suddenly the whole idea of heroic ethics is turned on its head. Heroism is reduced to fame. Honour is transformed into the recognition of loyalty to the group. This is an expression of conformity — the precise opposite of the uncertainty which ethics requires.

Such marginalization of ethics is based on an illusion: that the true heroism of a Socrates or a Moulin belongs to another time — to another reality. Ours is a society of measurement, of observation, of facts and calculations. We have a firmer grasp on our reality than any preceding civilization. The Greeks were asking almost innocent questions about themselves as humans. We know too much to be innocent. We know more than any civilization has ever known. And that is why these founding mythologies of ethical heroism must lie romantically in our past. Harmless reflections of a simpler time.

Why then do concrete facts relating to contemporary ethical crises have no effect on our actions? For decades now, daily military and civilian war casualties in the world have been running close to those of the French army during the First World War. This violence closely parallels the decision by Western democracies to use weapon exports as a standard tool of national economics.

Like Socrates, we have had the time to consider the ethical implications of our actions. Everyone in positions of authority knows. Yet knowing has had no ethical effect. Instead, it has provoked a long litany of managerial explanations that short-term need overwhelms all else. This is the marginalization of ethics.

●

THE ETHICS OF MOURNING

Marginalization is tied to our idea of progress. And progress is tied to our idea of knowledge. But knowledge is meant to draw us closer to an integrated view of reality. Knowledge which distances is what Socrates called "the ignorance that causes bad things... the most disgraceful sort of stupidity".[9] And what is that ignorant stupidity? It belongs to "those who don't know but think they do know". This is what Canadian philosopher Thomas de Koninck calls *The New Ignorance*.

In 1993–94 a genocide in Rwanda took the lives of some 800,000 to 1 million people; either that or some 500,000 to 800,000 people. Note, in passing, the profoundly non-ethical nature of knowledge built around fact. The factual variance here is twenty per cent, thirty per cent or fifty per cent; that is, somewhere between 200,000 and 500,000 human lives.

A tiny United Nations peacekeeping force was present under the command of Major-General Roméo Dallaire, a Canadian. General Dallaire, an experienced field officer, saw himself very much as a man of honour and a man of action. He repeatedly asked UN headquarters in New York for reinforcements. He reported that all the warning signs of a catastrophe were present. To be precise, on January 11, 1994, he faxed his superiors that a mass killing was being planned. The peacekeeping department at the United Nations in New York forbade him to intervene. The Security Council ensured that nothing was done. The United States and France were key in this. No more troops were sent. He was ordered not to raid weapon caches. Once the killing started he continued to ask for reinforcements and was refused. Three times he avoided orders to plan the pullout of his peacekeepers, hoping that, even preposterously outnumbered as they were, they might be able to slow the massacre.

Dallaire was unable to make his reality real for the managers who populated the UN structure and for the representatives of governments. Their logic related to budgets; to the need to convince countries to commit more troops; to whether, if more troops were available, Rwanda was the trouble spot most in need; to what was the relative 'fashionableness' of the Rwanda situation versus other situations. And how would it play at home? And what was the least that governments could get away with doing, given the number of choices? And what was the specific *realpolitik* view of each member of the Security Council when it came to that part of Africa? And so on.

Eight months after his original declaration of urgent need, Dallaire received 2,548 troops, far fewer than he had asked for. Murders were already widespread and the genocide was about to begin. Most of these reinforcements — a phantom battalion from Bangladesh — had no equipment and no training. They were an encumbrance and a danger to everyone. The general felt obliged to send them home. By the third week of April he was down to 450 soldiers, and the genocide was well underway. He managed to get 12 Canadian officers to help with organization, but 10 Belgian peacekeepers were killed, along with the 500,000 to 1 million Rwandans. And then it was over.

Dallaire came home to a good posting. He could have got on with his career, as his superiors at the United Nations had done. After all, his then boss is now Secretary-General. They proceeded as if nothing had happened which could or should affect their future contributions to society.

Gradually the ethical weight of the catastrophe overcame Dallaire. He began to resemble a tragic figure from Greek mythology. Having been unable to convince his superiors of the reality of the situation, he felt he must bear the responsibility. He never suggested that he was bearing it in their absence or on their behalf — Sophocles might have written such concepts into this drama — but only that he must bear it for having failed to convince them. All the same, what he had witnessed in the most intimate manner imaginable was the very real failure of our civilization to understand ethics and to act as if ethics mattered. In Jung's words, "nothing has a more divisive and alienating effect upon society than...moral complacency and lack of responsibility."[10]

The very fact of the event and the unwillingness of those responsible to take responsibility — which in existential terms amounts to complacency — seems to have drawn him to fill the vacuum which 'civilization' could not admit, let alone fill. Perhaps in his own way he was embracing the Socratic truth, that it is virtue which gives value to life.

In Dallaire's words: "[T]here were more people killed, wounded, or made refugees in less than four months in Rwanda than in the long Yugoslavian war. And we poured tens of thousands of troops into Yugoslavia.... And so I came to the conclusion that the world's response is fundamentally racist.

"I cannot, as many people urge, just put it behind me, get a new life. I can't wash my hands, like Pontius Pilate, of 800,000 dead. I can't forget...the people with all the hope they had, and then watching them as displaced people, seeing them after they had been chopped up — and when the survivors saw the blue beret, there was just bewilderment. What had happened? And seeing the terror, the horror in the eyes of children.... You don't, you don't just say...*damn, I did what I could, and it's too bad*. Not this stuff. I don't think I'm allowed to do that, morally."[11]

Instead of slipping away with his tragedy, he spoke publicly of twice attempting suicide in his despair. The despair of feeling he was unable personally to assume such a great tragedy. That he has pointed no finger at his superiors, that no promotion has been missed among them, merely reinforces the Rwandan genocide as a founding myth for contemporary ethics. This happened yesterday. Not in some other time in some other civilization. Here. To each of us.

THE NEED FOR CONSCIOUS UNCERTAINTY

In early 2000, I heard the head of a large Australian corporation declare that the Internet is erasing racism because we cannot know the colour or any other characteristic of the person with whom we are in communication. This is an astonishing idea: that ignorance could mean we are more consciously inclusive. I suppose we could add by extension that, having seen a few photos and some film footage of thousands of corpses, we understand about these deaths.

The question which lies behind all of this is: how are we to normalize ethics? How are we to carry it into the actions of our everyday lives? Socrates, Moulin and Saro-Wiwa are there as heroic models. But you cannot live your life on the model of a martyr, any more than you can on an example of astonishing purity, such as Aung San Suu Kyi, or of tragedy, such as Dallaire. To become obsessed by heroic actions is to slip into Hero worship and passivity. It is to marginalize ethics, as if it were proper only to extraordinary people.

We don't live out our days in an atmosphere of grandeur and choice. And yet both grandeur and choice are with us every minute. The philosopher George Steiner writes of a professor on his way to class who reads by chance a description of torture in the Algerian war. He abruptly announces to his students — "We will now put Immanuel Kant aside." He could only teach Kant "if an authentic relation could be shown between the monstrous [in the torture] and Kant's ethics".[12]

Let me draw the focus in a little closer. Statistics tell us that one in five American children lives in poverty. This is announced once a year, groaned over and put aside. It is a statistical event. Again, the precision of the facts — of the understanding — distances us. We have the numbers. We therefore think we understand, when we have no sense of those lives we are not leading. We confuse understanding and doing. Somehow this precise information actually seems to make us think we cannot act. Understanding does not naturally or automatically lead to ethics. Understanding without ethics is a demobilizing, even destructive force. The two must be consciously and intentionally put together.

When those numbers on child poverty appear, many leap in to debate the current definitions of poverty, as if precise calculations might alter the situation. Others are convinced that the solution is the exploitation of a 'natural' link between ethics and self-interest. Children are poor. We have ways to make them rich. According to this theory, we must convince ourselves that ethics does not drain the economy. To the contrary. Ethics pays. We will all benefit economically from fewer poor children.

This is the final degradation of what began in the eighteenth century as an honest and optimistic rational argument about social structures. Every enlightened person shared its intentions. Earlier, I quoted Watkin Tench, a young Marine officer with the original expedition to settle convicts in Australia: "The first step in every community which wishes to preserve honesty should be to set the people above want."[13]

I spoke of the shared knowledge in this phrase. There is also an ethical focus — a concentration on the obligation to create an inclusive society. If you confuse self interest with ethics, you stumble into a false rationality — instrumentalism — in which ethics is meant to be profitable. So Tench's phrase is taken to mean, 'The upfront sacrifice will be worth it.'

But if you believe that ethics pays, what are you to do if it doesn't? Marginalize it? Abandon it? Fall back on charity and pity?

Take another aspect of child poverty: child labour in the developing world. Our expert understanding concludes that child labour is inevitable. 'Otherwise how would they eat? Ethics is all very well. It's fine for you, with your comfortable middle-class life.' These phrases sound familiar because they were used a century ago, by our own industrial leadership and their supporters to justify extreme poverty in our own societies.

As you say 'ethics pays', step back mentally from this instrumentalism and ask yourself — What if this theory is wrong? What we are talking about here is a child, whether a hundred years ago or today. Look at your own child. Immediately it is obvious: to say 'ethics pays' is not ethical.

What about the down-to-earth question: 'How are these children to eat if denied the right to work?' This sounds like the voice of sensible compromise. But all you need do is pay the parents proper wages and their families will have enough to eat. How can we do that, when the factories are in the Third World? That is false naïveté. Production may be in the Third World; the market is here. Nothing would be easier than to organize access for Third World production in such a way that it neither exploits cheap labour nor prices its products out of the market. Here is a matter of utilitarian organization waiting to be shaped by ethics. Not ethics shaped by utilitarianism. Any fool — or group of fools, since we are talking about international arrangements — could organize and manage a fair system of that sort.

Steiner's story and that of Tench remind us of just how inconvenient ethics can be, and usually is. It is about constant choice as life moves on. We are both spectators and participants. The choices we make require a balance of both roles. In other words, ethics taken seriously means living with uncertainty. 'Embracing ethics' means putting uncertainty at the centre of our lives.

It's not surprising that most of us prefer mental comfort — a sort of emotional and intellectual stability — at the centre of our lives, even if it is only an illusion of stability. Few of us are born anarchists. We want something to hold on to.

How can we deal with such contradiction — our desire for certainty, our need for uncertainty? That surely is the essential dilemma of our society and of ethics.

The partial answer is that the very stability of democratic society — its slow, stolid nature — allows it to embrace large elements of permanent instability. Political doubt is one of those elements. Ethics is another. The basis of that stability is our belief that legitimacy lies with the citizens, not with the élites. And that ethics is an expression of responsible individualism.

The mentality which requires certainty on all fronts tries to frighten us with the dangers of uncertainty in a world of unforgiving inevitabilities. We are told that only by using our utilitarian skills to fit into the structures of society can we weather the storms of great inevitable forces. That is glib nonsense.

The built-in instability of debate, doubt and ethics is precisely the key to our success. The more we marginalize them, the more fragile, that is, unstable, democracy becomes.

THE MARGINALIZATION OF ETHICS

How then can we reverse the distancing of ethics from our lives — our normal lives? Four precise problems come to mind.

There is the ever-growing difference between theory and practice — that is, between theories of ethics and the ethical reality we know and understand. The result has been "...the irrelevance of much of ethical theory to the ethical lives that people are actually striving to lead".[14] The ever-increasing 'professionalism' of philosophy resembles that of any other corporation.

It shuts the subject in upon a dialect of narrow use. This accentuates the distance between the language which is supposed to help us out ethically and the choices we have to make.

Of course the Sophists were accused a few millennia ago of accentuating the same distance. And Jefferson said: "State a moral case to a ploughman and a professor. The former will decide it as well as, and often better than the latter, because he has not been led astray by artificial rules." Jefferson's point is that shared knowledge — common sense — also has ethical value. That of the jury is a perfect example, as they ponder probability and justice, rather than truth through exact measurement. Surely memory also plays a role in ethics. Perhaps imagination as well. Perhaps instinct. So the reflection of our other qualities maintains our ethical reality.

But there is also the very real fear that, if you let ethics off the rational leash, it will turn into ideology. Certainly it can and has. That fear is a second distancing factor. Our histories are full of romanticism and good intentions which turn into ethically motivated injustice, violence and murder. And these are highly personalized whenever ethics is confused with morality. Of all our qualities, ethics slips the most easily into extremism. There is a Christian or Islamic fundamentalist, a witch-hunter, sometimes even a führer, lurking in the shadows of every ethical principle. As if from nowhere, good intentions are converted into misplaced certainty as to moral rectitude. This certainty convinces the holder of the *truth* that he has the right to harm others.

But then ethics is not about good intentions. It is not moralistic or romantic or wishful thinking. "The trouble with transcendental good intentions…," Joseph Conrad wrote, is that they "cause often more unhappiness than the plots of the most evil tendency."[15] That's why it is so important to anchor the ethical reflex in normal life, where it can be exercised daily.

We exercise it with our reason, but equally with our common sense, imagination and memory. These three maintain the daily existential nature of ethics. How? They give us context and the ability to imagine the consequences of an action. Why? Because we know what has happened before and this helps us to consider what might happen in this case.

Ethics on its own is a justification for almost anything. On the eve of the NATO bombing campaign against Serbia, Christopher Hill, the U.S. Ambassador to Macedonia, met with Slobodan Milosevic, the then President of Yugoslavia. Milosevic said to the Ambassador, "You are a super-power. You can do what you want. If you want to say Sunday is Wednesday, you can. It is all up to you." Justice Louise Arbour, then the Prosecutor of the International Criminal Tribunal for the Former Yugoslavia and for Rwanda, pointed out the implications of Milosevic's statement. He believed that if you have the power to control understanding, then truth is whatever serves your cause.[16] This is pure isolated ethics.

The job of an international war-crimes tribunal is to establish justice beyond causes. But in wider terms it is to moderate the extremism of pure ethics by holding this quality up to reflection before our other qualities.

A third distancing factor is the fear that if ethics is embraced by any one party, then the differences between the many religions, groups, societies, indeed within the societies, will be accentuated. Ethics seen this way is a source of division, because each major group appears to believe in different basics.

But what are these different basics? There are virtually no major ethical differences between the basic texts of Judaism, Christianity, Islam, Buddhism, Confucianism and Greek and Roman applied philosophy.

The four Confucian qualities are goodness, conscience, reverence and knowledge. You may debate these, but they reflect the same concepts, and, when carefully translated, the same words as the various European traditions. Phrases generally attributed to the Buddha can be used interchangeably with those attributed to Christ. Most of the Koran is a direct reflection of Judaic and Christian texts.

The standard cliché has it that Islam is violently militant, promotes its martyrs to paradise and admires revenge. But Christianity has precisely the same tendencies within it. In both cases these are their expressions of "transcendental good intentions", not of their ethics. And if you look at the sweep of history, Christian militancy has wreaked far greater destruction than anything managed by Islam. There are continents of people who were subjected to Christian soldiers marching onward and who are therefore not terribly sympathetic when we complain of Islamic militantism.

The meditative, reflective, social tendencies within Islam reflect the equivalent tendencies within Christianity. Sufi meditations bring to mind those of Asian and European monks, filled with peaceable thoughts and ethical justice.

I might add that it was Islamic respect for the differences of the *other* which led Spanish Jews to flee to North Africa in the fifteenth century, along with most of the defeated Moors, rather than stay to be butchered by the victorious and monolithic-minded Christians. I sometimes feel that European and North American aggressivity towards Arabs over the last half-century has had less to do with Middle Eastern politics and more to do with an almost psychotic attempt to forget that it was the Christian civilization and no other which massacred six million Jews.

What about the daily questions we must deal with? How many are ethically unresolvable within the Western tradition? Very few. Of course there is endless room for disagreement and debate, but not to a degree which must fracture societies.

The profoundly unresolvable issues are so few that they can be listed. Two famous questions come to mind. The death penalty and abortion.

The first is a false debate. Throughout history the higher the civilization, the more reticent it has been to use the ultimate power of state violence. The most visible power of the leader has usually been that of commuting death sentences. To commute was to demonstrate the power of grace — a godlike power — which was ranked much higher than those of punishment and revenge. Why higher? First, punishment and revenge are expressions of fear and insecurity. Both rightfully exist, but both, if allowed to lead us, are signs of social failure. Second, the higher the civilization the more the citizenry as a whole is considered to be responsible. To commute was to express the confident cohesion of the society.

This is not an idea proper to democracies. Only in the most brutal societies did — or indeed does — the leader lead and the people submit. In tribal societies and sophisticated monarchies the concept of grace meant that the leader accepted that there was a more important level of judgement than his own. The more complex the society or the more ethically conscious the leader — whether absolute monarch, prelate or soldier — the more he wished to act as if with a wider consent. This idea of the consent of the populace has taken on hundreds of slightly different forms over the centuries. Once you reach the democratic idea of legitimacy rooted in the citizenry, an execution implies that the populace not only consents, but assumes responsibility for the decision. You, as a citizen, are no less directly responsible than a president or a judge or the jury on which you do not personally sit.

Democratic consent means that you would be prepared personally to act as executioner. Execution is not an abstract theory. It is an existential act. To be for the death penalty is to consider the convicted one by one and answer affirmatively the question: Am I personally prepared to kill that man? Consciously or unconsciously that final level of responsibility explains why Western democracies, with one exception, have ended the practice. The citizenry found themselves face to face with the combination of an ethical reality and their personal responsibility and decided that legal murder was ethically unacceptable, whatever the conditions. That the death penalty has returned with such a vengeance in one Western society tells you more about the social crisis that place is experiencing than the meaning of ethics.

Abortion, on the other hand, is one of those rare issues over which we will be unlikely to find an ethical response. It involves a deep, unresolvable confusion between morality and ethics; between personal belief and ethical principle.

Since no agreement is possible, structured choice is the only viable response by the state — that is, let the citizens' idea of the good life guide their own decision as it applies to them. Those against would reply that choice is precisely the problem, as it legalizes murder.

Curiously enough, a sizeable percentage of those against abortion tend to be for the death penalty. Thus their point is not whether the state should legislate murder, but simply who the state should use this power against. They might reply: against the guilty not the innocent. But that would be slipping into Conrad's transcendental good intentions.

The point is: this is one of those rare issues on which agreement is virtually impossible. That there are periodic unresolvable issues does not mean that ethics doesn't work. And why should an unanswerable question be treated as the most important one? The few unresolvable issues are an indication that ethics works most of the time.

The fourth distancing factor is the dominant role of reason. Again and again over the last 2,500 years we have been subjected to the assertion that reason alone allows us to identify and use ethics. The intention has often been good. But the effect, each time, has been to turn ethics into a creature of reason.

If anything, it is reason which can be made reasonable if seen in the reflection of ethics. Am I exaggerating the problem? Here is the philosopher Stuart Hampshire:

> There are two faces of morality: the rational and articulate
> side and the *less* than rational, the *historically conditioned,*
> *fiercely individual, imaginative, parochial, the less than fully*
> *articulate* side.[17]

Note how ethics, memory and imagination are presented by Hampshire as being inferior to reason. Note how imagination is paired with parochial, an astonishing idea; how only reason can make ethics articulate.

And here is John Rawls, the American theorist:

> Having defined a person's good as the successful execution
> of a rational plan of life....

This is embarrassing in its naïveté. For example, how would Rawls explain the rational plans of the Nazis or of apartheid? Instead of instituting a "less than rational...less than fully articulate" dictatorship, the South African regime was able to institute a rationally articulate and articulated system, down to the smallest legal details: the Population Registration Act, the Group Areas Act, the Native Labour Act, the Black Affairs Administration Act, and so on and so on.

Jürgen Habermas, conscious of this contradiction, has tried to reconstruct "an ecumenical conception of reason" by arguing that it is not instrumental but *communicative*; a way of explaining that we would be in ethical agreement if we were able to fully explore our ethical doubts together. The problem is again the obsessive desire to approach ethics as a sub-genre of reason. It is this assumption about intellectual form which is central to distancing ethics from real use.

Compare these three philosophers to Voltaire's prudent,

> It only remains therefore to use our reason to discern the
> shades of goodness and badness.

In other words, reason is one of the tools which can help us deal with the shades of ethics. It is not the source of truth. It is not therefore liable to deform ethics, as if manipulating a plaything designed for rational pleasure.

"Reason alone no longer suffices," Jung said. With hindsight we can see that it never did. Reason is not a filter through which to shape ethics. To treat it as if it were is to go down the road of relativism, where there are no choices, only process and interest. It leads you to U.S. President John Kennedy's disastrous formula of "situational ethics", which perfectly described the new managerial, instrumental approach towards power.

All relativism can do is deform ethics. Reality is the solid base from which we choose in the context of uncertainty. Context and reality help us to understand the real costs of striving to live in an ethical manner. They are part of knowing and choosing.

THE COMMON SENSE
OF ETHICS

Once distanced from our real lives, ethics can be presented romantically in a Manichean manner. Either it is Heroic, terrible and solitary, like an avenging god who may choose at will to do great good or great evil. Or it is a fragile, obscure quality which can only find strength and clarity through the lens of reason — by becoming its creature and losing its contact with real life. What I keep coming back to is that ethics is the exact opposite of a romantic tendency. Nothing could be more diamond-like, more unforgiving to our weaknesses, more humiliating to our secret self.

From the beginning there has been an assumption that ethics would always have to be advanced against opposition from interested parties or ideologues. From many, yes. Much of the time, yes. But then, as Adam Smith put it, "To act according to the dictates of prudence, of justice, and proper beneficence, seems to have no great merit where there is no temptation to do otherwise."[18] This was part of his argument for the centrality of ethics and against the dominance of self-interest in *The Theory of Moral Sentiments*.

It may often seem that everything from survival to self-interest argues against the use of ethics. Yet this quality is not about sacrifice *per se*. That would be self-indulgent. Nor is it a denial of self-interest as a necessary subsidiary characteristic, but one which has nothing to do with either ethics or freedom. "Liberty without justice is a veritable contradiction,"[19] was how Rousseau put it. The ideological right may quiver with indignation, but no major religion or philosophy, and certainly no real conservative, has put it any differently. Rousseau's formula summarizes the essential element which binds together conservatives, liberals and social democrats while separating them from ideologues, whether of the right or the left. And this formula is shared across cultures. Confucianism assumes that man is ethical by nature, and not just to save his soul. Even though it may ruin his life, he will act properly for its own sake.

If not central to our daily life, ethics is nothing. The quality which reinforces that centrality is common sense. And the very idea of shared knowledge suggests why.

If common sense is profoundly complex, ethics is inescapably disturbing. It is not about analysis or argument or resolution or style or comfort or manners. As Camus put it, torturers "know how to give up their seat in the métro, just like Himmler". It is inescapably disturbing because it assumes that freedom — freedom with justice — comes before any form of authority. This is where the neo-conservative argument turns into simplistic comedy, calling for non-ethical freedom on the one hand and moralizing constraint on the other.

It is commonsensical that ethics may be expressed in many ways, for example, through forgiveness. That was one of the great revelations of the South African Truth and Reconciliation Commission. At stake were thousands of cases of murder and torture carried out by officials. The need was to establish a personal and national sense of justice. Intellectuals, power-brokers and journalists were at first cynical about a non-punishing process. But then they saw the importance which unknown victims gave to being heard and to having their experience fully explained. The pain of the evil done to them or their families seemed to come in large part from its invisibility. Public exposure converted the pain to ethical self-respect.

The simplest of village people participated, not in order to extract revenge, but to meet the person who had tortured and killed their son or daughter or husband. They wanted to hear them questioned or to question them themselves in order to understand what had happened and how the perpetrator felt, and then to say they were satisfied or that they forgave. Or not. It was Elias Canetti who pointed out that "an act of mercy is a very high and concentrated expression of power, for it presupposes condemnation" and that the inability to forgive reveals that that person suffers from a "paranoid structure".[20] You could say that the South African victims were exercising that *grace* of Kings which I spoke of earlier. And that those obsessed today in the West by the need to execute criminals suffer from a paranoid structure.

One of the most surprising elements in the hearings was the desire of both the tortured who had survived and their torturers to meet, as if in search of a relationship which would allow both to regain their virtue; that is, their reason to live. The society itself seemed to need these meetings and revelations in order to find a "communal starting point". That is, they needed to create a conscious shared memory in order to shape an ethical relationship.

There is no clear intellectual explanation for the success of this process. Archbishop Tutu, as the Chair, brought Christian and humanist roots to the table. He also very consciously evoked pre-European African concepts such as *Ubuntu*, which could be summarized as "I am because you are" — a non-exclusive, societal form of individualism, which seems to me far more sophisticated than the rather crude and egocentred formula: I am because I think. But you could also argue that, in the end, the relative success of the reconciliation process was an expression of the people's ability to marry ethics and common sense. They established a shared knowledge.

The Commission was also a direct illustration of an argument made by Sophocles. The great bowman Philoctetes, banished to a bleak island by his allies, writhes in pain from a poisonous wound which will never heal. He writhes in both physical pain and bitterness. Finally, he is able to free himself of the hold this grievance has on him. The wound then heals, not miraculously, but as a direct result of his ethical resolution of the wrong done him. He is then able to serve his people.[21] Sophocles was dramatizing reconciliation with oneself, and thus with others, as an exercise in ethics. To remind ourselves of how hard-edged and unromantic ethics is, we need to focus on just what has happened here. This is reconciliation, not closure. Nothing is forgotten.

Let me contrast the Truth and Reconciliation Commission with an opposing example that shows how, by avoiding common sense, highly educated people can pretend they are acting in an ethical manner.

There have always been courtiers. Thus, in modern terms, there have always been lobbyists and consultants. This is now one of the most respected of professions.

By pretending to see themselves as modern professionals, they avoid the mirror of history which says a courtier is a courtier is a courtier — whether at Versailles or on the doorstep of a ministry. Their job remains the same: to deform the public good in order to serve the self-interest of their employer. The traditional term for this is influence-peddling.

Our new difficulty comes with the "situational ethics" of the public technocracy, who have sought a structural solution to the lobbyist problem. And so, in most countries, they have normalized the courtiers by the simple act of registering them. Theoretically, lobbyists are now under observance, monitored and controlled. In reality they are now part of the structure of government. What is the message to citizens? Since lobbying has been normalized, ethics must be marginal. This is relativism, which is, as I said earlier, a denial of reality and therefore of ethics. However, the technocrat can pretend that her duty has been done, because a visible embarrassment has been so integrated as to make it invisible to the general public.

ETHICS DOESN'T PAY—ONE

While ethics is useful, it is not utilitarian.

Is that true? Could ethics be useful on a daily basis and not be utilitarian? How strange that that question need even be treated as a serious matter. After all, the utilitarian is little more than that — a creature of utility. It can indifferently serve any force, from mass murder to feeding poor children.

The starting point for ethics is very different. It does not 'pay'. To be precise, ethics may pay sometimes, sometimes not. And a particular ethical action or position which pays today may cost you your job or your life tomorrow. In other words, there is no measurable, sustainable relationship between ethics and interest.

When ethics is focused on the *other* — the neighbour, the fellow citizen, the unknown — it represents an obligation. That is, ethics is the precise opposite not only of interest but of charity, which grows in societies where ethics has been marginalized.

"All charity is humiliating,"[22] was how Strindberg put it. "I'd rather be hated than pitied. It's easier to fight," are the phrases of Joe Garvey, a paraplegic activist.

What about the great tradition of charity attached to all religions? Remember that it was based on the concept of the tithe — the *obligatory* giving of a fixed percentage of each person's income. Thus the giver was not to have the self-indulgent pleasure of self-satisfaction or the power of choosing. It was not a concept of noblesse oblige. In the absence of this sense of obligation, what remains? Michael Peers, Primate of the Anglican Church of Canada, preaches that "faithful giving is to offer the first fruits. To offer the last is not faithful giving." You could say that it is charity as self-aggrandizement. This is very close to Saint Vincent de Paul giving advice to a young woman about to make her first visit to the poor — "It is only because of your love that the poor will forgive you the bread you give them...."

In other words, if there must be charity, it is the giver, not the receiver, who is under obligation. Vincent de Paul, like Archbishop Peers, set impossibly high standards. Who, in this society, will give their first fruit? Few enough happily give their last, mollified by the presence of a tax receipt. Who will have enough love in themselves to give it to all who are in need? What Peers, like Vincent de Paul, is talking about is the need to replace the ego of giving with the obligation. If not, the idea hidden deep inside charity is far worse than humiliation. It is punishment — we who have will decide what those who do not have deserve.

Is this too severe? I repeat — ethics is the least romantic of human qualities; the one with the hardest edge; the most demanding.

What we have seen over the last decade, as democracies have gradually abandoned public services in the hope that private money will take their place, is that the effort required by disinterested bodies to raise the funds is enormous. It can cost six times more than tax-based government funds to raise and administer charitable funds. This applies to traditional charities as it does to the arts and other non-profit causes. Charity is an expensive and inefficient way of dealing with the needs of the public good. But there I am dangerously close to the "ethics pays" syndrome.

The point is that the private approach fails by its own standards. It is wasteful. It requires an inordinate amount of expensive time to raise the funds. And these do not replace the funds lost from the public sector. Charity doesn't produce enough funds.

In the United States — the model for modern charity-giving — some $150 billion is raised annually. This is wonderfully generous. It is also peanuts when measured against public programming. What's more, the private sector — a theoretically bottomless well of money for replacing that public sector — in fact only gives some eight per cent of the total and foundations another seven per cent. Finally, it's worth remembering that any money available through private fundraising is, by definition, available through simple, efficient, inexpensive taxation.

Our reversion to charity has brought with it, to a degree not seen even during the Renaissance, an indulgence of the ego of donors. Their names are on programs, usually above that of the cause or event. People sing, dance, skate, run in their name. On public stage after public stage, thanks are sonorously given, before a sullen or uneasy audience, to the technocrats managing joint-stock companies. People are thanked. People thank each other to ensure they will be thanked in return. Where a century ago their names went onto buildings, or four centuries ago their little faces peered out of the corner of paintings which had Christ at the centre, today every wing of every building has been christened with the name of a donor. Increasingly the same is true of university lecture halls, dining halls, lobbies, waiting rooms, the tiles on the floor, the seats in which we listen to Mozart, the beds in which we lie ailing, the benches in citizen-owned parks. The oxygen mask clasped to our face may well have a plaque on it in memory of some donor's favourite child, dog or husband. And where once a name on a hospital or theatre or other public structure meant that that person had paid for it, today the common pattern is that citizen tax-payers fund eighty or ninety per cent. Then, in return for kicking in the last ten or twenty per cent, an individual gets his name on the front of a citizens' building.

"I felt the need," Tolstoy said of an early period in his life, "to be known and loved of all the world; to *name my name*, the sound of which would greatly impress everybody, so that they would troop round me and thank me for something...."[23]

The classic socialist view of charity draws obvious conclusions from all of this. Giuseppe Mazzini, the conscience of Italian reunification: "You have taught the rich man that society was constituted only to assure his rights, and you ask him then to sacrifice them all for the advancement of a class, with which he has no ties either of affection or custom. He refuses. Will you call him bad? Why should he consent? He is only logical." Interestingly enough the classic conservative, Adam Smith, says the same thing: "[H]e is certainly not a good citizen who does not wish to promote, by every means in his power, the welfare of the whole society of his fellow-citizens." Note the inclusive terminology: "good citizen", as in public good and not as in generous donor; "by every means in his power", not as he sees fit from time to time; "the welfare of the whole society", not a personally chosen charity; "his fellow citizens", and not a less fortunate and thus less important class.

Charity will always exist and, as always, will do some good. But in citizen-based societies such as ours it is only ethical when operating in the strictest of conditions. These could be summarized as an acceptance of obligation to society and therefore a removal of ego.

The point of this argument is not to demean those who give generously above and beyond their taxes, often with great modesty. And some do pay for the whole building. I am not even hitting out at the easy target of hungry self-esteem among those who are not so modest.

My only point is that charity fails as a social project. And it fails as a utilitarian methodology. It cannot be an expression of public ethics. Yet increasingly there is a consensus among technocrats, social scientists and the private sector that 'universality' or 'inclusion' is not working. That we need more *efficient*, narrowly focused systems which target some specific needs, and leave the rest to charity. This 'targeting' is a curious return of nineteenth-century poorhouse moralism combined with the most outdated managerial micromanaging of the lives of the poor.

Moralism has found a natural friend in managerialism. Both are top down, judgemental and exclusive. They impose a modern version of noblesse oblige. They happily abandon the real strengths of democracy — the real ethical strengths — which are inclusive. The efficiency proposed is false efficiency because such targeted programs, while theoretically cheaper because serving fewer people, actually tend to be more expensive because they require heavy and constant administration and monitoring. Because these are targeted, their primary obsession is control of access. Only the needy will be allowed through the gate. Need must therefore be strictly defined and monitored, case by case, minute by minute, over the years. And the greater the need of the people or structure targeted, the greater the control this approach demands.

Whatever problems our larger programs may have today relate to the confusing details of incremental laws and administration. These are not the product of universality. Simple, transparent, all-inclusive public policies set us free from bureaucratic interference, the self-interest of élites, the need of the corporations for conformity and loyalty, and of course from paternalism.

What is being suggested everywhere is the exact opposite — a reversion to old-fashioned, multitiered programming; the charitable patchwork of class-based societies. Those who have will give themselves the best tier money can buy. Having opted out, they will resist, from their positions within the power structures, the taxes and investments necessary to fund the lower, public tier of services. Not because they are bad people, but, as Mazzini pointed out, because they are logical.

Again, the temptation to cry out — ethics pays! — is very strong. Every study shows that two-tier services are more expensive — whether in Britain, Australia or the United States.[24]

Iceland has a single, all-inclusive health system and education system. The result is record-high literacy, remarkably high life expectancy and a lower percentage of GDP in taxes than countries with two-tier systems. It is the identification of tiers and the maintenance of such differences which costs money.

But again, the issue is not cost. It is ethics. There is an obligation to serve all citizens. It is not for one class or corporation to decide how the others will be served.

ETHICS DOESN'T PAY—TWO

I am not simply referring to the classic divisions between have and have not. Take a completely different example. What I call corporatism has gradually been undermining the idea of participatory democracy. We belong to our corporations. We are loyal to them.

Yet, at the same time, a new, enthusiastic sort of participation has flowered through parallel voluntary groups whose members see themselves as disinterested and driven by ethics.

They are apolitical in the sense that they function largely outside of the structures of representative democracy. With a few exceptions — the Greens in Germany, for example — they do not seek formal endorsement of the citizenry. Their approach is in the populist tradition, with all its strengths and weaknesses. The central weakness we know from history is that populism gone wrong turns into false-populism.

The generic term for these groups is NGOs, or non-governmental organizations, although not all are organized in such a formal way. Many do not see themselves as part of a parallel power structure. On the other hand, many do.

What has been exciting for democracies over the last decade has been to see tens of thousands of mainly younger citizens engaging themselves in public debate through these voluntary groups. This is their way of saying that they will not submit to what much of the official political, administrative, economic and intellectual structures insist are inevitable forces. By refusing this ideology of inevitability, they are asserting the idea of individual responsibility.

The real initiative for debate, indeed the true alternatives on environmental issues, biotechnology, human rights, transnationals, the return of monopolies and oligopolies, unregulated markets, international debt structures — in fact, pretty well every major issue of today — comes from outside of the normal democratic organizations. That means outside of the political parties or parliaments, as well as outside of the normal academic and think-tank structures.

The problem is that the NGOs tend to be specialized. They pursue issues within their particular area; you could even say within their corporatist structure. Why? Because most NGOs have defined themselves as the shadow of the corporatist structure which they oppose. Thus, they are doubly corporatist and profoundly reactive. Nevertheless, they dominate the media on those subjects, precisely because they are addressing the issues, while the corporations, whether public- or private-sector, are obscuring them.

In spite of this domination, they cannot set the agenda. The power of initiation belongs to those they oppose. The ethical good feelings they bring out in many of us mask the secondary nature of their argument.

Forty years ago they would have gained the primary initiative by carrying their issues into mainstream elective politics. Today this happens in Germany; elsewhere, scarcely at all. Parliaments used to be filled with lawyers, because in the nineteenth century we needed to create the legal infrastructure of an increasingly inclusive democracy. That was done. Now lawyers represent scarcely fifteen per cent of the elected. The same was true of teachers and education. The women's movement has slowly — all too slowly — moved into democratic politics.

My point is that the people who have set and who continue to set the ethical agenda of our time are absent from the chambers to which the citizens send their representatives. They don't want to be there. When pressed, they tend to respond that elected officials have no real power. But if they don't believe it is worth being elected, then they don't believe in democracy. If they don't believe in democracy, what do they think should replace it? And however much they believe they are right, do they not believe that the citizenry have the right to make the final decision? If so, how, since they themselves have rejected the legitimacy of the legislature? If not, how do they differentiate themselves from others who believe that it is they who are right, also reject democracy, and happen to disagree with the NGO in question? The growing neo-fascist movements, for example.

Let me come back to a central confusion which surrounds the work of these public-interest groups. Why is it that they can capture the news and block policies, yet can't set new policies? Isn't it because in democracies policies are decided in assemblies, in legislative committees, in party caucuses, in offices, in endless discussion between a multitude of elected groups, one-on-one, in small groups, formally and informally, in ministerial jockeying and argument, in the endless debate and pressuring between the elected, the ministers and the civil service? The levers of power are inside. If you're not there — elected and present — your only hope is to influence those who are. Suddenly your role is not that of a public person, but of a courtier — a lobbyist. You are on the outside, lobbying for change. Even if the cause is good, a lobbyist is a lobbyist is a lobbyist.

I'm not saying that work in parallel voluntary groups is bad. To the contrary. This is a remarkable new form of public engagement by citizens. And it is a remarkably clear response to those who say humans are driven by self-interest. The presence of thousands of citizens in the street is a sign of democratic health. All the same, there is an ethical problem and a structural problem. You could say that the more the parallel method succeeds, the more corporatism is reinforced, the more democracy is undermined.

None of which means that the NGOs necessarily fail. They can certainly stop things which appeared to be inevitable. And they can change the atmosphere. Suddenly political leaders, who for more than a decade have talked at the international level almost exclusively about inevitable economic forces, are beginning to talk of social issues.

Coming out of the G8 Summit in Genoa, Tony Blair of Britain protested angrily that he was elected by the citizenry and the protesters were not. True and untrue. The unelected nature of such a

powerful movement does threaten democracy. But that threat is itself
created when political parties and their leaders do not articulate the
concerns of the citizenry in order to lead. Citizens are not very interested in leaders who say they want power but protest they cannot
actually use it because they feel victimized by forces of inevitability.
Their passivity promotes parallel groups up to a role of leadership.

And yet, Prime Minister Blair is also right. The NGOs are nearing
an intersection where the forces at play cancel each other out. It
would be difficult for them to have more power to stop things and less
power to make changes in public policy. The result is that governments and corporations now want to talk to them. To consult them.
This is the Sirens' call to influence change. But in what role? The more
the NGOs slip in the direction of the non-elected insider, the more
they will lose their public support.

What I am suggesting is that each generation has limited opportunities to improve its society. A few succeed. Many have an impact. Many
more miss their opportunity, in spite of expending great, well-
intentioned and intelligent efforts. The European reformers of 1848
marched up a steep incline to a mountaintop from which they dominated the continent's imagination and political structures. Then,
abruptly, unable to convert this power into mainstream structures, they
plunged off the other side into failure and left their societies with terrible
unresolved ethical issues. These led, in part, to the First World War.

The success and failure of the reformers of 1900–14 was even
more dramatic. They were convinced of their grasp on the situation.
This is an interesting example for today's NGOs, because the basis of
power — or rather influence — for the early-twentieth-century
reformers was the union structure; in other words, well-intentioned
corporations which were shadows of interest-based corporations.
Unions a hundred years ago filled almost exactly the same space as
NGOs do today. And those unions had a fervent, well-structured,
well-organized membership of many millions. These individuals had
a real experience of difficult public demonstrations. They had

stubborn persistence. Their élite was tightly linked to the mass of their members. They were far more profoundly anchored in society than most contemporary leadership-driven NGOs. Even their most interest-driven campaigns were part of inclusive, clearly expressed, ethical arguments. What's more, they had great confidence in their international structures. They were constantly meeting on a pan-European level. They had developed clear, solid strategies to oppose any continent-wide conflict. And these strategies were repeatedly supported on all sides. Bluntly put, they were all agreed that should war be declared they would not fight. Given their numbers, war would therefore be impossible.

Then the crisis came. War was declared, and to everyone's astonishment, their strength dissolved, slipped away, and one of the most catastrophic bloodbaths of history began.[25]

In other words, there is an intimate relationship between ethics and responsible individualism. Yes, elective politics is often unpleasant, destructive of personal lives, and of families.

But if you live in a democracy and believe legitimacy lies with the people and want to see changes in society, getting elected is the ultimate way to ensure that society will act ethically. I'm not for a moment suggesting that those involved in NGOs transform parliaments into a bric-à-brac of interest groups. I'm talking about the need for each generation to integrate its ethical causes into the mainstream of public debate.

THE ETHICAL IMPERATIVE

According to Aristotle we do have a sense of the just and the unjust. And that quality — in part ethics, in part instinct — makes us a whole.[26] A *polis*. A common understanding of people.

John Rawls, in his typical combination of good intentions and utilitarianism, concludes that that common understanding is about fairness. Well, if justice were only that; if ethics were merely fairness, we could have ended this debate shortly after it opened a few thousand years ago.

Fair or unfair, the foundations of ethics are under constant attack from two forces. The first — ideology posing as truth and the accompanying inevitability of belief — I have already dealt with. The second is the constant ambition of self-interest. In Wilfrid Laurier's words, "this leads to venality, to the flattening of consciences, to this infamous behaviour that surrounds us." Laurier was simply reformulating what lies at the core of all our ethical philosophies:

Buddha:
: "[E]conomic and material happiness is 'not worth one sixteenth part' of the spiritual happiness arising out of a faultless and good life."

The Koran:
: "Your hearts are taken up with worldly gain from the cradle to the grave.

But you shall know. You shall before long come to know.

Indeed, if you knew the truth with certainty, you would see the fire of Hell...."

Euripides:
: "[I]nside the souls of wealthy men bleak famine lives...

How then can man distinguish man, what test can he use?

The test of wealth? That measure means poverty of mind."

Sophocles:
: "Money, gentlemen, money! The virus That infects mankind with every sickness We have a name for, no greater scourge Than that! Money it is that pounds Great cities to piles of rubble, turns people By the millions into homeless refugees,

> Takes homeless citizens and corrupts them
> Into doing things they would be ashamed to think of
> Before the fee was mentioned...."

Harry Truman: "Glenn Martin was making B-26 bombers, and they were crashing and killing kids right and left. So I said to Martin, 'What's wrong with these planes?'
— He said, 'The wing-spread isn't wide enough.'
— So I said, 'Then why aren't you making it wider?'
— And he said, 'I don't have to...and besides, I've got a contract.'
— So I said, 'All right. If that's the way you feel, I'll see to it that your contract is cancelled and you won't get another.'
— 'Oh,' he says, 'if that's the way it's going to be, we'll fix it,' and he did.

Aung San Suu Kyi, still under house arrest, while American, British and French oil companies feed the junta's bank accounts in order to build and exploit a pipeline through the jungle with what respectable people say is slave labour:

> If they think there's a chance to make money, they are not
> very concerned about the political situation — unless, of
> course, it affects their business.

The message would appear to be that, in Aurel Kolnai's words, "attending with care to one's business is not an outstanding moral merit." Solon's warning two and a half millennia before comes floating back into mind: "The public evil enters the house of each man, the gates of his courtyard cannot keep it out...."

The point of this litany is not to argue that self-interest or business is bad; but that they cannot lead in a decent society. Society must lead them.

This leadership serves society, but may well come at a price. There is a German phrase, *Die Gerechten müssen viel leiden. The just must suffer a lot.* Well, only a few among us are up to being that just. And often (again the tempting 'ethics pays!') our ethical policies may produce prosperity. The Marshall Plan is the standard example. "Our policy is directed not against any country or doctrine," General Marshall said, "but against hunger, poverty, desperation and chaos." The point is, this was public policy, not economics. Neither ethics nor responsible individualism nor democracy is about prosperity. You can have prosperity without any ethics, responsible individualism and democracy. Or indeed you can have it with. As usual, Socrates said it with the greatest clarity, "Justice is virtue and wisdom" and "injustice is vice and ignorance." But, he added, "injustice is powerful."27

And that is why, in a sensible society, ethics is more likely to cost than to pay. To cost a life or a career. Certainly to cost time, to leave scars. It is inconvenient, often embarrassing. It means standing out, taking the marshalled criticism of well-organized conformists who see ethics as a threat to their self-pride. Why well-organized? Conformists are the natural men and women of structure. It was easy for a man of Confucius's ethical strength to say, "One who is free to choose, yet does not prefer to dwell among the Good — how can he be accorded the name of wise?" That is choice, stated with unforgiving clarity. Hiding behind a bit of irony, Voltaire claimed only, "J'ai fait un peu de bien, c'est mon meilleur ouvrage."

What makes it possible to choose and to pay the cost? Sensible thinkers have repeatedly referred to something which could be called 'ethical insight'. This is the muscle which must be exercised if we are to deal with myriad tiny daily ethical tests and the periodic larger ones.

●

NORMALIZING NO

How then do you exercise that muscle? How do you make it as normal as possible to exercise? Note that I didn't say, 'as easy as possible'. Ethics has never been easy, but it can approach normal behaviour.

And so there is a permanent tension in ethics between normal and difficult. You can see this in our legal systems. "In a legalistic society," ethicist Margaret Somerville says, "...the law replaces morality and ethics."[28] That is, the law converts our knowledge of standards into enforceable standards. And these standards — these laws — are designed to create a solid wall of ethics which will protect us. That is what we mean when we talk about *justice* being the enforcement of *the spirit of our laws* as opposed to *the letter of the law*.

The letter of the law is understood by citizens to mean the betrayal of justice; that is, the betrayal of ethics. Utilitarianism and corporatism are dependent upon law being reduced to its letter at the expense of its spirit.

So the law in its spirit is intended to provide enforceable standards. But that protection also weakens the citizen's reflexes. After all, a law can only work if individuals believe it is an expression of justice, and so wish it to be enforced. If we do believe, then we let down our guard and begin to forget that ethics costs. Like all living things, ethics also requires constant attention and consideration. If we forget this, then a social crisis will follow. The clearest example of what happens can be seen in the state of our commercial laws.

We have now severely confused the law of the public good — the spirit of the law — with that of commercial law; the social contract with the commercial contract. That is why we slip so easily towards an unsatisfactory reliance on utilitarianism, as if believing it was part and parcel of ethical behaviour. The confusion is so great that theoretically intelligent people, such as John Rawls, devote themselves to arguments which treat this confusion as intentional. And as in any argument which attempts to equate civilization with contractual arrangements, he unintentionally opens up the door to those who believe that society is merely interest-driven.

The heart of the confusion between the social contract and the commercial contract lies in an intriguing, old legalistic fiction: that a company is a person before the law. Of course we all know that we are people and a company isn't; that we are incredibly complex humans, and they are merely banal linear devices to advance commercial interests. That they are driven by self-interest and we are not. To believe that a company is a person has required from us an incredibly sophisticated — to say nothing of indulgent — theatrical suspension of disbelief.

The British more or less came up with this theatrical device two hundred years ago in the early industrial revolution. Its purpose was to facilitate the creation of debt in order to encourage the creation of larger joint-stock companies. This brilliantly imaginative gamble accomplished what it was intended to accomplish.

We are now surrounded by large joint-stock companies. In fact, the fiction of their corporal nature is now damaging the healthy market it was invented to create. It is helping the largest of these *people* — the transnationals — to avoid competition, in part by engaging in a sort of ethnic cleansing of the medium and small companies. What began as an incubation tool for undersized, premature, commercial babies has become a mechanism of ferocious cannibalism, in which the obese consume everything small, and to no good economic purpose.

In fact, this device is now used in a wide variety of ways to limit free markets. Take the libel laws — an ethical tool for citizens to use to protect their freedom of speech. Today the fictive corporate humans are able to combine deep pockets and these libel laws in order to discourage, even prevent, real citizens from questioning the companies' methods and products, to decrease transparency, to discourage debate, to hide errors and to justify price-fixing.

It isn't surprising in an increasingly corporatist society that more and more individual citizens — the flesh-and-blood sort — feel obliged to turn themselves into a fictional person — a personal company. Fictional people have better tax rates than real people. And, while the law is strict with real people, it is virtually impossible to hold private-sector technocrats, public sector technocrats and all sorts of non-profit agency technocrats responsible for their actions. Thus, by becoming a legal person, a real person protects himself from much of the law.

Nothing prevents us from suspending our willing suspension of disbelief. This wouldn't be complicated. And such a small legal change would, quite suddenly, release us from much of the corporatist stranglehold. The human status conferred upon private companies has had a structural effect on all corporations, from government departments to professional associations. It has created the context for aggressive loyalty to the group, which has done so much damage to ethics as a daily reality.

Tied to the fictive legal person is an astonishing legal/administrative/managerial control over knowledge and ideas and, as a result, over the freedom of speech of employees. This control is maintained through the legal structures of employment. You could call it the tyranny of the employment contract.

We take these banal employment contracts for granted. We believe they work for all parties as the legal guarantor of our relationships. And in some ways they do. But if you examine the utilitarian wall which separates the corporation — private, public, non-profit — from society, it is the employment contract. Ethics is publicly silenced behind these walls.

How? Well, this is the contractual mechanism by which the employer purchases the knowledge of the employee, along with her skill to explain and apply that knowledge. And yet this knowledge and these skills are not primarily utilitarian. They give form to important — often the most important — contributions the individual has to make to society, including ethical contributions.

Instead, abruptly, through a banal interest-based contract, these talents are legally removed from the commonweal. Of course, corporations and governments have a right to something for their money. They pay the wages. But they don't have the ethical right to literally purchase the copyright of a citizen's potential contribution to society. In a democracy they should not have the legal right to silence the quasi-totality of the functioning élite in order to satisfy a managerial taste for control and secrecy.

Silence? Surely there is a great deal of public debate. Yes and no. There is debate. But the people who have the specialist skills and knowledge on any side of a debate are not free to take part. Why? Because they are contracted to one side or the other. And employment regulations determine the nature of their public involvement. If they are present, it is only as 'spokespeople' for interests. There is almost no possibility of disinterested participation.

In short, our society has structured itself to prevent most people who know something about a given issue from expressing their concerns, their disagreement, even their real agreement. We have created a structure which removes ethics from our daily life and makes it abnormal to flex our ethical muscle, abnormal to say no. Loyalty replaces ethics. Only through heroic opposition, which will probably damage her career and the well-being of her family, can a citizen express concerns in the areas she knows best.

This raising of her voice may or may not be as heroic as the good deaths of Socrates, Moulin and Saro-Wiwa. It may or may not require the courage of Aung San Suu Kyi or the ethical stubbornness of Dallaire. But the point is not to measure each person's contribution. Rather it is to ensure the constant flexing of the ethical muscle.

It could be argued that today's equivalent of the Athenian debts faced by Solon is the employment contract. After all, here is the chief structural limitation on the citizen's normal, daily freedom to participate in public affairs in an ethical manner. Compare our legal theories of free speech to the very real constraints which now exist.

Just as Solon's solution to an impossible situation was relatively simple, so it would be relatively easy to create employment arrangements which are more 'minimalist' — which are designed to encourage rather than limit and control citizen participation. The normalization of ethics is dependent upon that participation and upon the normalcy of saying no.

These legal changes could be as simple as the decision two centuries ago to pretend that companies were people. The effect could resemble a "breaking of the chains", as Solon once put it.

Democracy can provide the kind of profound stability which allows us to engage in a permanent and happily unstable examination of our ethical choices. I would call this the common-sense view of ethics. The imaginative view allows us to project possible ethical realities. Our memory of what has turned out to be right and wrong, of what has led us astray or helped, is another element. As is that of the practical, instinctual reflex. To say nothing of the rational analysis which, if used properly, will help us understand the shading of our unstable reflections, instead of trying to control them.

If you fold all of this together it produces a culture of ethics which can help us at each instant. Making an ethical choice depends on how we imagine ourselves, what we admire, how we are willing to be admired, what we are prepared to say we admire.

Few would deny that a million daily habits can inextricably lead us deep into utilitarianism and conformity. We know this about ourselves. We have always known it.

But utility and conformity don't need to be the norm. Certainly, marginalized ethics is not normal. It's just that utility and conformity are easy and apparently simple, while the assumption of our own ethics is complex, costly and difficult. Which is why the first step for each of us is learning how to say no. The habit of refusal breaks the pattern of linear conformity.

No to what? In general, no to the facile whenever possible. And to the inevitable.

The capacity to do that, today as before, urgently requires the demotion of self-interest and utilitarianism — in our imaginations and in our structures. How could we describe its replacement? To say that a sense of the public good, of social responsibility, of ethics, belongs at the core of society may seem too earnest for some. Perhaps a better way of putting it is that we need to admire and encourage the individual courage or unpredictability of non-conformity at every level — not just the heroic, but also in the repetitive minutiae of our lives. You might call this the capacity to say no as a normal reflex of daily life. The first step beyond no — not towards acceptance, but towards consideration — would be to strengthen our desire to participate in the formulation of the question.

CHAPTER FOUR

IMAGINATION

Kindly control your imagination.
That is what makes men beasts.

August Strindberg[1]

Or romantic fools. Or plain fools. Or so the *responsible* argument goes. Imagination is useful for diversion, for the tired in need of distraction. And useful also to society, if properly organized, directed and licensed. Apart from that, it is troublesome, dangerous.

But if that is the case, how do you leap off a cliff and fly? First you imagine you can do it. Then, in some combination of memory, instinct, common sense and rational analysis, you work out how to do it. And, all the way through that often long and twisted process, you keep on imagining it happening. Or rather, you reimagine it in evolving forms as you progress. Then, in the twinkling of an eye — less than a century in fact — you can do it seated uncomfortably with hundreds of fellow passengers in a jet, or alone, on the cliff, with a simple apparatus of kite-like wings.

This suggests that imagination isn't really a means of distraction. Nor is it an unquantifiable wild card which needs to be saved from itself by responsible organizers. This is the quality which most naturally draws all of our other qualities together. But it does so in a swirling uncertainty — a prolonged swirling uncertainty. It is that uncertainty which makes progress possible.

Imagination protects us from the temptation of premature conclusions; the temptation of certainty and the fantasy of fixed truth. What's more, it seems to draw us forward by using this prolonged uncertainty to alternately leap ahead and then enfold our other qualities — our other means of perception — into a new, inclusive vision of the whole. Then, just as we *think* we understand, it leaps ahead again into more uncertainty. And so imagination appears to be naturally inclusive and inconclusive.

As an inclusive quality, imagination is thus our primary force for progress, whatever progress is. That has never been very clear, except that it doesn't take itself too seriously. It doesn't know enough about where it's going to claim solid respectability. Jump off cliffs? How? Why? To save people? To transport them? To visit the one you love? To impress her? To have a look around? For sheer pleasure? To drop bombs on people from above? The inclusive nature of imagination accepts naturally all of the above. One purpose does not exclude another, unless ethics intervenes or memory, for example. There is no natural order of precedence. The market 'need' for faster transport is not necessarily the driving force either of the original idea or of the process; that is, the progress. Neither is love, although it might as likely be.

Certainly no concrete difference — and therefore order of precedence — has ever been established between imagining for one purpose or another. The ability to perceive a machine which doesn't exist — a printing press, for example — is like the perception of a society. Both involve imagining relationships.

And being so uncertain of itself, so unwilling to lock itself into truths, imagination quite comfortably interlocks with irony, a form of humour which leaves doors open, evolution fluid. It is irony which makes the managers of power most uncomfortable. They will attack it as scepticism, even cynicism — neither of which it is. But then, the way they see life — their lives — the assurance that they are being taken seriously is one of the necessary burdens of authority.

The great Austrian novelist Joseph Roth poked away at such self-importance in his masterpiece *Flight Without End*: "I have invented nothing, made up nothing. The question of 'poetic invention' is no longer relevant. Observed fact is all that counts."[2] Irony is our instrumental protection from false certainty. It keeps our imagination free to function. This is not about being elusive, Northrop Frye argued, but about avoiding unnecessary answers. "[T]o answer such a question is to consolidate the mental level on which the question is asked. Unless something is kept in reserve, suggesting the possibility of better and fuller questions, [our] mental advance is blocked."[3]

Let me go back to the idea that imagination is the force of progress. We are more or less capable of moving through time, propelled by common sense and memory. But what stops us from bogging down?

Imagination energizes the norm. This suggests it is not merely contemplative — though it needs contemplation. And it certainly isn't secretive. It is perhaps our most aggressive quality. Yet this ambition is not based on self-interest. One of our most beloved clichés is that we need self-interest to motivate ourselves. Well, we certainly have self-interest. No doubt we need it. But not to motivate us. If anything, self-interest slows us down because it most often focuses on accumulation and on the short term.

If anything, imagination is more likely to serve disinterest. After all, being naturally inclusive, even more than ethics, imagination enables us to conceive of the *other*. This will not automatically produce empathy. That will depend on the degree to which our swirling, uncertain imagining draws in other qualities.

But the inclusiveness is there. And that makes imagination the source of public policy and public programming. The impression today is that these two things are the children of specialists and analysts and managers, and so perhaps of reason. But public policy is driven by ideas — incomplete, aggressive, inclusive ideas. That is the nature of the public good. And once in place, these policies can only survive if they continue to be led by ideas — by the imagination. The moment their direction slips into managerial logic, they begin to fall apart, because they are no longer linked directly to the reality and the collective unconscious of the society.

The point to be drawn from this is that imagination propels itself. And not in some mystical way. Imagination is encouraged by the habit of imagining. You see here the return of the theme of balance and of normalization. Because to imagine without the context of our other qualities is to decline into fantasy.

●

"FEAR FIRST CREATED GODS IN THE WORLD."

Statius, *Thebaid*, AD 93

Gods to protect us from fear are gods to protect us from the necessity of imagining our long past and the probability of tomorrow. Gods give us truth. We can deny all the rest.

And what is a god? Rarely the complex figure imagined in most religious texts. Usually a certainty. A totem of some sort. A structure. A way of doing things. Something asserted to be progress, or efficient. Something asserted to be the way things are done. All that such belief requires is a willingness not to imagine. You may continue to think, but in a linear manner from the base of truth, not in a lateral or a pre-objective manner.

Not to allow yourself to imagine is a choice. It is choosing not to have a choice. In a sense, that is your problem. Although to choose not to choose can quickly take on a force of its own. Because we live in societies, it means that you must then discourage others from imagining. How else can you live with them? That is the story of religious or racial wars. Or of self-destructive social attitudes.

●

COWS AND SHEEP

In 1996 in Britain there were clear public rumours of a new disease afoot. Bovine spongiform encephalopathy, Creutzfeldt-Jacob disease, mad cow disease. In some cases it struck cows, in others humans. The rumour was that the cow variety could leap to humans if you ate the meat of a sick animal. And as the incubation period was thought to be up to a decade, the farmer would have no direct warning before he sold his animal. The rumour continued that authorities had known about this for years and had hidden it. The cause it seemed was commercial feed which contained dead sheep. The resulting disease led to a particularly humiliating form of death.

Interestingly enough, this rumour seemed to have been started by the expert scientists in the public service. It was the managers — technocrats — of government, industry and agriculture who denied it. They said there was no scientific proof that such a leap was possible.

The scientists on the other hand were saying something very specific, something filled with imagination. Their argument was a force of progress. It was that they didn't need proof. They knew enough. They were capable of lateral thinking. They could imagine the probabilities.

In other words, the non-scientists wanted to apply the false science of absolute proof, which does not exist in the real world of scientific work. They didn't want to think about reality. They wanted truth. Religion. Absolute belief. They wanted a god. They had no sense of the imaginary nature of science. "No scientific theory," Jacob Bronowski said, "is a collection of facts. It will not even do to call a theory true or false in the simple sense in which every fact is either so or not so."⁴ Or "In the language of science, every fact is a field — a crisscross of implications."

Why is this such an interesting story? Because the denial of imagination is so central. Why did those who administered public policy, along with the cattle industry and the fertilizer industry, defend something so desperately which any fool could see was slipping towards disaster? The easy answer would be that public policy had been captured by industry; that self-interest mainly exists in the short term; and if left to its own devices it is usually self-destructive. This answer is partly true. All parties in charge were deeply committed to a minor god called economic certainty.

But the major god here is the one most animated by fear: the desperate belief that humans can order and reorder nature as we wish. For those in authority, the very idea that nature might not passively respond to their ideas of structure is terrifying. It suggests they do not have the power they need to believe they have.

The quality which most naturally undermines their assertion of certainty is imagination. They know that the best way to control it is to insist on belief. Belief in what? Why, in truth of course. The modern truth of utilitarian structure. Northrop Frye's suggestion that you should always avoid unnecessary answers, avoid making up your mind too soon, would be terrifying to them. And so they leapt upon a new, if minor, idea — feeding dead sheep to cows — proclaimed it a truth, and so consolidated their understanding at an infantile level. I say infantile both because the idea was in its first stages, unfit for general application, and because the untamed curiosity and imagination of any child past infancy would have seen through their posturing if given a chance.

Humans generally eat the meat of herbivores. Cows have always been herbivores. Wouldn't it have been worth wondering whether turning herbivores into carnivores might not have some side effects on the cows, let alone the humans?

Such simple questions would have suggested that there were not even the beginnings of a truth to be established and declared; that authority could not maintain a structure on the basis of this new idea. As I said, enforced loyalty to declared truth is the way to marginalize the imagination. There is a certain irony in this case that the basis of our conformity was to be unquestioning belief in the adaptability of sheep.

THE NORMALIZATION OF IMAGINING

To normalize imagination is not to quantify it. Nor is it to structure cultural industries or build cultural buildings. These may be good things, but they are part of a separate issue.

Normalization means creating the social conditions which will allow imagination to flower for whatever reason.

The most obvious form of normalization is social context. It is no accident that great creators often begin from a context in which originality of thought or creativity is the norm. The father of John Cage, the modern American composer, was a successful inventor, which was where the son learnt that it was good to think what no one else was thinking and necessary to fight for your ideas. Mozart, with a highly professional but mediocre composer/performer father, was brought up with the skills. All that was needed was genius, or even talent, for those skills to spring to life. Of course, both Cage and Mozart are examples of creative privilege. Equally great genius can pop out of totally unsympathetic surroundings. Whatever its origins, creativity is not meant to be an heroic model. That would be an invitation to passivity — a false populist trap set through romantic Heroism by philosophers such as Schopenhauer and Thomas Carlyle with models such as Napoleon.

Normalizing imagination may mean a family pattern, or a school atmosphere or the respect in which public debate is held. These may be broader, less intense versions of what Cage and Mozart experienced, but they are part of a context which releases imagination by encouraging and admiring it.

How can the imagination play a role in our societies? Look at those communities where conditions most discourage its normalization. Strindberg would point to the upper-middle-class neighbourhoods in each city, arguing that imagination could only endanger what has been amassed, and so it must be controlled. Yet, to the extent that that might be true, it would be a situation of choice and therefore capable of reversal.

Look instead at the most isolated communities in our societies. The aboriginal settlements in Australia, Canada and the United States come to mind. But look at the other isolations — the small towns deep in the hinterlands; the nineteenth-century industrial centres without economic purpose in parts of the old East Germany and northern France; the poor shapeless suburbs which lie on the edge of our cities; the slums which surround most developing-world cities, modern versions of our nineteenth-century industrial revolution slums. Each of these is different, yet each is faced by the same problem: how to imagine itself.

The utilitarian will say of the people in these communities that if they got jobs they wouldn't have their problems of alcoholism, drug addiction, violence and suicide. And that a proper education — by which they usually mean training — would get them a proper job. But every study done shows that the real barrier to academic success in these places is social inadaption. And what are these barriers? Essentially that the old industrial centres, the isolated towns and the aboriginal communities and the new slums, have lost a reflection of who they are and why. Or they have had it smashed by others. And so they can only imagine themselves in models delivered by civil servants, economists, businessmen and television from elsewhere. And these models, if people in East Germany or Labrador or central Australia try to fit them into their imagination, make no sense at all.

For a start, the chief effect of the education offered is to oblige the person to leave where they live. Alienation at its most essential level is not poverty or unemployment. It is the inability to imagine your society and therefore to imagine yourself in it. No quantity of commonsensical or ethical or rational activity, no matter how well-intentioned, can lessen the alienation of being unable to imagine yourself. The core of the problem again is how to normalize imagination as an expression of each community, in a way which makes sense for itself, in the same sense that John Cage, growing up with an inventor, saw how he could, in normalized terms, imagine new music.

This is tied to the built-in aggressivity of our qualities. Cage described his mentor, Arnold Schönberg, as "a fighter from the word go".[5]

Consider this in the context of ethics. It is one thing to have the sense of a non-conforming act and its relationship to other people. But the act itself must still be imagined. You must imagine yourself in the mirror of society. Immediately after the last World War, Albert Camus attempted to explain in a public argument why he had chosen resistance over collaboration or, as was most common, over abdication and personal survival. "The question makes no sense.... I couldn't imagine myself elsewhere, that's all." And then added something damning for those who think that all imagination needs in order to become helpful and not dangerous is organization. "Then I understood that I detested less the violence, than the institutions of violence."[6]

What keeps getting in the way of our imagination is the stubborn Platonist conviction that the intellect — reason — "is so much more powerful than the imagination". That is the fifteenth-century formula of Marsilio Ficino.[7] It was 'modernized' through Descartes's insistence on the separation of understanding from imagination, with understanding dominant. By the eighteenth century, many had begun to feel that this Platonist approach led nowhere. It was dependent on the institutionalization of imbalance — one quality would dominate all others — which in turn institutionalized the idea of opposing qualities. Thus the greater the reason, the less the imagination.[8]

How then could imagination do its job? For example, how could imagination whip reason out of its satisfaction with the present, which, given its belief in answers and truth, it mistakes for the future?

There is a flatness in the "immortality of the present," George Steiner writes. What is missing is imagination: the unverifiable or poetic, "...the potentiality of fictions [which] leap into tomorrows without end..."9

The theoretically scathing response from those who feel a constant need 'to get on with things' would be that intellectual disorder is unhelpful romanticism. But it is they who are genuinely surprised when their idea of a clarified future turns out to be a misidentified present — for example, those uncooperative dead sheep. What I am describing is an incapacity to live inside a necessary fiction; one in which you imagine in order to understand the real risks involved in your metaphysics. If you can't live with the implications of uncertainty, you lock yourself into the old conundrum: logic is the art of going wrong with confidence.

Not that reason can't play a positive role in helping imagination to fill its normal role. It is there to encourage further questioning by regularizing the process of dissent. But to play this role, reason must be kept in discomfort; kept away from its taste for self-satisfaction; balanced with imagination in order to enjoy the uncertainty of dissent.

We cannot live this uncertainty to its full every moment of our day in every area. We must — there's no denying it — get on with things. But the reflex of uncertainty and dissent must be there, to be flashed out at any moment. What do I mean? That today we have the reflex of certainty and conformity on any issue that matters. Put aside our celebration of non-conformity on marginal self-indulgent issues. Examine the questions that shape our lives and our society. You'll see that certainty is the admired reflex. If not, where were the voices through the 1990s which could easily have been raised, from a thousand directions, to question the process which led to mad cow disease? Each of us can identify quantities of other examples around us.

"Science has bred the love of originality as a mark of independence," Jacob Bronowski wrote. "Independence, originality, and therefore dissent."[10]

Where is that independence today? Where the dissent? Not the independence and dissent of a few brave souls. Where is the normalized independence and dissent which you would expect in a free, developed, educated, prosperous society?

Instead, we are taught that public — even privately expressed — disagreement is unprofessional, romantic and disloyal. Besides, it will damage our careers. "Has there ever been a society which has died of dissent?" Bronowski asked. "Several have died of conformity in our lifetime."

I am not suggesting a celebration of disagreement and refusal for the mere pleasure of it. Although better to celebrate the pleasure of dissent than of conformity. There is the need, as Camus put it, "to balance the real and the refusal which man asserts against this reality". Why? Because it is this act of agitating which makes us function. It is a form of progress. Strindberg, in his non-ironic voice, put it that "Water which has remained stationary and silent for too long becomes rotten." Or, Bronowski again: "Dissent is not itself an end; it is the surface mark of a deeper value. Dissent is the mark of freedom, as originality is the mark of independence of mind!"

The final element in this constant rebalancing of our need for uncertainty versus our weakness for certainty is the ability of imagination to bring memory into the present and the future. It allows us to tell the stories which link our experience with our ongoing life. Vico wrote of a necessary *fantasia*. Not fantasy — and I will come back to this — but the ability to actualize our memory; to bring it alive, in the present tense, into today's world.

The Truth and Reconciliation Commission in South Africa allowed people to do just that. Some activists had wanted clear decisions on guilt versus innocence, and punishment versus freedom. This was the standard managerial élite position: what was required was a linear process with measurable outcomes. Innocence or guilt.

And if the constituted structures had committed errors, the structure itself would not have to admit to it.

An admission of fault is taken to be weakness. Real men may accept adjudicated guilt, but they don't apologize.

Others, like Baba Sikwepere, who had been shot, beaten to disfigurement and blinded, wanted something quite different.

> I feel what has been making me sick all the time is the fact that I couldn't tell my story. But now I — it feels like I got my sight back by coming here and telling you the story. [11]

He is still blind. What is the sight he has regained? The ability to imagine himself and his experience as a public part of a society's experience; its self-declared reality. His sight is that he can now be seen by others through his story. For them he has become part of the empathized *other*. You might say his self-esteem has been re-established through his imagination and that of others.

This reimagining — reconfiguring — of memory is a key element in the absorbing of all our qualities into the creative process. You could say that this is one of the toughest artistic creations: to look at a past which is known and to give it a new life. Painters capture images up through the ages, reinterpreting them in each era as something new. Arguments, phrases, dramatic situations, are reinvented dozens of times, each successful version being a reimagining of the past into the present. Novelists are perfectly conscious that they are working with the material of others, as are philosophers or poets.

We are not all great or even good artists. But we are all intrinsically part of the imagination's inclusive nature. Those who believe in the dominance of understanding and methodology seem to miss the obvious. The tools they consider marginal — those of the arts — are in fact the tools of storytelling and reimagining ourselves which all humans use. And why do we use them? In order to convince ourselves that we exist as humans and as individuals in a society.

TRANSCENDING THE SELF

I said earlier that imagination was the most inclusive of our qualities; that it could effortlessly draw all of the others together in a balanced manner. Not surprisingly it also has the ability to draw together humans — all of us — who are separated by our limited perceptions of reality.

God knows there is great value in our concrete differences. They are our daily primary identity and comfort. But a human who knows only his personal or local reality may be tempted into thinking that the *other*, the human across the street or in the next town or of another colour or language or social condition, does not really exist. Not as a human.

Transcending the self is about imagining the *other*; not to weaken the self, but to be capable of reaching beyond it. No convincing argument has yet been made which limits you or myself to our self-interest. In "Ethics," I quoted Adam Smith, the supposed philosopher of self-interest, repeatedly arguing the exact opposite. His approach takes on its full sense in the context of imagination. Throughout *The Theory of Moral Sentiments* and its subsidiary volume, *The Wealth of Nations*, he very carefully placed the selfish within us on a lower, less interesting level than qualities such as ethics and imagination. The opening sentence of *Moral Sentiments* summarizes, with irony and understatement, what he will show over hundreds of pages:

> How selfish soever man may be supposed, there are evidently some principles in his nature, which interest him in the fortune of others, and render their happiness to him, though he derives nothing from it except the pleasure of seeing it.[12]

However selfish we are supposed to be! Smith then sets out to explore how we can learn to transcend ourselves. We can't have an "immediate experience" of what others experience or feel. We can only try to conceive what they experience and feel. "[I]t is by the imagination only that we can form any conception of what are his sensations. . . . By the imagination we place ourselves in his situation."

Here is the heart of how our societies function. The jury — for example — struggles with its shared knowledge. Its common sense. What is the element — the quality — which allows it to reach beyond itself to a sense of the *other* and therefore of justice? Imagination. And what is it which allows us to reach beyond our personal comfort to support universal public programs such as health care and education? Not pity or noblesse oblige or charity. Rather it is our ability to imagine the *other*.

Any marginalization of this central role of the imagination is an attempt at dehumanization. The denial of imagination as a central quality in the conceptualization of societies is an attempt to deny the *other*.

What are the signs of such a denial? First, a belief in the primacy of self-interest. Then there is the belief that a healthy imagination is reserved for a few superior people. That is the Heroic model. A variation on this is the belief that imagination is strongest, in fact only really functions fully, in marginal, rather unstable people. Pure scientists and artists are the usual examples.

Related to this is a belief that the imagination, and the use of the imagination, is fundamentally romantic. This is one of the most dangerous mechanisms of marginalization. If we say imagination is wonderful, essential even, but its source is limited and unstable, then the door to power is opened wide. To whom? To those with the least imagination. They come patronizingly through, announcing that they must therefore structure the inspired babbling of the imaginative.

Listen to Schopenhauer, so often wrong, here both right and wrong.

> The man who is endowed with imagination is able, as it
> were, to call up spirits, who at the right time reveal to him
> the truths which the naked reality of things exhibits only
> weakly, rarely, and then for the most part at the wrong time.
> Therefore the man without imagination is related to him, as
> the mussel fastened to its rock....[13]

He stabs at a description of the imaginative process with all his talent, but can only see it as an élitist privilege. Only some are blessed. And even then the process of imagining is mystical, almost religious. He who imagines is a priest-like figure, able "to call up spirits". They "reveal" "truths". This is not someone capable of playing a normal, central role in society. The imagination belongs to the oracle or the sage; the one "endowed"; the strange figure living in isolation in the cave or out in the desert. We are dependent on him, yes. This is an élite, yes, but a marginal élite. The artist as religious prophet.

Here in sum are all the elements of the romantic slur. As with ethics, imagination has been romantically ennobled in order to get it out of the way of real life. Of business. Of self-interest. Of looking after ourselves. If it is romantic, the property of a difficult élite, something which takes place at inaccessible levels, well then we don't have to imagine the *other*. We needn't bother "by the imagination [t]o place ourselves in his situation". Instead, in our own romantic way, we may feel superior pity or wallow in a desire to be distracted, and so extend our charity — our noblesse oblige — to those in need, whether the suffering or the artists.

It is difficult to adequately express the damage done to our use of ethics and imagination by the romantic movement of the nineteenth century. This romanticism was basically a reaction to the dominance of rationality in the arguments of the eighteenth century — or rather to the impossibility of actually living with such a high level of abstraction.

The arrival of Goethe's *Young Werther* in 1774, the first modern romantic hero, angst-ridden, weeping, suicidal, was just what was needed. And the genius of what was said and written by many of the romantics over the next century speaks for itself. But the movement was one of reaction; a shadow of the phenomenon it opposed, drawing its life from the apparent. And so romanticism is the shadow-life of reason. This is an inextricably entwined love affair, full of battle and built upon the fundamental dependence of the romantic. Put another way, the more remarkable the romantic expression, the more it reinforces the ideology of a rationally led world.

It isn't surprising, therefore, that the rise of romanticism led to attempts at defining and measuring the imagination. What could be more romantic than the idea of measuring imagination? At the same time the idea that imagination was full of uncontrolled emotion, swooning, tempers, congenital instability, made its way. "Kindly control your imagination. That is what makes men beasts."

I spoke of the romantic slur. In a corporatist world built on self-interest, romanticism is the ultimate false compliment, designed to increase marginalization. Yet if you were to look for the equivalent of Young Werther's uncontrolled passion today, where would you find it? Put aside *first love*, which always exists and which wasn't really the subject of *Werther*. You certainly wouldn't find it among artists or scientists. Their minds and lives are more likely to be driven by uncertainty. The most obvious equivalent would be the marketplace, with its romantic obsessions. Think of its newly discovered truths which must be pursued until fortune or bankruptcy. Or consider the juvenile pure truths of neo-conservative economists, with their belief that they are "endowed" of a mystical ability "to call up [the] spirits" of inevitable forces and natural non-human balances which will "reveal to them the truths", as Schopenhauer put it. Here you see romanticism as the natural shadow of pure reason.

Romanticism has often tried to portray, as its own, imagination's great strengths of inclusiveness and openness to the *other*. In the first instances of the romantic perception, this can be true. But because the romantic is so profoundly obsessive and operates in a shadow-life of rational methodology, it is not naturally inclusive or open. Left to its own logic it quickly becomes exclusive and closed in upon its particular truth. That was the story of *Young Werther*, as it was of Romeo and Juliet. The romantic leaderships of the nineteenth century became dictatorships. We saw the worst modern form of this with Mussolini and Hitler. The romantic nationalisms became terrifying forces. The 'romantic impulse' justified every action, from imperial conquest to sacred borders to racism.

The idea that the imagination is romantic or romantically inclusive was not at first consciously ill-intentioned. Coleridge, in 1808 in London, gave a series of lectures which many consider the manifesto of the romantic movement. He argued that creative imagination was part of the "balance-loving nature of man". But then he sold the poetic imagination "as a single unifying force within all creative acts". This was to be "the 'one power' of Imagination".[14]

How could you possibly juxtapose "balance" with "one power"? In these few words you can see how the romantic argument would become the enemy of the imagination. What's more, it would become pretentious. For example, Coleridge's interpretation of a Shakespearean couplet describing the flight of Adonis is described as "a historic declaration of the Romantic principle of the Imagination".

Shakespeare:	"Look! How a bright star shooteth from the sky So glides he in the night from Venus' Eye."
Coleridge:	"How many Images and feelings are here brought together without effort and without discord — the beauty of Adonis — the rapidity of his flight — the yearning yet hopelessness of the enamoured gazer — and a shadowy ideal character thrown over the whole — or it acts by impressing the stamp of human feeling, over inanimate objects..."[15]

Shakespeare's couplet is imaginative genius. Coleridge's analysis is wonderful. But what makes either romantic? What is the romantic principle in question here?

Take a related bit of poetry, this time by Skaay, one of the great Haida storytellers of the late nineteenth century. In the ancient oral-bard tradition, he reimagined verse for his generation. "Raven Travelling" is an "Homeric" epic poem of 1,400 lines.

> Then, when he had flown a while longer,
> something brightened toward the north.
> It caught his eye, they say.
> And then he flew right up against it.
>
> He pushed his mind through
> and pulled his body after.[16]

Skaay didn't know about Shakespeare. He was dealing in his own way with similar concepts. He had a multilayered creative imagination. He brought the images together rather more intellectually than Shakespeare, with the mind preceding the body through the eye. His style was closer to twentieth-century surrealism.

My point is that the imagination is no more romantic than ethics. And neither is. Certainly there is nothing romantic about the ability to transmit a multitude of images, ideas, emotions, actions, in one or a few words. That is a sign of talent, perhaps of genius. It is certainly the opposite of linear rational thought. And to a manager wedded to the linear, anything lateral is frightening. So the ability to express several elements at once can be most comfortably discarded by describing it as romantic.

Like ethics, the imagination is central to our lives in a way which is useful, not utilitarian. As for the poets, Skaay is a reminder of their historic role. In Shelley's over-the-top description, they are "the unacknowledged legislators of the world". In the classic Islamic formula the same thing is said without the romanticism: they were "the men of knowledge for their people".[17] Of knowledge, not of understanding. This suggests they were — are — driven by some combination in which imagination is buttressed by common sense, ethics, intuition and memory. They were part of a process of imagination throughout their civilization.

What drove the imagination? In good part curiosity, which Vico called "that inborn property of man, daughter of ignorance and mother of knowledge".[18] As you see, my argument turns in a circle. What is "this activity of imagining"? Michael Oakeshott asked. "[I]t is not a condition of thought." What I describe as prolonged uncertainty, Oakeshott called conversation. "What I have called the conversation of mankind is the meeting-place of various modes of imagining."

So the circle in which we turn is indeed the process of transcending ourselves through our imaginations. Adam Smith called this a matter of "sympathy" for the *other*. He consciously paused to point out that this sympathy had nothing to do with pity or compassion or benevolence. Today we might call it 'identification' with the *other*. This is the tool which allows societies to imagine that they exist and that the *other* exists, both firmly attached to reality. You might say that imagination is the key to the reality of responsible individualism.

From the local to the universal

Reality? A dangerous word to invoke. You approach it and it fades away. Which is why imagination must be so useful, so central.

Take the difference between a good doctor and a great doctor. Obviously there are dozens of more or less calculable factors — intelligence, training, rapidity, care. But even among doctors, most agree that the best of them are somehow healers. They have the ability to heal. It's a bit like great generals. There are lots of smart, well-trained, tough, intellectual or hands-on generals who tend to lose. Napoleon said what he looked for in a general was luck. He meant the talent for winning. He didn't really mean luck. And he didn't mean the skill for winning. He meant a general who, in addition to all the measurable prerequisites, was able to win. The same could be said of the doctor who can heal.

Nothing romantic or irrational is being suggested here. In a sense, it is the healer-doctor who is most profoundly grounded in reality — in the reality of the patient's life — or rather her internal balance between the forces of life and of death. You see how local this is. How precise. These healers are fully equipped with Smith's *sympathy*. They are able to imagine beyond themselves, beyond what they know as experts, beyond what the procedures say and what it is normal to do.

And what do they imagine if not the *other*, the reality of the *other* — the patient? This is not about defeating death, but, in Conrad's formula, about finding a way for the patient to live. This requires a savage, terrible eye for a specific reality, combined with that sense of the ever-tipping balance between the forces of life and death. And so the word 'healer' may at first seem to refer to a past world of superstition and miracles, when it refers instead to the power to transport yourself into the *other*. To imagine yourself into the *other*.

I quoted Schopenhauer earlier on the power of a few to imagine. All of us imagine. And all of us can imagine the *other*. But the doctor who can heal does belong to Schopenhauer's élite.

Napoleon looked for lucky generals. Sun Tzu said battles were won and lost in the minds of generals before they were fought. He didn't mean that one had imagined how to win. That would be the mediocre, competitive interpretation. That is probably how they now teach Sun Tzu in management schools. What he meant was that the winning general has accurately imagined the conditions of reality. The one who best imagines these conditions will be able to use his more ordinary skills and talents to win.

The point here again is just how localized that imagination is. How focused on a certain reality. The romantic may fantasize about great universal clouds of imagination. Reality has our imagination grounded in the local. If we are accurate or true, then what we have imagined may indeed be universal.

Skaay and Shakespeare created eerily similar images. No traceable tradition linked them. André Malraux would describe this phenomenon as a specific but universal idea or force of beauty, leading to objects and images around the word, linked somehow to each other through their expression of local conditions. I would call this a universal undercurrent, or collective unconscious, of beauty. Vico described the phenomenon in a matter-of-fact way, long before Malraux was imagined:

> [U]niform ideas, born among peoples unknown to each
> other, must have a common ground of truth....

This is not such a strange idea. Think of our intellectual traditions. It is this commonality of local realities — almost local truths — which explains why we are still invoking Solon to discuss our current political and social dramas.

"[T]he first fables," Vico said, "must have contained civil truths." But a local truth can also stop us from movement, can freeze our thoughts, can serve power in its desire for immobility. It is imagination which can protect us from this. It can disturb, as Bronowski put it, and encourage dissent. How? Quite simply by imagining differently. Coleridge and Schopenhauer — opposites in many ways — had a vision of imagination as a great arm of truth. But each of us imagines and does so differently. And so there is a constant delicate balance between the universal truths which local imagined realities produce and the universal dissent which that same imagination produces around those same realities.

Words, sounds, images, actions

There is an assumption that the imagination is a product of the brain. Perhaps that explains the recurring fear of 'uncontrolled' imagination — it is a form of brain fever. Unpredictable. Dangerous for all of us.

Let me come at this question of what we now tend to call creativity in a roundabout way.

One of the central creators of modern individualism was Elisabeth of Hungary, daughter of a king, wife and then widow of the Landgrave of Thuringia.[19] She and Francis of Assisi were, in contemporary terms, the most famous of the twelfth-century activists, calling for an interpretation of Christian faith as one of obligation based on the recognition of the *other* and, therefore, on a form of responsible individualism.

To a great extent they laid out the modern democratic model of inclusion. More precisely, their relationship with the *other* was an important step in our acceptance of egalitarianism. They rejected charity as traditionally conceived, with those who *have* choosing to help those who do *not have*; and helping as it suits them, not those helped.

Slightly in the shadow of these two remarkable figures, others — John of Salisbury, Aelred of Rievaulx, John of Paris, to name only a few — were putting in place the ideas which Thomas Aquinas, Petrarch, Dante, again to name only a few, would later pick up and develop.

While others wrote or acted personally, Elisabeth used her position as a member of the ruling class to put the ideas into action. Like many others, she created a hospice. Hers was in the valley at Marburg. But unlike others, she went well beyond pity and charity. In an ultimate illustration of imagining the *other*, she herself washed the sick and buried the dead. It is hard to imagine now the public impact of a royal figure washing the bodies of the homeless dead. Imagine the

American Vice-President, not visiting or holding hands with street people, but washing their bodies for burial. Elisabeth supplied the poor with agricultural tools and shoes and clothes, so that they could create and live normal lives.

That is, she treated exclusion and poverty not as an inevitability, but rather as a socially constructed form of suffering. And she treated a normal life as a right. She visited prisoners, which today sounds fairly innocuous. But the concept of prison in the twelfth century had none of the false moralism that was attached to law in the eighteenth to nineteenth century. Those locked up in the twelfth century were largely those who fell on the wrong side of power, little more. And so to visit prisoners was to make a statement about public responsibility and individual rights.

Elisabeth died young. Within four years she was a saint and a cathedral was being built over her tomb — the Elisabethenkirke. This was one of the great European pilgrimage sites until the eighteenth century. The cathedral was the first German Gothic church, and became the model for all the other churches that followed.

You have never heard of her? The way in which she has been forgotten reminds us of how male-driven the rational nation-state was.

Elisabeth and the other 'activists' took the elements of personal responsibility, which had been set out tantalizingly in the New Testament, and imagined a social model which would come more or less to fruition seven hundred years later. They imagined a way of living, of acting, which would require thousands of written and visual expansions in order to capture our imaginations enough to change our societies.

This social idea and the pilgrimage church in which it was physically grounded were at the centre of the European imagination for a long time. Remarkable twelfth-century stained-glass windows in the chevet lay out graphically Elisabeth's actions. The windows are the visual equivalent of a revolutionary manifesto. In this context of conscious avant-garde representation, the two major chapels of the church are placed opposite each other. One contains her tomb. The other has the ten raised tombs of the Landgrave of Hessen, the local rulers. They lie carved, life-size, on the top of their stone coffins. On either side of their carved heads are small angels, coming out of each ear. Sometimes a larger angel is pulling them out. These little angels are the soul, leaving the body. By the ears. From the brain?

Is this a reference to the means by which the holy word has been heard? Who knows? But you might also say that the ears and the eyes are how people were exposed to Elisabeth's ideas. And the soul was somehow an evocation of those ideas, in the sense that they were recognized to be holy. So the soul was an imagined ethical idea. Or ideal. An imagined ethical idea of the *other*.

Of course the concept of the soul has rather lost favour these days in favour of the brain. But if that is the case, where precisely do we put Jung's archetypes and their effect on us? What I mean is: the soul is a relatively vague concept which could probably accommodate the idea of archetypes. But the brain is another matter. So where precisely in our brain are Jung's archetypes physically lodged? Most of us accept that there are archetypes which have survived thousands of years. And somehow they mark our characters. Fine. If our imagination is a sub-product of rational process or, alternately, a marginal, romantic, uncontrolled indulgence, where precisely is it lodged? After all, the concepts of measurement and definition would require as a minimum that we know where to find the thing we define and measure. And if there are eternal archetypes, this business of identifying their actual location would seem even more self-evident.

Is there a corner of the brain set aside? I mention this as the archetypes seem to have more effect on our real actions in the real world than, say, economic charts projecting the future.

Let me put it another way. I recently watched Ali Rajput — one of the world's leading researchers on Parkinson's disease — dissect a brain. The size is disturbing. It seems larger than a head. It was sliced in thicknesses which kept reminding me of a chef's preparation of calves' brain or large puff-balls to fry in a saucepan. In his understated but magical way, Dr. Rajput explained what we know about the brain and how it functions. We now know quite a bit. We know precisely where the problems of Parkinson's and Alzheimer's are located. You can see these tiny areas.

But at the end of the day, the outside limits of what happens between the brain and the body remain unclear, as do the means of internal communications by tens of thousands of blood vessels and nerves.

After all, we have had perfect dissections of the human body from the sixteenth century on, and therefore a relatively clear understanding of what you might call functions. In the seventeenth and eighteenth centuries, artists in Italy were creating perfect, life-sized reproductions of the body, differentiating all of the nerves, blood vessels and, of course, bones.[20] It took almost three more centuries to begin making creative or imaginative sense of the physical evidence provided by this first breakthrough.

The point is that these early dissections and re-creations of the body were tied to art and to a belief in the humanist code of "know thyself". They were the beginnings of a certain flowering of the imagination. The idea that medicine could make use of such information came slowly out of this imagining of ourselves as something — a partly physical *other*. The interesting thing is that still, today, our most definitive medical progress is limited to the most mechanical of elements — the heart and bones. The common cold continues to run ahead of our ability to conceptualize health and sickness.

I am turning around the question: where is our imagination lodged? It can be argued, more convincingly today than in the Middle Ages, that the adrenalin glands play a role in the shaping of our imagination. Or our glands in general. Or our nervous system. Of course it could be argued in reply that these feed back into the brain. Perhaps. But that is a theory based on intellect as the core of imagination. I return to the archetypes. Is there any proof at all of any sort that the structured archetypes, which we have been unable to shed over thousands of years, are directly related to brain activity?

The point is that we do not know a great deal about the true nature of our imagination. Endless time has been spent by philosophers attempting to prove that what we imagine is processed via images, and more recently that it is not. Neither of which has been particularly helpful or relevant.

Some thinkers, like Mostyn Jones, have attacked this narrow, scholastic approach — led in the twentieth century by Sartre and Wittgenstein — and called for a return to the "broader perspectives" of Vico, Collingwood and, yes, Marx. Jones calls this a return to the idea of *creativity* in its fullest sense — "a dynamic, evolving synergy whose powers have been transformed and expanded across history".[21] And in this he is surely right. Although devoting yourself to the idea of *creativity*, as opposed to *imagination*, may simply be a technical way of escaping the damage done to the idea of the imagination by a century of academic philosophers. After all, the idea of creativity has already been recuperated by the same forces of narrow expert definitionitis that marginalized imagination. It is now *taught* in dozens of areas, including 'creative' writing classes, as if it were a subsection of instrumental reason.

Still, Jones's is a healthy voice that takes us back to Coleridge's idea of the imagination as something which "dissolves, diffuses, dissipates, in order to recreate!"[22] A great, continuing swirl of prolonged uncertainty.

Perhaps it would be enough to suggest that imagination is a form of perception which allows us to progress. That may be what the French philosopher Merleau-Ponty meant when he wrote of the need to explore the "pre-objective realm" within us. You could say that imagination is a heightened quality of consciousness. Or that it causes words, images and sounds to tumble about in our unconscious and our consciousness in a multitude of ways.

There is no defined process. There is nothing definable or measurable. There is no order of importance. The tumbling will more often produce sexual fantasies than architectural creativity or literary

masterpieces. But then there is more sex in life than there are buildings and books.

Bark-biting is a rather rarified art of various aboriginal nations in
the near north of Canada. Women fold small pieces of a particular
layer of under-bark from birch trees into different patterns and then
bite them, using a single, particular upper and lower tooth. The result
in certain hands — or rather teeth — is both intricate and beautiful.
It is done by very few, in part because the imaginary abstraction is
so extreme. There is little repetition in the results. I asked a new-
generation bark-biter at Pointe Bleu on Lac Saint-Jean in Québec
what she thought of as she did it. She replied "the forest". She was not
biting images of the forest. What did she mean? I have no idea. What
I do know is that Picasso said much the same thing when asked
what Delacroix would have thought of what he was doing. "I would
say to Delacroix: You, you were thinking of Rubens and you produced
Delacroix. And so, I, thinking of you, I produce something else."[23] In
other words, in the process of creating, the imagination often uses
one image to get to another, which has not yet been imagined.

What I also know is that many visual artists need music to work,
as do some writers. This does not function as an image generator, but
rather as a key, unlocking their imaginations. Many musicians need
words. If I sit in a live concert, after almost exactly twenty minutes
words and phrases will begin to tumble into my consciousness,
unlocking different ongoing problems of writing. Angus Wilson felt
that it was Zola's love of the Impressionists which gave him another
sense of how to write. Here truly images were producing words.[24]

David Malouf has made an even more direct connection, pointing
out that, until Australian writers dropped specifically British images
and took up specifically Australian, they could not imagine where
they were. There were no trees, flowers, birds of Australia, in early
Australian verse. "This is not because they were not there in the land-
scape, to be seen and appreciated, but because there was as yet no
place for them in the world of verse. The associations had not yet

been found that would allow them entry there. They carried no charge of emotion." So these trees, flowers, birds, landscapes, climates had first to enter into the imagination of the immigrants. It wasn't a question of nationalism or of excluding others, but of imagining being at home there themselves. Then it happened. And it was as if the people had "come at last into full possession of a place".[25]

The opposite can just as easily happen. Police and courtroom dramas set in New York, Los Angeles, Chicago have become so common around the world — they are America's most common expression of itself — that many people in other countries now think their own legal system is like that of the United States. German youth have no other legal image, unless they are arrested. And then they ask to be read their rights and later ask for trial by jury, as if their system worked that way. There is a sentiment in Germany that more locally produced television police-court dramas are needed to create vaguely relevant images. Without the images, they cannot imagine themselves.

But let me suggest something quite different about the imagination. At the Modern Art Museum in Frankfurt there was until recently a room devoted to Gerhard Richter's paintings of political terrorists, the Baader Meinhof Gang, before and after their mass suicide in prison on October 18, 1977. The paintings were done from police photos. I didn't know of the paintings. I walked into the room and was immobilized by the atmosphere. I hadn't yet looked at a picture. The force which he somehow put into his paintings overwhelmed the space. And it remained when you examined the paintings one by one. That force is virtually impossible to describe, except to say that Richter is a great painter and he has the genius to create something like a force field which connects him with the viewer.

This is not emotion. Is it an image? If so, then the police dramas I mentioned a moment ago are not images, since their power is dependent on their being seen in the most direct manner. Richter has touched something in our imagination which is only secondarily about visual perception.

Take John Ruskin's description of St. Stephen in Carpaccio's paint-ing in the Brera in Milan. After pointing out how Carpaccio has not bothered with any of the tricks or traditions of imagery, has even placed Stephen off in a corner of the painting, he comes to the real point — "Stephen's face, radiant with true soul of heaven":

> For the heavenly look on the face of Stephen is not set off
> with raised light, or opposed shade, or principality of place.
> The master trusts only to what nature herself would have
> trusted in — expression pure and simple. If you cannot see
> heaven in the boy's mind, without any turning on of the
> stage lights, you shall not see it at all.[26]

Is this an image? Again, if so, what is an image? Or here is David Malouf again, on how we read:

> ...reading is itself an interiorising activity, a matter of
> 'taking things in', perhaps because language, with its
> combination of image and rhythm, its appeal to the eye and
> to the way our bodies move, is continuous with some activ-
> ity in us that involves, in the most immediate way, both
> body and mind. [27]

So there is an image in our imagination, but only as part of something else — a rhythm of the body. The imagination is caught up in many things — intellect, perception, our body as a whole, our relationship to others, to what we create, to rooms, to atmospheres.

You see, the point of it is not what it is but what it does.

One last example: a few years ago in a hill village in Corsica I attempted to help a friend rebuild his old dry stone wall — that is, a wall without anything except the placement of the stones holding it together. In Corsica these are particularly wide and therefore compli-cated. My friend is a well-known professor of law, highly intelligent, open to culture and different ideas. We worked at it for some time on a hot day and got nowhere. Every five minutes we had to take down what we had put up. The stones have to fit — all of them, all the way through the thickness — like a tight, balanced jigsaw puzzle — or the whole thing collapses.

Then his neighbour came by, returning from the hill above with his donkey. In the proverbial manner he began offering advice. He touched nothing. He didn't even approach. He simply pointed at a stone in the pile and pointed where it should go on the wall. With minimalist finger gestures, hardly moving the wrist, he indicated exactly which way up, which edge forward, which way in. Each instruction was given before the stone was near the wall. He never had to adjust his directions. Each stone slipped precisely into place. My friend and I were reduced to semi-automated machines.

What was this? Memory in the form of experience? The neighbour had certainly done it many times, but that is an insufficient explanation. This was not merely a learnt skill. There was no fixed set of variables. The stones were whatever shape they happened to be.

Was it reason? Instrumental or other. Not at all. We were the ones attempting to apply reason and failing badly.

Intuition? Not really. He was too certain, too rapid. He knew.

Common sense, then? Perhaps to some extent. There was a shared knowledge of shapes — a spatial sense of shapes — without any artificial need for understanding.

But above all it was an exercise in imagination. He was placing the rocks the way a poet places words or phrases, word by word, yet in an uncontrolled flow, like floating atoms. He imagined the wall, then the stones tumbled out of his imagination into place. No doubt he was helped by a lifetime of using his imagination in this manner, just as a writer's imagination is helped by his experience manipulating language.

But do I mean that he imagined an image of the wall? No. He didn't have an abstract, analytic, linear view of what a wall is, he had a spatial view, exactly as a good novelist or poet does. Perhaps that acceptance or capacity for the spatial is the central characteristic of imagination. Perhaps that is what Merleau-Ponty meant by the "pre-objective realm" within us.

Now, on a computer you can revolve objects in a spatial manner. And in the process of day-to-day design this is a remarkable process. Yet at the same time it is heavy and pedantic in comparison to the imagination of a normal human. It is a stolid image — a representation — of an object; a manual version of Aristotle's imagined image, a laborious reduction of the spatial to a 3D form of the linear.

It can be measured. That is useful. But there is none of the fluid, unfixed rapidity of the imagination; none of Coleridge's dissolving, diffusing, dissipating in order to re-create. None of the swirling prolonged uncertainty.

Of course there are morphing capacities and a dozen other technological tools, improving every day. And that is wonderful. But again, these are manual tools in electronic guise. The dissolve is decided. In the imagination it is not.

It is the spatial without conscious process which makes our imagination so frightening to those who see society as a measured construct. This is a higher form of consciousness than anything we can reproduce. Even in the case of a great painter or writer, what is actually produced is only an incomplete manifestation of the imagination's capacity.

We all have this spatial capacity. Some have more of it; and if they can combine it with other qualities they may become great creators or inventors or leaders. Many of us are frightened of the uncertainty or instability this spatial force implies and so find ways to shut it down. In a society as linear and structural as ours nothing could be easier. We have only to act as the structures expect us to act.

If you consider the greatest music or words or images, what seems to set them apart is their ability to literally rotate creativity into a shape not perceived by others. And yet the tools are the same. They have access to the same memory and structures. Like a remarkable plane, they then spin out of the known formation into another, and so reinvent what we already know.

Take Picasso. Throughout the twentieth century he had an ability, the moment others seemed to be catching up, to simply spin out of whatever form represented contemporary control. The world of official art history spent much of its time intellectually — artificially, in fact — trying to attach his innovations to the Western tradition. From time to time they would reluctantly offer a little tip of the hat to the influence on Picasso of creative traditions from what they considered to be Third World societies. They couldn't pretend that the painter, and other painters, hadn't taken notice of these theoretically lesser traditions in Africa, the South Pacific and the Canadian West Coast.

Why were they lesser? Because they had not entered into the artistic evolution of Western society. Their art was therefore 'naive' or 'brut' or 'primitive'. But it was also good. It was art which had remained in a spatial, non-linear mode. What's more, it had links to the creative roots of imagination — that is, right into the animistic reality. And it had the imaginative aggressive drive to reinvent itself constantly. The Western tradition, having cut itself off from the animist, found it difficult to spin into reinvention.

What made the art world so nervous about Picasso was that he seemed to look at Western imagery with the eye of an anthropologist. Meanwhile, he related to the art of that other world — let's call it the animist — with the imagination of a participant.

It is not accurate to say that he was influenced by the images of Africa, Western Canada and Oceania. He had actually spun out of the Western linear tradition — cut free — and entered right into the spatial world of the *other*. He took a tool bag of Western techniques and conventions with him. But he was actually ensconced inside the other imagination. He merely used the various Western forms. You could say that he had entered into the spatial, animist world and was merely influenced by the Western tradition.

How did he do this? As always with the imagination of a genius, we don't know. But the point is that he gave our imaginations access to great animistic forces at a time when the Western tradition could do little more than fiddle, yet again, with the shadow and light and the geometric forms in our well-established images.

●

Fear of the Unpredictable

Aristotle more or less set in place the idea of imagination as an imitation of something, and it is. You could almost call it a constant repetition. But if it were only that, it would be memory, not imagination. I spoke earlier of the oral poet Skaay and the continual reinvention of the Haida myths. The Homeric myths still guide us in thousands of reimagined ways.

"One of the first things I noticed about literature," Northrop Frye wrote, "was the stability of its structural units; the fact that certain themes, situations and character types, in comedy let us say, have persisted with very little change from Aristophanes to our own time.... This quality of repetition is essential to myth in all its contexts. A society...cannot keep its central myths of concern constantly in mind unless they are continually being re-presented."[28]

You might expect then that imagination would be predictable, since it reinvents what already exists. But we have no idea what effect will result. Who would have imagined the Nazis using ancient German myths, brought to life by a great composer, to justify killing millions? Or Elisabeth in that same geographical place of German culture using thousand-year-old Christian myths to construct the beginnings of modern social justice? Stable and unimaginable. That is how these myths can have a social function. As Frye puts it, they are "a program of action".

Now step back and consider this same imagination — yours —

from another point of view. There has never been so much creative production of every sort. And yet the imagination is considered more marginal today — when it comes down to how we consider programs of action or reaction to real events — than through most of our history. The very idea, for example, that language, words, real arguments are to produce debates and then action is very far from how we now imagine our progress. Thomas Paine came to believe that the "three great faculties of the mind" were memory, judgement and imagination.[29] We are far today from accepting that to imagine is as important as getting on with the theoretical practicalities of life. Our fear of the unmeasurable continues to push our imaginations to the margins.

Perhaps the consciousness with which it is marginalized suggests the exact opposite: that fear of the imagination means we believe in its power. Ken Saro-Wiwa, during his last long period in jail, wrote that the Nigerian dictators "... are so scared of the power of the word that they do not read". At first you might think that this is a specific comment on violent dictators. Think of it instead as a generic characteristic of people frightened by their own imaginations and therefore by that of others. Wander up and down the business-class aisles of airplanes throughout the world — the floating club of our contemporary élites. You will be hard-pressed to find anyone reading anything more than a magazine or a Robert Ludlum thriller.

This could be put down to the burdens and fatigue of leadership. But are they any harder worked than the rest of the population? And in what conditions? A more convincing argument would be that our system cuts our attention span into small structural bits; that the higher our rise, the more it is cut up into yet smaller pieces; that literacy is not admired as a leadership quality in the managerial world; that there is indeed a fear of words, particularly words as a force of imagination and thus as a method of change, rather than as slogans and screens of obfuscation. And then there is that most peculiar of fears: that the certainty made possible by high-level functional illiteracy will be rendered less certain by any unleashing of the imagination.

You might say that what we are dealing with is intelligence reduced to creative agoraphobia.

Paul Valéry used to argue that "a work of art should always teach us that we have not seen what we are seeing."[30] What then are all of these fears if not a negative reflection of imagination as a source of uncertainty.

THE CREATIVE INTERVENTION

[T]he progress of an artist is...a continual extinction of personality.

T.S. Eliot

This is a strange sort of life. Solitary. Often, the greater the talent the more solitary. And all of that avoiding experience.

Perhaps it is the aggressive nature of the imagination which creates this effect. There is also the uncertainty. "An artist shoots in the dark," Mahler would often repeat, "not knowing whether he hits or what he hits."[31] The idea of purpose is always incomplete.

It isn't surprising that the artist often seems odd. Marginal. The tendency of a highly structured society, in which the appearance of conformity is so important, is to leap upon visual or superficial oddities as a proof of the marginality of the content.

At the same time 'artistic' mannerisms are sometimes adopted by others to suggest non-conformity. In fact, some middle-class people believe the age of conformity is over. And structuralism with it. They talk of new technologies and the end of classic employment. They point at Microsoft in Seattle — 15,000 people in T-shirts and jeans without apparent structure. But 15,000 people wearing T-shirts and jeans are 15,000 perfectly regimented people. As for the apparent lack of structure, it is built upon a quick understanding by the employees of what the structure is. An effective army or ideology or one-party state does not need to give orders.

The psychological principle of, say, the Khmer Rouge was that, in the absence of visual differentiation, order is more easily maintained. This may seem an unfair comparison. There is no mass murder at Microsoft, except perhaps of syntax. But the question here is the nature of ideology, not a particular outcome.

Believers believe they have made a creative decision. Their conformity appears to them to be an act of imaginative individual commitment. It is a remarkable trick. You can see the emerging shape of this modern marginalization of imagination as early as Marsilio Ficino, partly responsible for the Platonist revival during the Renaissance. He criticized the "crude powers of sensibility" and "fantasy mixed with natural instinct".[32] And he defined fantasy as made up of desire, pleasure, fear and pain — a sort of creative delirium. Imagination is thus not only marginal, it is destructive.

Colin Davis has said that, "When you are conducting [the third act of *Tristan*], it's touch and go. You're just holding on." What does he mean? Well, in part the music is a perfect example of the intellect and the body combined. The imagination is not lodged in the brain. The result, as the Wagner expert Owen Lee puts it, is that with this music we come "closer than many of us would like to what is repressed and potentially threatening in ourselves".[33] This is the inverted argument of art as a solid continuum in need of reinvention. We already know what there is to know about ourselves. Yet we do not know how to express it, how to really know it. And so we are hidden from ourselves. Only art can reveal to us what we already know.

Some might argue that we have grown beyond such fears of uncertainty. Why then is there nothing in our society to suggest this? Think of how we are constantly reassured that there are no problems. The fear from our managerial élites is that we are too fragile, too excitable, too impressionable to be told the truth. In this exchange from Strindberg's *The Father*, you, the citizens, are the husband:

Doctor:	Avoid touching on any subject that
	might excite your husband. In a sick
	brain, fancies grow like weeds, and can
	easily develop into obsessions or even
	monomania. You understand?
Laura:	You mean I must take care not to awake
	his suspicions?
Doctor:	Exactly. A sick man is receptive to the
	slightest impression, and can therefore
	be made to imagine anything.[34]

A conformist, structured society sees imagination as "the sick brain". The curious thing is that when we do find out about such terrible errors as mad cow disease or floating radiation clouds from Chernobyl or tainted drinking water in public systems here and there throughout North America and Europe, our fancies do not "grow like weeds". We do not slip into creative brain-fever and go out of control. If anything, we put our imaginations aside and react with what I would call the solid common sense. We know the system has broken down, so we boycott the system.

The public reaction to mad cow disease has in general been to stop buying beef. What could be more sensible? We are under no obligation to further risk our health by believing in a system which has demonstrated it isn't to be believed. We are informed too late of exposure to an unnecessary risk, so we sensibly cut our losses and change our diet.

What instrumental reason condemns as uncontrollable imagination is often ethics or intuition or memory or common sense moving into action. Where the creative act is most feared by a conformist society we often have the least need of our imaginations.

INFLATION OF THE IMAGE

It's hard to know exactly how people imagined before 1850, before the photograph. What was the impact of a word before many people could read and before the mass production of magazines and books; of music before recordings; of an image before there were many images?

As late as the early 1970s, I knew peasant farmers in the Sologne in France who did not have a television. When you called on them, they took you into the kitchen, sat you down, talked, told stories and, yes, sang. I should add that a highly effective system of universal public education had been in place for seventy years. That is to say, these people were well educated. They were not picturesque relics of our former selves. The day the television arrived in their kitchen, the talk, the storytelling and singing ended. I don't mean they had stopped imagining. Or started. I do mean that the natural aggressivity of the functioning imagination had, at least temporarily, disappeared from their relationship with the *other*. Now they received images and sounds while emitting few themselves.

I began this chapter by talking of our imagination's naturally inclusive nature, of how it somehow gathered elements together and then sprang ahead, dragging the rest of our qualities on towards new or reinterpreted imaginings.

For a millennium this had been based on a fairly standard quantity of images, sounds, words. Suddenly there were immeasurable quantities of these. We know that the multiplication of books, thanks to the printing press, made an explosion of reading possible. But reading is an active form of participation and so you could see a positive effect on the normalization of imagining at a new level.

Only 150 years ago there weren't many images, apart from statues in squares and paintings in churches and various hand-painted or carved popular objects. Few people had images in their homes. The use of time was also different. Few people rode past a statue. They walked. They were in its presence much longer. We can only imagine that the relationship with these images was different. I said there had been relative stability in external images for a millennium. Suddenly there was an explosion in the reproduction of images. For a century and a half this has been an exponential explosion. The pace is, if anything, quickening. What is the effect on our imaginations? We have no real idea.

You can easily follow our society adjusting as fast as it can to these technical explosions in multiplication. The painted image leapt forwards from exactitude to impressions to both the surreal and the abstract. I spoke in the beginning of the imagination's ironic nature. The irony of René Magritte was among the most popular imagery of the twentieth century. Think of the years just before the terror of Nazism, when Magritte was painting "The White Race" as a balancing act — an eye up on top of an ear on top of a mouth on top of two noses, like elephants' feet. You could sense that our imagination was finding ways of staying ahead and dealing with reality.

But the ironic technique of Magritte was quickly taken over by the sceptical, indeed cynical, tool of public relations. The very technique of disconnecting the pieces to unleash the imagination are now used to exploit it. And so the smile of an athlete and the chiselled body are used to sell soft drinks which rot teeth and put on fat. Why does this method work? Precisely because it reduces irony down to scepticism and scepticism down to cynicism. And so, creative humour is deformed into destructive self-loathing. It's a clever trick; exactly the 'cleverness' traditionally proper to the courtier class.

But how then can the imagination free itself? Our partial reaction has been to take refuge in the fantastic — in generalized fantasy — as if to drown out the specific, goal-oriented world of fantastic advertising. You might say that we have embraced the double-edged sword of Vico's *fantasia*, with its positive and negative connotations — imagination and fantasy — in an attempt to reanimate our memory.

Where once the fantastic was a marginal distraction in paintings of hell and gargoyles, it is now as common as apples. The very explosion in the role of the fantastic — monsters, outer-space monsters, monsters or apparently real animals fighting humans — in everything from cartoons to films could be taken many ways. One is that our imaginations are still leaping ahead. Another is that, overwhelmed by the passivity which the new waves of sensations impose, we are escaping into precisely the marginal, self-destructive fantasies which the imagination was always accused of encouraging.

What do I mean by passivity? Think of the rapidity with which business, advertising, government, film, television, commercial music — the organized structures in our societies — have discovered how to use all of these same sensations in a controlled way. That is, the explosion in images has been captured for linear use. Fractured into thousands of unreliable elements, it prevents our imaginations from getting access to enough sensations to imagine what reality resembles.

Take a very specific example. In the 1960s and 1970s these image systems gave the American people access to their war in Viet Nam. And they used what they saw to imagine themselves out of it, against the wishes of their functioning élites. The new imagery served the imagination. Less than twenty years later that same élite conducted a war in Iraq in which, according to the technology of sensations, no one died, suffered or even sweated. It was virtually impossible for any American citizen, let alone any other Westerner, to gather even the fragments of direct images or sounds in order to imagine what was happening. And old-fashioned print journalists were simply kept out of the way.

So it was a very new kind of war. Not because of smart bombs, but because it was isolated from the imaginations of the citizenry. I'm not referring to a victory for propaganda. I'm not even judging the actual events. I am describing two opposing realities. One in which we are overwhelmed by a multiplicity of fractured sensations. The other in which there are no sensations at all.

How in such an atmosphere can our imagination operate as an

inclusive, ironic force of progress? How is it to leap forward except through the mediocre world of technological progress? As technology, and with that economics, has become our obsession, so our imagining of conscious, intentional human development and relations has become more difficult.

If I were to force my optimism, I'd imagine that we live in a period of adjustment; that we are working out how to use our qualities in a changed atmosphere. Earlier, when discussing ethics, I pointed out the contradictory situation of those working in parallel volunteer organizations such as NGOs. Look at their activity from yet a different angle. You could argue that those hundreds of thousands of young have disconnected not from democracy, but from the tidal wave of shapeless sensations constantly breaking over us and, indeed, from the quicksand of broken-up self-absorbed administrative and specialist structures.

Had they disconnected simply in frustration, the result would be classic alienation. But they are engaged. They have recentred their imaginations on something real — the environment, the conditions of life of the marginalized, the rules of international engagement, global warming and so on. These areas represent the basic realities in which we live and function. This is where our imaginations must work.

Let me put this in a larger context. In spite of sophisticated universal public education systems throughout the West, we continue to see a growth in functional illiteracy. Some of this is due to deregulation and cutbacks, which favour those who can afford private schools. But the numbers go beyond that. Calculated and counted in myriad ways, the percentages of illiteracy, functional and complete, keep turning up at more than thirty per cent.

What can this possibly mean? In part it seems to be a shutting down of our affect — our inclusive imaginations — when faced by a combination of exclusive, controlling forces: those of a civilization obsessed by structure, accompanied by an explosion in shapeless shards of technological imagination, which in and of themselves are meaningless. No doubt we can and will do something with these shards. For the moment we are either passive before them, or we are actively, aggressively even, mixing together fantasy and utilitarianism in the interests of profit.

These terrifying levels of functional illiteracy tell us only a part of the problem. After all, the functioning élite suffers from its own form of functional illiteracy — one in which literacy is limited to ever-narrower specializations, which discourage lateral thinking. And lateral thinking is one sign of a functioning imagination. Voltaire used to joke about the illiterate aristocracy of the eighteenth century that they didn't need to read or to know things or to imagine. They had power and certainty. They could hire people to read, to be expert, to be uncertain. Illiteracy was a medal of superiority.

It is common now to talk of ours as a society of spectators seeking passive distraction. A more sympathetic interpretation would be that the myriad shapeless managerial or specialist truths, combined with a shapeless mass of technological details, create great noise. Like the Romans at the Coliseum, we are distracted by this cacophony; often rendered passive. Is it possible that this noise so distracts us at our various levels that many of us, each in our own way, are effectively rendered illiterate?

S H E E P

In October 2000, four years after the mad cow disease scandal began, the British official report on what had gone wrong was finally published, under the signature of Lord Phillips. He put the blame more or less on intensive farming methods and was relatively kind to the public officials involved. He confirmed that there had been "a total suppression of information on the subject for some time", but seemed more upset by the methodology involved. "There were, however, mistakes in the way the risk was communicated to the public and there are lessons to be learned from this." The tone here suggests a continuing belief in the need to 'manage' the public. For example, he wrote of the public "feeling of betrayal" when the truth came out. But there was no "feeling" of betrayal. It was not an emotional reaction. They *were* betrayed.

The strange element was that, despite his one clear criticism of intensive farming, this did not provoke a wider debate about other animals raised in similar conditions. You might have expected speculation on battery hens, pig-factory farming or fish farming. Many use the same sheep-enhanced feed. You might have expected more general questions, beyond CJD; for example, about the effects of bending the rules of nature. Our linear, blinkered approach, which marginalizes 'imagination', meant that no attempt at speculative extrapolation took place. The very idea that speculative thinking is a sign of responsibility and intelligence did not occur to anyone in a position defined as responsible.

Within one month sick cows were found in France, precisely where official voices had been loudest over the four previous years in proclaiming purity. The first reaction of French officials was identical to that of the British. Denial. Threats of unbearable economic costs, of a loss of competitiveness. Protests of quality. And, of course, the public was reassured.

But it was not 1996. There had been four years of experience. Enough people allowed their imaginations to roam in order to reveal the shape of these events. And yet for days the official refusal to think dragged on, reinforced by four years of pseudo-rationalist posturing.

Then abruptly, the French political class sensed the full issue and tore the whole question out of the hands of the professional administration and the industrial structures. They more or less made a clean breast of it and switched from the defence to the offence. This meant that people tended to forget the relative inaction of the preceding four years. Suddenly there was pressure on all of Europe to ban the meat-laden feed and intensify testing.

One week at a time, other countries went from embarrassing imitations of the original British claims of innocence and purity, to an admission of doubt, to half-actions. It began with the German political leadership who — pushed by the presence of the Greens inside the government — became as offensive as their French equivalents. It's worth noting in passing the ability to create policy of the environmentalists inside governments. One by one, the other countries followed Germany. Of course, they were not so much leading or thinking or imagining as they were by now being driven by the progress of a five-year-old public debate.

Nevertheless they remained terrified of their own imaginations and that of the public. There were regular moaning references to the costs of destroying the feed containing meat, and niggling arguments over which animals and what feed and for how long. There was still more accent on the fate of feed producers than on the health of citizens. There was no thought that the utilitarian industrial costs might turn out to be peanuts compared to the long-term medical costs. No references were made to the underlying problems of intensive farming.

And there was no discussion of what had actually happened: that the European cattle industry had been destroyed, not by sheep-laced feed, not by a panicked public, not by disloyal scientists, not by a disease which came from somewhere else, but by a public-private sector élite which had refused from beginning to end to use their imagination to understand what was really happening. Instead, they locked themselves up inside their abstract, linear structures and followed short-term self-interest. This is what happens when we marginalize the imagination; that is, refuse to consider the usefulness of the imagination, because it fills us with uncertainty and therefore fear. Instead, we cling to the truth of the gods.

THE FOOLISH ACT

And so the suggestion is, do not control your imagination. Controlled, it will make men beasts. Or romantic fools. Or plain fools. Lord Phillips could have titled his report any of the above. *Beasts* after those who, for a mess of potage, hid what they knew even though it would endanger other people's lives. *Romantic Fools* for those who desperately believed that linear, fact-based progress had to be all right. And *Plain Fools* for those political figures and risk managers who believed that the right thing to do was to pretend you were certain that things were all right. That was the manly thing to do. The plainest of fools are of course us — if, that is, we have decided not to doubt the truth of the gods until no other path presents itself. Why would we cling so desperately to unquestioning belief? Why, if not from a fear that we will have to live with uncertainty.

And yet we do live with it. We force ourselves. Serious scientists, for example, argue that the scientific imagination is like that which writes novels or poetry. Certainly all three take permanent uncertainty and the preobjective realm and lateral thought as givens. Anything clearer would indicate fraud.

Which brings us back to the Schopenhauer dilemma. Yes, there are great imaginations. Imaginations of genius. But then there are also great tennis-players, which doesn't prevent tens of millions of people from playing decent tennis. There are great cooks, yet a billion-odd people cook for their families. And their families seem as happy and as healthy as the supply of food permits.

Great tennis and cooking may not be at the level of great imaginations, but the parallel is nevertheless there. It is the strange élitism of a Schopenhauer and the Hero worship of a Carlyle which have made it seem that imagination is unlike other qualities. Far rarer.

Most can but follow, depend, worship, because their absence of imagination makes them incapable of deciding sensibly.

"In most men," Schopenhauer claims, "the faculty of judgement is only nominally present.... Ordinary men show even in the smallest affairs want of confidence in their own judgement, just because they know from experience that it is of no service. With them prejudice and imitation take its place."[35] Schopenhauer is by no means alone in thinking so little of himself and therefore of the rest of us. He is expressing a received wisdom of contemporary society.

Why has imagination been so marginalized, unless the underlying assumption of our society is that the citizenry are too weak to be left to ponder. Note that Schopenhauer ends his comments on our incapacity to judge with a mixing together of what he says we sink into — "prejudice and imitation". In other words, he has chosen Aristotle's definition of imagination — that is, imitation — as an indicator of our incapacity. Because we have our imagination, our judgement cannot be trusted.

What about our very real marginalization of the imagination. We all know it exists and that we have it. In a sense we are awed by it, which is a polite way of describing fear. But if you stare in an unromantic manner at how our lives are organized and lived, how our societies are organized and function, you realize just how far we have gone in forgetting the central nature of this quality. Yet imagination remains exactly where it always is, right at hand, ready to be used as we wish.

After all, those characteristics which are seen as most admirable in our society by the functioning élites may simply be a self-indulgent confirmation of their own weaknesses. De Tocqueville pointed out how the self-indulgence of the eighteenth-century aristocracy reinforced their unquestioning certainty while destroying them from within. "The taste for luxury, the love of war, the rule of fashion, and the most superficial as well as the deepest passions of the human heart seemed to cooperate to enrich the poor and to impoverish the rich."[36] These tastes, not talents, in Edith Wharton's words, are the hallmarks of today's false imagination. They are therefore reminders of the fragility of our functioning élites, certainly as they are currently constituted.

And what are the talents of imagination itself? Tocqueville talks of science, new ideas, "poetry, eloquence and memory, the graces of the mind, the fire of imagination, depth of thought, and all the gifts which Heaven scatters at a venture". These, he said, "turned to the advantage of democracy".

He is not simply referring to those formal political acts we call democratic. He is talking of a type of society, essentially egalitarian, in which there is an assumption about the talent of all citizens to imagine, live with uncertainty, question and judge.

We must never forget for a moment that this sense of a great, shared, human quality, inclusive, pulling us forward, has always been rejected by what you might call the 'eternal, governing party' of Western civilization. The Platonists. In his late, anti-Socratic years, Plato clearly laid out the party platform. He called it his "strongest accusation against *imitation* [that is, imagination]. For it is surely monstrous that *it* is able to corrupt even the decent people with very few exceptions." You can almost hear Plato whispering strategy into the ears of the CJD crisis 'risk managers'.

And to use the creative imagination as a positive, active mirror of our own uncertainties is, for the Platonists, even worse. "[W]e must give poetry entry into our city as far only as hymns to the gods and panegyrics of the good are concerned. But if you receive the honeyed Muse in lyric or epic, be sure that pleasure and pain will be kings in your city, instead of law and whatever reasoned argument the community shall approve in each case to be best."[37] Again you can sense the fear — that fear which demands certainty.

But uncertainty and comfort with our own speculations and judgements are not such a difficult matter. We reassert our uncertainty and therefore ourselves more often than we realize. The great

American Justice Learned Hand spoke of democracy and the citizen as a combination of tolerance and imagination. He saw this — and the real but essential need for courage — as the norm of a successful society. What did he mean by courage? His reference was to another great Justice, Oliver Wendell Holmes. Courage was risking life "on a conclusion that tomorrow may disprove".[38] So courage is also in part an expression of our imagination.

In these few words you hear the essential democratic expression: an ability to imagine the whole, to accept uncertainty, to draw in our other qualities. And so you also hear hints of the essential scientific or creative expression.

Foolish things are said about why we want democracy despite its imperfections. The essential reason is that it is not a political system apart.

As a political system, democracy is a failure. But as an approach which lives off the expression of our imaginations, it is a success. It permits us to live with a continuing, prolonged swirl of uncertainty. To use our creativity. In other words, it is a success because it allows us to drag ourselves forward through the expression of our imaginations. This is a pre-objective process of folding considerations together. There is no proof. It is an uncomfortable, inclusive way of life. It is an enormous success.

To marginalize imagination in order to give comfort to rather simplistic linear methods and certainties is to undermine our strengths and discourage a dynamic use of our other qualities. In other words, do not control your imagination, unless you wish to make men beasts.

CHAPTER FIVE

INTUITION

AN EXISTENTIAL QUALITY

The problem is our tendency to confuse imagination and intuition. To run them together. Much of what we call imagination is really intuition.

Perhaps this happens because imagination is such an aggressive, offensive force, while intuition is essentially defensive — a reaction to the need to choose: to choose to act and to choose how to express ourselves. In our imaginations we have the courage, the strength, the aggressivity to juggle uncertainty. But we also need to make decisions. Periodically, we wish to or must make sense of the swirling forces of imagination in which there are elements of memory, common sense, ethics and reason. Like a god, we send our thunderbolt of decision and hope it strikes. This is the intuitive moment.

It may not sound defensive, but it is. The offensive force is the swirling uncertainty of our imagination. Intuition is our reaction to that movement.

In other words, intuition is the most practical of our qualities. The most useful, verging on the utilitarian. This is the essential existential quality.

It comes in two forms. First it is the basis of action which does not have the luxury of slow consideration. And very little of what we do is truly the fruit of careful consideration. Second, in a more passive form, intuition is the manner in which we choose to express ourselves.

All around us reality swirls. Within us, among us, our imagination swirls. Permanent movement and uncertainty. Movement is life. Certainty is death. Movement and uncertainty is reality.

Is it fear of this uncertainty which makes us not so much marginalize as deny intuition? At least in what passes for serious thought. Denial, you might say, is one of our endearing characteristics. We look in the mirror. We see right through what is there. We see things that aren't there. Is this self-deception? Or a desire to avoid the troublesome, the somehow embarrassing?

Because we intellectually deny its importance, we have to use it as if by accident or with subterfuge. And so it is difficult for us to make sensible use of our intuition. How could we, when it is treated as a human weakness, like unto an addiction — a Sirens' Isle waiting to lure us to lowly acts?

Our denial of intuition is driven by a fear of it. A fear of what? Perhaps first that to normalize a non-intellectual, indeed anti-intellectual function might open the door wide to the worst in us — a celebration of ignorance, a wallowing in superstition. And from there despotism, whether in personal relationships, social structures, private or public power, is but a step away.

Is there any justification for such fear? We actually know a great deal about how intuition functions and how we use it. This is an area in which we have made real intellectual progress over the last hundred years. I'd be hard pressed to demonstrate that there has been as much philosophical innovation in other areas, because most of the twentieth century was taken up with testing nineteenth-century ideas. And in our classrooms much time has been spent counting angels on pinheads; doing credit and debit columns of fragments of ideas.

But if there has been progress in our idea of intuition, there cannot have been complete denial. In fact, the blockage has been only on the structural side of our lives, education, careers and society. The rest has been remarkably open to intuition. So much so that it sometimes seems the Greek tragedies were written just yesterday.

And so as a professional, rational people we deny intuition. But when it comes to our lives and our destinies, we openly flaunt it.

How do we flaunt it? For a start, through the normalizing of psychology, the psychosomatic and the acceptance of archetypes. Through an explosion in the arts along lines which reinforce the intuitive underpinnings of creativity over thousands of years. And the effortless integration of imagery from animistic societies has infused new creative strength into the anaemic linear evolution of Western images.

Think of the ease with which Jung's formula — the collective unconscious — has reinjected non-rational forces into our civilization. Jung wrote of "inherited thought patterns", a concept in which intuition is implicit.[1] He knew it would bring on accusations of "fanciful mysticism", yet those accusations have disappeared into obscure scholastic texts, while Jung's idea has been integrated into our civilization as almost self-evident.

Into our civilization, but not into how we run our civilization. Our education and our structures are obsessed with linear progress. And that progress is presented as a function of knowledge, proof, understanding, verifiable truth. Yet how could anything so complete be reasonable, commonsensical, even rational? It is an approach which misses the non-linear nature of progress.

The scientist Henri Poincaré used to say that "intuition is the instrument of invention." I'd settle for 'one of the instruments of invention'. It may appear and reappear at any stage of the creative process. These appearances or interventions are neither vague nor irrational. They are specifically non-rational. The key point is what the scientific example suggests: that intuition is central to civilization, not just to intellect or methodology.

Jung understated our reality. "The primary function of intuition," he said, "is to transmit mere images or perceptions of relations and conditions which could not be transmitted by other means or only in very roundabout ways."[2] But these are not mere images or perceptions. They are the fruit of our imaginations. And the roundabout way is the best way if reality permits. It will marry imagination and reason with common sense and ethics, in order to produce policies, products and theories, paintings, music.

Jung again: "Intuition seeks to discover possibilities in the objective situation." "[I]t is also the instrument which, in the presence of a hopelessly blocked situation, works automatically towards the issue, which no other function could discover." So it is the instrument of need and of limited time.

Our problem remains that, while we have integrated intuition into our civilization in an almost self-evident manner, it remains technically excluded from how we run our affairs. This creates a conflict between reality and the way in which we pretend to manage reality.

How are we to admit in our organized life that intuition exists? That we use it. That we need to build in space for it. How are we to do that? For a start, by developing questions which are not designed to reward essentially rational or linear answers.

THE INTUITIVE ACT

Take a general in battle. He has the shared knowledge of common sense — so he understands the terrain and his opponent's techniques. He has his memory — his knowledge of precedents and current practice. He has his analytic rational thoughts and those instrumental structures which lie below reason. If he is talented and can put these three qualities together, he will be able to function in a perfectly competent manner, deploying his men and equipment professionally.

What does that mean once a battle starts? Suddenly all overriding structure disappears. If he has only these qualities — the qualities of professionalism — he will be thrown into a reactive mode.

Only his imagination can keep him moving with the fluidity of battle. With his imagination he can draw other qualities into a swirling sense of continuous movement involving both armies. He must be able to imagine the *other*. More to the point, he must imagine his army and the enemy's as one — a single field of positive and negative forces. Then, as the swirling mutates from one form to another, he will be able to conceive of his place within the whole. Henri Bergson, the early-twentieth-century advocate of intuition: "We grasp at the same time how the two are opposed and how they are reconciled."[3] It is from that imagining of the whole that he must decide and act.

This action is not rational. It is beyond common sense, free of memory.

This is the intuitive act. The imagination swirls and leaps. It contains the patterns of forward movement. The general, deep within his imagination, seizes upon these patterns and turns them into reality. He appears to have acted or to have created the circumstances for action. He has simply seized upon the patterns which existed in the imagination. The general himself will only be able to justify his intuitive action — that is, explain it intellectually — long after the battle is over.

Napoleon won the battle of Austerlitz on December 2, 1805. If you stand on the hill from which he directed the fight, two hundred years of carefully analyzing his great victory melt away. Because the outcome was so clear, historians and strategists have attributed his success to his formal — rational — plan, perfectly executed. But from the hill you can imagine how fluid the situation was. His victory was overwhelming because he was able to imagine the whole and then intuitively act as the movement swirled.

In the classic formula of Sun Tzu, it was a battle won and lost in the minds of the generals before it was fought. The Russian commander Mikhail Kutuzov could not imagine how he would win. He could not make the *whole* swirl in his intuitional favour. The apparent ease of the victory was the expression of a one-sided advantage of imagination and intuition, not of men, equipment and professionalism. You could say the same of the German advantage in May 1940. The most extreme expression of this deception is again from Sun Tzu: "The supreme art of war is to subdue the enemy without fighting." Napoleon was never quite able to rise to that level. He had to fight his battles. But on a good day he could win in a manner which appeared effortless, by combining most of our qualities into a force which wheeled on imagination and struck with intuition. The opposing general, no matter what he did, was no more than a passive, reactive shadow.

None of which means that Kutuzov was not a great general. In the monumental tides of civilization, this was not his moment. He waited and waited until his imagination could enfold the whole. He was remarkably conscious of what he was waiting for. It was seven years before his moment came in the second half of the 1812 Russian campaign.

In *War and Peace* Tolstoy captured this bizarre *floating in context* of the old Marshal, as he was carried to and fro through the endless campaigns, hunched forward on a horse, rocking in a carriage, somnolent on a litter, his eyes closed or half-closed, hardly speaking, seemingly hardly able to speak, apparently floating passively with events. He seemed to drift with his army, a thousand miles one way. A thousand the other. Asleep? Senile?

The others — the Tsar, his officers and men, his enemy — wait and wait and wait for him to do something. To take control of events. To freeze time. To organize a victory. Instead, he is deep in his imagination, trying to build a sense of the great tides of power and climate and geography, floating on them like a Delphic muse, waiting for the tides to favour his combination of qualities.

Then, abruptly, somewhere well to the east of Moscow, which he had refused to defend, Kutuzov sensed — intuited — that the uncertain swirl of events was his to grasp. The old wreck of a man slipped from apparently inert uncertainty and intuitively seized the moment. You could say he clambered onto a surfboard to ride a wave of fate all the way back to France.

In Western Europe this is called the retreat from Moscow, as if the world were a fixed place with its centre in the West; as if the defeat had been an error which would be corrected later on. In fact, Kutuzov chased them across the continent, with blow after blow seized from the swirl, driving them panicked through the snow. He annihilated Napoleon's great force.

The old Marshal, like an Australian aborigine, dreamt the songlines of the universe in which these events were taking place. These are "the inherited thought-patterns" Jung spoke of. Napoleon had done the same at Austerlitz. But, lulled by years of success and coddled by the inevitable courtiers, he had slipped out of imagination into mere talent, and so could not seize upon his intuition.[4]

In a very different style, Garibaldi went through the same evolution. There has always been something mysterious about his ability to defeat any force, almost without fighting, using a weak and motley crew of volunteers. The mythology surrounding the reunification of Italy, and the rise of Hero-worship to unprecedented heights, caused people to slide over the reality of what happened. Instead, they focused on the man as icon.

Perhaps the great liberal historian G.M. Trevelyan came closest to understanding Garibaldi. He described his "ubiquitous personal energy". The "ubiquitous" was Garibaldi's ability to imagine when others could not and then act intuitively while they were frozen in place. A few years later, the mission which drove him completed, he lost that energy or sense of movement and suddenly seemed to have become a bumbling old fool.

Kutuzov at Austerlitz, Napoleon in Russia or Waterloo, Garibaldi a few years after his victories. History loves a concrete explanation for these sorts of failures. Blame it on haemorrhoids if you like. But what happened was not concrete. Great general though he was, Napoleon allowed his imagination to freeze-frame, as if he could fix reality in place. And so his intuition could not function.

Bergson said this sort of situation was "...largely the result of our applying, to the disinterested knowledge of the *real*, processes which we generally employ for practical ends".[5] The phrase may seem rather cool and abstract for such a situation. But think of the First World War generals turning from cutting-edge theoretical strategists into butchers; of their inability to imagine the swirling whole, let alone to act through their intuition as the movement continued.

The greatest of hockey players, Wayne Gretzky, put it that "you must skate to where the puck is going, not to where it is." But where is it going? As you move, the whole pattern of people and energies moves about you. You might say the same of a great chess player — Karpov, for example — but he deals with the swirl in slow motion and on a limited space — a narrow field of complexity. However varied, the options are definable. A great player may multiply the options, but they are still, at best, scarcely out of the world of logic. The intuition used to judge his opponent is there, but overwhelmed by the limitations of the chessboard. Compared to Gretzky, Karpov operates on a lower plane of imagination and intuition. In a way our fascination for chess comes from its narrow focus — a few qualities intensively applied.

A hockey rink has some of the limitations of a chessboard — shape, lines, rules — and most players move about on it in an entirely predictable manner. But the possibility of great and continual fluidity with incalculable movement is there, in part because of the astonishing speed and manoeuvrability which skates give to the game. The same could be said of the potentially incalculable fluidity of soccer, with its lesser speed compensated for by the almost continual movement.

To understand the greatest of hockey players you had to be in the arena. Television is painfully linear. It follows the puck like a mediocre chess player. Most of the time Gretzky was not even on camera. He was hanging around the edges of the movement, watching it. Watching like Kutuzov. He was not calculating his moment, but imagining the shape of the whole in an almost detached Buddhist manner, making himself part of the past, present and future of the flow. It was a curious combination of passive and active, unconscious and conscious imagining. His interventions, when they came, seemed to materialize out of nowhere. He did not create or shape logic. He seized upon the shape of the movement in a way no one else could predict. Often he simply passed the puck to someone who only then saw his opportunity. Sometimes the opportunity was two or three passes away. Gretzky had not created these situations. He had imagined these movements coalescing. He had seized a moment in the imaginary flow. It was a high form of intuition.

The hockey rink does not have the battlefield's degree of the unknown and the unmeasurable. You can call a general's choice what you will — existentialism or even a hunch. This term — a hunch — is often used to denigrate intuition. But this is not the punter's hunch. The hunch of the card game or the stock-market gambler is a parody of intuition. The intuitional choices made by Kutuzov and Napoleon on an unlimited field of swirling forces were instants of reality seized out of undefinable circumstances.

ACTIVE AND PASSIVE INTUITION

Here is how intuition works. First it is about choosing a moment: either an instantaneous, urgent moment of action, or a moment in which we recognize and express some aspect either of ourselves or of a larger context. In both cases, intuition is a way of increasing our effective consciousness by non-rational means.

In other words, while intuition is always defensive, it comes in two forms — active and passive. The active I have just described through Napoleon, Kutuzov, Gretzky and Karpov. That is applied imagination.

The passive is quite different. I would call it applied animism. It is less about decision and action and more about discovering how to live in a larger reality — the synchronistic whole in which our lives are tied to a great sweep of time and of people and of place.

The first form — active — is instrumental, it is a way of describing the choices we make as reality flows unrelentingly about us. We stop imagining for that moment. We opt to move in a specific direction. We risk a certain action.

There is no point ignoring — as so much of social organization and indeed formal philosophy does — the real circumstances in which choice normally takes place. Choices of all sorts, big and small. To pretend that immobile conditions leading to clear, conscious decision-making are a reality available to any of us at almost any time is simply naive. To refuse to deal with how we have made choices over thousands of years and millions of occasions is to abandon philosophy to marginality by fixating on the imaginary ideal of "certainty" or "complete knowledge" — to use Descartes's term. Or, in an even more obsessional manner, to believe — as he did — that intuition itself is "the indubitable conception of a clear and attentive mind which proceeds solely from the light of reason".[6]

The very idea of *intuition* induces therefore a certain fear. And in its passive form it provokes even greater fear because it is tied to the concept of *animism*.

Why then insist upon describing passive intuition as 'applied animism'? Because animism is not and never has been about talking to rocks. It is about having an integrated sense of the whole, therefore of our place in it. You could say that animism is about having a sense of our actions in the context of the whole. Why do I call it passive?

Because this is not about choosing in the context of swirling forces and events. It is about trying to express our understanding of our context — that is, our place within the whole.

The result, as with the intuition of applied imagination, will be a form of choice. That is, we discover exactly how to express our understanding. A particular sort of painted image, for example.

You might say that this passive applied animism is timeless. Or that it helps us to understand a whole aspect of ourselves which is timeless. This is the exact opposite of our mortal lives in which a finite amount of time sweeps on to its end and we must choose — ethically, intuitively, rationally — all along the way. With passive applied animism we are part of the synchronistic whole.

Think about the sorts of difficulties we have dealing with our reality — our personal reality and that of our society. Much of that difficulty comes not from reality but from our denial of its existence. And why do we deny it?

Well, in part, because we believe that humans are superior to the other elements on the planet — a harmless enough conviction. But from that superiority we draw a false conclusion — that we are set apart from all the rest and driven independently by linear, rational forces. This sense of apartness feeds our conviction that progress is a rather straightforward and inevitable human force.

This makes us see ourselves as entirely time-sensitive. You might say that our superior apartness makes us time-sensitive in a rather rudimentary, naive way. There is only life and death. We are constantly rushing forward. Towards what? Death? A linear idea of progress accentuates a fear-laden obsession with mortality. It isolates us in a desperate way from the context in which we exist and from the timelessness of that context.

Emile Durkheim, with the best will in the world, celebrated society as a force which liberates us "from blind unthinking physical forces"; in other words, specifically from nature, generally from context and psychologically from mortality.[7] In this approach, nature and context are things which subject us. We must free ourselves from our subjection to the forces of nature. They fill us with fear.

Here you see our weakness for ideology. If we live in a context, we believe we are subjected. If we can free ourselves from this context, well then, we are free. For some reason, the idea that we might have a bit of both seems extraordinarily complicated. Why not have the ability to act in a manner which other animals or rocks cannot, while still seeing ourselves as part of the unthinking physical forces? Quite simply because it would imply living with complexity and uncertainty. We must have one or the other — freedom or subjection.

But if we cannot accept that we are both rushing forward and yet part of a synchronistic whole, what are we doing if not condemning ourselves to an isolated stance of denial?

What is there in our passive animism which is essentially timeless? Dreams are the most obvious example. Jung talked of "Ancient images...restored to life by the primitive, analogical mode of thinking peculiar to dreams".[8] These are inherited time-patterns. But Jung's desire to reconnect us with a deep past accidentally creates a false sense of progress — we must reconnect ourselves with and through the primitive. We must therefore make an organized effort to do what exactly? Become primitive?

But are these elements primitive in any way which we understand that idea? Is there, for example, anything primitive about *The Epic of Gilgamesh*, at least five thousand years old? It strikes me as having a more modern feel and sound than most management theories of twenty years ago. More precisely, it delivers a clearer understanding of human reality than these management theories.

Take the description of the great flood. Gilgamesh had been King of Uruk, which lay between Babylon and Ur on the Euphrates. Here, in what we call the cradle of civilization, the story of the flood was clearly told on clay tablets long before the Old Testament, fifteen hundred years before Homer. It is worth making this point because Homer and the Old Testament have theoretically provided us with the formal elements of modern mythology and archetypes. Yet they were themselves built upon an equally, if not more sophisticated, mythology, itself with deep historic roots. The warning of the disaster to come was delivered to the original 'Noah' — that of Gilgamesh's epic — in a dream. "Tear down your house and build a boat, abandon possessions and look for life, despise worldly goods and save your soul alive."[9]

The practical message is obvious: build a boat and stay alive. But the real message is quite different. It is timeless. Synchronistic. It could be written today. Indeed it often is. We must die. Our house, our possessions, our worldly goods cause us to live in denial. The boat is life and all that matters. It is our "soul alive". It is the timelessness of life, the essence of it, as opposed to the linear, material, short version, which leads to extinction.

And as the narrator of *Gilgamesh* points out: "The wise man learned it in a dream." Earlier in the epic, before the flood incident, Gilgamesh himself says, "The dream was marvellous, but the terror was great; we must treasure the dream whatever the terror; for the dream has shown that misery comes at last to the healthy man, the end of life is sorrow."

The dream links us both to our mortality and to the immortal nature of our timelessness; that is, to our collective unconscious. These personal points of access to timelessness — dreams and the collective unconscious — remind us that we are surrounded by many versions of synchronicity. Art, stories, music, sounds, myths, actions, courage, fear, the physical nature of our relationship to the non-human. We are never liberated from the physical forces. And we don't need to be. We need to be conscious of reality and how to live with it. We do not need to rediscover the primitive. It is no more primitive than it ever was. Rather we need to accept that both mortality and timelessness exist. Earlier I quoted Jung's idea that we function in part with "inherited thought patterns". These are not intellectual patterns, although they contain elements of the intellectual. Our brain functions as it has always functioned. It is our brain or our soul or our qualities in some sort of equilibrium. We progress in one sense, yet in another we react to apparently eternal images, myths or choices.

I said that intuition comes in two forms: active and passive; applied imagination and applied animism. But they don't stand on their own, separated one from the other. Deny the application of imagination and you deny the existence of a synchronistic timeless whole, even though the evidence of its existence is all around you. Intuition is one of our most practical qualities. Deny its function and you set yourself up for utilitarian mysticism and Hero worship. Deny the animist and you deny both the roots of imagination and its application. In fact, you deny the very idea of swirling uncertainty as a human strength.

A DEFENSIVE QUALITY

Intuition is defensive because it is how we actually live, whether on the practical or the metaphysical level. On both we choose, we act, we express ourselves by reacting to our contexts; that of time passing and that of timelessness.

I can think of three ways to express the defensive nature of choosing. First take the practical question of choice. There is nothing intellectual about it. As Thomas de Koninck puts it, "we are not in possession of a direct intellectual intuition of our own".[10] Our choices emerge out of a personal and general jumble of events and people, involving elements of the shared knowledge of common sense and the abstraction of reason, and a great deal more.

Second, there is the uncertainty surrounding how we choose. This complexity of the context means that intuition tends to conservatism. Take the emergence of the environmental movement over the last quarter-century. In political terms it is on the cutting edge of ideas and debate. Those in power — whether political, administrative or corporate — think of the environmental movement as radical because it does not fit into their own linear logic, which they call progress. Certainty and inevitability — utilitarian determinism — are its anchors.

The arrival on the scene of the environmentalists has been frightening to these people. Why? Because the foundation of the apparently new environmental arguments is neither linear nor utilitarian.

Not that the environmentalists don't tend to play it both ways. They often slip into the language of the day, phrasing their interventions in an apparently linear, quantifiable, even utilitarian manner. At first, those in power are reassured. They can hire their own expert environmentalists to concoct a reply. They can hold consultations or stakeholder meetings in the classic corporatist manner, as if only rival views of self-interest were at stake. This leads to the classic corporatist stand-off in which everyone has his reason.

But the environmentalists may then switch from their own blinkered utilitarianism to timeless arguments without formal intellectual shape. They then remind the authorities that the primary fiduciary trust of those with any responsibility over a society is to take contextual precautions before action. They talk of our general need, in Canadian philosopher Charles Taylor's words, to "recover a sense of the demand that our natural surroundings and wilderness make on us".[11] Why? So that those with political and economic power will act in a careful, precautionary manner. The need is not for someone who thinks he is courageous because he is sure enough of himself to press on regardless. Far better to have someone who wonders whether he is not wrong, than someone certain that he is right.

To act in contextual terms involves lateral thinking and consideration of our uncertainties. If you look at environmentalism in common-sense terms or those of ethics or imagination, or reason, you realize that it is both conservative in practical terms and profoundly conservative in general terms. Conservative in the true meaning of the word — that of contextualization and timelessness married to those choices which appear with the passage of time.

This has nothing to do with the false conservatism of ideologues who are obsessed above all by a curious combination of moralism and absolute economic truths. Rather, environmentalism at its best implies an awareness of both mortality and timelessness. What do these two factors suggest? That we need to be careful. "Since our ignorance about the natural world which sustains us is vast," David Suzuki argues, "everything we do ought to be done cautiously and conservatively."[12]

Seen in this way, you realize that much of our devotion to absolute truths and linear progress is actually a formalization of rather juvenile determinism; a determination to deny mortality and timelessness; a desperation to push naïveté at least into middle age. Intuition, on the other hand, has a defensive precautionary air about it when faced by environmental choices, because it is restrained by a sense of uncertainty combined with a need to choose.

A third and more basic explanation of intuition's defensive nature is mortality itself. Birth and death are the underpinnings of the collective unconscious. Here is the great source of fear; the fear which makes us deny death so actively. Witness how much of scientific and medical progress is based on the idea of a war against death. Against mortality. The intention is good, but the reality is an encouragement of denial.

Again, we have always struggled with the implications of our mortality. Gilgamesh wished to be eternal, just as we do. One of the great experts on this epic puts it that the gods cannot be tragic as they do not die.[13] Gilgamesh's first hint of tragedy comes with the agonizing death of his great friend, Enkidu. He then makes an impossible journey across the earth to reach the Underworld in order to gain the secret of eternal life — to defeat death.

When he finally reaches the other side, he begins: "I wish to question you concerning the living and the dead, how shall I find the life for which I am searching?"

And the reply comes back: "'There is no permanence.'"

Gilgamesh was able to accept that the ultimate choice is to admit that there isn't one or to live in denial. And so he became our first tragic hero. A real hero; because he refused the myth of immortality. He accepted that tragedy is only bearable if we make ourselves conscious of it.

Here is the ultimate reminder that intuition seen as choice must be defensive. Here the pretensions of linear progress are revealed as tragicomedy. False individualism comes from a false sense of how we might fulfil ourselves. Self-fulfilment does not come from setting ourselves apart. It is a result of accepting our context. Or, in Charles Taylor's phrase: "[S]elf-fulfilment, so far from excluding unconditional relationships and moral demands beyond the self, actually requires these in some form."[14]

The point is that the tragedy of mortality is tied to the tragedy of choosing. If we deny our context and see ourselves as primarily free agents set apart from all others, or even as set apart from most others, except a small group — our family or race or community or nation — or set apart from the other elements with which we survive, whether animal, plant, physical or climatic, well then, the context will simply impose its version of the choice upon us at a time which suits it.

If we deny the tragedy of our mortality, we are well on the road to denying intuition; well on the way to blustering about truth and control. In other words, intuition is not about the helpless acceptance of mysterious external forces. The active part of it is about an intelligent exercise of our real options. Our choices may be limited and fundamentally defensive, but using intuition intelligently, we can make enormous changes which do not produce a whiplash effect that erases our accomplishments, leaving us worse off than before our brilliant initiative.

As for the passive part — applied animism — it also is a defensive expression of our context. But passive does not mean helpless. As with Gilgamesh, our tragedy must be expressed. Our force is our ability to express our context. Our consciousness. That is the application of creativity, of art.

"When I was writing down these fantasies," Jung remembered, "I once asked myself, 'What am I really doing? Certainly this has nothing to do with science. But then what is it?' Whereupon a voice within me said, 'It is art.'"[15]

THE COMEDY OF DENIAL

The more sophisticated we become, the more eager we are to deny the importance or even the existence of intuition. We are eager to believe ourselves in control of our lives in every way; to have explanations and to be able to apply them.

John Stuart Mill: Intuition and unconsciousness are "the great intellectual support of false doctrines and bad institutions.... There never was such an instrument devised for consecrating all deepseated prejudices."[16]

Here is the fear of anything not clearly demonstrated to be true through a linear process of proof.

John Rawls: "Our dependence on intuition can be reduced by posing more limited questions and by substituting prudential for moral judgement."

But intuition is not about questioning or judging. It is about choosing or expressing. These choices, driven by time-sensitive needs, are usually very specific. Nothing could be more prudent than intuition. As for morality, intuition is not particularly marked by it. It is either practical or contextual. There is room for religion or moralism in the expression of a context. But more fundamentally it is a phenomenon of myth and of art. And the greater the quality of the art, the more it expresses reality in a manner free of perspective.

Rawls is so busy fearing intuition that he doesn't examine what it actually does. "No doubt any conception of justice will have to rely on intuition to some degree. Nevertheless we should do what we can to reduce [its use in] our considered judgements." Why? Because, if we don't, we will all end up with different "final principles" and so with different "concepts of justice".

He is so obsessed with a standardized analysis of justice tied to contractual obligations that he misses the central role of intuition in the choices made by juries and judges. When committees or cabinets or juries intervene, they rarely have the luxury of considered understanding upon which to reach a clearly proved conclusion. He sees intuition as a threat to reason because he imagines that reality is at the beck and call of rational methodology. To pretend it is, is to emulate King Canute walking into the sea and ordering the tide to halt.

Why quote Mill and Rawls? Because they remind us of our continuing intellectual denial of intuition; a fear which persists although, in fact, we make regular use of it. But this denial prevents us from using it sensibly. Instead, we must repeatedly be surprised to find ourselves in its grip and then erase all memory of our misdemeanour as quickly as possible. At worst, we believe that to use our intuition is to reveal a weakness. At best, we are encouraged to see it merely as an aspect of something else. For example, it is often presented as no more than an aspect of intelligence. In that case, so is ethics — the intelligence to know what is right. And so are common sense and our other qualities.

What then is intelligence except a grab bag? And we are back inside the ideology of all-inclusive reason, attempting to categorize the non-rational in a rational cage. The humanities, for example, are now suffering from pedantic attempts at categorization and measurement. But, as George Steiner points out, they "... are susceptible neither to crucial experiments nor to verification".[17] Rather they are "narratives of intuition", what I would call the expression of context; a way of touching much of what cannot be calculated in our experience. "[T]here are things in the psyche which I do not produce," Jung said, "but which produce themselves and have their own life." We are constantly struggling to gain access to these "things", "this function". We do not really succeed because our approach is essentially one of denial.

Our best hope is first to accept the existence of intuition as a quality in its own right. And then to avoid attempts at analysis, proof and definition. We are better off attempting to describe intuition in action.

Here are two particularly peculiar examples. During the South African Truth and Reconciliation Commission, the idea of the humanities was taken back to its source as a lived narration of intuition.

"This thing called reconciliation," the mother of a victim said, "if it means this perpetrator, this man who has killed Christopher Piet, if it means he becomes human again, this man, so that I, so that all of us, get our humanity back... then I agree, then I support it all."[18] Here is an expression of passive intuition in context in its fullest sense.

Now put aside our accepted notion of humanism. Perhaps the most famous of the torturers — Captain Jeffrey Benzien — was known to be capable of getting the information he wanted from anyone within thirty minutes. This was not a matter of machines or technique. He understood the psyche of each victim. You might call such a talent intuition gone wrong. During his examination before the Commission by those of his victims who had survived, what surprised the observers was the desire of each victim to understand his torturer. Only that way could they understand themselves. Before packed courtrooms, many reverted to the tone of victim, often revealing themselves in a way which was harmful to their reputation and their career. There was no other way through for them.

Christopher Piet's mother and the torture victims would probably have found Immanuel Kant's ideas on intuition or those of Bertrand Russell rather naive, even silly. Kant tried his best to link sensibility (intuitions) to understanding; to argue that you must combine them to make proper judgement. This simply isn't true. "Thoughts without content are empty; intuitions without concepts are blind." Well, yes and no. That all depends on what you mean by content and concepts.

In the *Critique of Pure Reason*, Kant subjected them to reason, not imagination, and so missed the point of intuition.

Russell goes on about "slow and fallible study" and so misses what intuition is and does.[19] Since it is not a product of this slow-motion analysis, he concludes that it must be a matter of "revelation" or "illumination" "as contrasted with sense, reason and analysis". In other words, if there is intuition it must be seen as mysticism — the enemy of human thought patterns.

The tendency then is either to deny intuition or to work it into an argument in a dependent position, as if it were a weakness rather than a strength, let alone a quality.

Deny intuition or denigrate it, neither really matters. We simply go on using it. The only pity is that by refusing to normalize intuition, to treat it as a quality and a strength not a weakness, we limit ourselves to less intelligent action than would otherwise be possible.

APPLIED ANIMISM

One way of approaching passive intuition is through beauty — that beauty which can be seen or felt, without being fully understood or owned.

Here is the eternal dilemma of any novelist or artist. Beauty may be a step away, all our life, in our bed, on our wall. We reach out to grasp hold and it seems to slip away. Of course you can see beauty another way, as the sum of the parts — the trophy wife, the painting — owned, possessed as utilitarian objects.

The first sort — beauty as truth, truth as beauty — fulfils David Suzuki's prediction. To grow, to enrich, to be enjoyed, the relationship must be one of care — a love which is a form of respect because it is only partially understood and cannot truly be possessed.

It was the Earl of Shaftesbury, in the early eighteenth century, who said "All beauty is truth." But not the truth of proof. Rather that of an "inner intellectual structure of the universe". This is a truth which can be experienced and intuitively understood, something which "...does not proceed from the parts to the whole, but from the whole to the parts". Only through art can humans express this on a sustained, organized basis.

By simply taking as a given that there is an inner intellectual structure, we can embrace the idea of something much larger than anything we can understand or construct. From that comes the need for us to act with precautionary care. This is an expression of our intuition. Shaftesbury's argument would be that "...real truth can no more exist without beauty than beauty can without truth."[20]

The average proponent of truth as proof would ask — 'What does that mean?' If you could ask Donatello or Piero della Francesca or Goya or Picasso, they would simply nod because they instinctively understood. They would not see this as erasing their need for training or specific knowledge, but as the key to that "inner intellectual structure of the universe" which makes the difference between a professional painting and beauty.

Carpaccio's cycle of paintings on the life of St. Ursula is now in the Academia in Venice. As he progressed through the scenes, he gradually found a revolutionary inner intellectual structure of beauty — a way of conveying the remarkable story and its religious and ethical force — its inner beauty. When you get to the best painting — that of Ursula's martyrdom and burial — you find the painting divided in half by her murderer. The saint, the pope and the other martyrs are on the left. On the right are the murderer's companions and, as in a cartoon, the next scene, the saint's future burial. As for the murderer, he has his bow drawn. He is about to loose the arrow into her heart.

The point is this: he has a perfect, elegant figure, a narrow waist, is poised in an artistic manner, almost as a dancer. He is wearing the most fashionable, colourful clothing — pleats, silk, slashed sleeves with linen puffing out, brocaded, red, gold and white, delicate.

He is the most beautiful person in the painting. He is the representation of corporeal perfection. Carpaccio seems to be saying something about the truth of the inner intellectual structure of the universe as beauty, versus corporeal beauty. And the murderer's back is turned to us so that we do not see his face.

This inner structure of the universe is all around us. In August 2000, I flew in a small plane up the Nahanni River in the Canadian Northwest Territories. We flew low, with the cliffs of the monumental canyon above us on both sides. This National Park is probably the most spectacular unspoilt watershed in the world. Partway upriver you reach the Virginia Falls, which are twice the height of Niagara Falls. You fly straight at their crest, crossing only a few metres above the waterline, and touch down on the pool above — the most astonishing way to land a plane I know of.

The problem is that the park includes only the Nahanni itself — the central line of the watershed — not the pristine rivers which drain into it.

You might say that at its most basic level the watershed system of the Nahanni is a physical example of the inner intellectual structure of the universe. Each of the parts can be looked at separately — the various rivers crashing through the mountains, the plateaus, waterfalls, wildlife — but the true beauty exists only as a whole.

We flew out along one of the tributary rivers which took us over a mining site, just beyond the park, built deep in a canyon on the water's edge. The tailings pond has been constructed according to the law. It meets all of the instrumental tests. It can be proved by every intellectual tool available that there is no calculable danger.

The intuitive point is obvious. The tailings pond is constructed of high gravel walls on the river's edge. The river is in a deep canyon. The tailings cannot go anywhere else. They can either stay in the pond for eternity, seep out by some undetermined means at some unknown date into the river, or be released by a freak accident, such as a storm which unleashes as yet uncalculated amounts of water.

Around the world over the last twenty years we have seen repeated uncalculated storms, leaks and burst dams. We are told that we are entering a period of increasing climatic instability, which may render safety calculations uncertain.

And in this particular case, what are the known factors used to establish the safety standards? We've only had the opportunity to measure the river system's daily levels for a few years. Until recently it was even more inaccessible. A proper calculation would include an element of timelessness — what do we know, what don't we know, what is the balance? What experiences have there been elsewhere? For example, the Durance in southern France has periodically over the last 150 years risen two to three times beyond its normal variations, crossing dykes, drowning numbers of people and flooding built-up areas. Carefully calculated dams and dykes have since been built throughout the area. Yet nearby, Nîmes, theoretically protected by long-established standards based on two thousand years of experience and measurement, was seriously flooded in 1988 by its much smaller and more controlled river. So the past, even known, is only that. Our survival has to be based on past, present and future, imagined and intuited.

What could be more romantic than the idea of a tailings pond on the Nahanni watershed? Why romantic? Because it assumes that — like love — gravel walls bulldozed into place are forever. This is the romanticism of thousands of emperors and kings, declaring that suns will never set and walls will always stand. But many of their carefully mortared fortresses and palaces last only a few decades.

The intuitive argument is very simple. The Nahanni is an irreplaceable marvel for which humans are responsible to the extent that they touch it. We have no real need to touch it. It is not a matter of our life or death. A few people in mining stand to make a bit of money which at most represents a drop in the sea of cash which finances society. On the other hand, should there be a single spill from a single tailings pond, the whole system will be changed, damaged, perhaps ruined. A great general would have no trouble understanding this. His profession is to combine the truth of a terrible beauty with its inner structure. Kutuzov and Napoleon were always looking for the unnecessary incalculable risk in order to avoid taking it.

On the other hand, the intent of civilization is very clear. Shaftesbury would have argued that "the purest harmony between man and the world is attainable only through beauty." More than three hundred years ago Spinoza made the same intuitive argument, which could just as easily act as a framework for the Nahanni watershed. Intuition leads "to the adequate knowledge of the essence of things".[21] To put a tailings pond on it is a romantic refusal of that knowledge.

This sort of argument is relatively straightforward. Why then do we have so much trouble with the idea of intuition and animism?

In part because our ability to believe ourselves to be creatures apart — a deformation of the idea of consciousness — does make us what Erich Fromm called "the freak of the universe". We alone "can feel evicted from paradise". What is this paradise? That of unconscious participation in the inner structure of the universe. Fromm called it nature. That would explain our ambivalence to the planet on which we live. We love it, moon over it, versify and paint it, yet we take great pleasure in raping it as if to teach it a lesson, as if demonstrating that the true beauty of the great synchronistic whole can be brought down to our level of psychic homelessness.

In mythological terms our eviction is that from the womb. And our loss is the loss of the matriarchal civilization. After all, the matriarchal model is all-inclusive and not tied to an obsession with dividing up power. Only the self-loathing of the evicted could make us want to believe that sticking a tailings pond on the greatest unspoilt watershed in the world is a good idea and worth the risk. And that not doing so would show weakness. Weakness before whom? Before a nature which first evicts us and then, while exhibiting its beauty, resists our control.

Since the industrial revolution the arguments surrounding the shattering of the whole — and our eviction from it — have been constant. What's more they have by no means been limited to the West and its use of rational domination.

Octavio Paz describes the Mexican view of life as combat. "The Mexican *macho* — the male — is a hermetic being, closed up in himself.... Manliness is judged according to one's invulnerability."[22] Invulnerable to what? To "...the world around us...." And why this obviously false pretense? Because, as the great Guatemalan novelist Miguel Angel Asturias put it, organic culture has been destroyed. Organic? Le Clézio: "[T]he individualist and possessive world of Hernando Cortès" had destroyed "the collective and magic world of the Indians." Suddenly, one of the Indian leaders said in 1520, "All that has value was then counted as nothing."

Magic? Obviously magic can be mere superstition. For example, to buy a pair of running shoes — because a famous basketball player says he wears that brand, having been paid to do so — in some vague hope of playing better or of being touched by the force of the Hero, is an acceptance of magic as banal superstition. If magic can be exploited in the most dishonest and superficial of ways, it must actually exist at some profound, unconscious level.

The organic culture Asturias spoke of was somehow more integrated. Magic could relate to the matriarchal idea of a shared world. The Iroquois used to carve masks to protect themselves against their plants becoming diseased — crop blight in particular. These were worn during false-face ceremonies before each growing season. The interesting detail is that they carved these masks on living basswood trees. Once completed, they held ritual ceremonies asking the trees permission to slice off the mask. The obvious idea was that this false face would hold the life of the tree itself, reaching down through its roots into the life of the earth. Think what you will of the practical argument. The highly sophisticated point being made lies in the idea of an integrated world view — an organic view in which each element is related to the other.

From the sixteenth century on, European societies were busy celebrating their subjugation of the matriarchal. I quoted Durkheim on the liberating effect of society as it theoretically frees us from "subjection to the world of nature". The ultimate expression of this freedom was to whirl about in order to subject nature. Better yet, punish it! Make the subjection felt.

The curious thing is that the inner structure of the universe isn't all that hard to get along with. It is capable of yielding up a great deal without a backlash. And we could, after all, easily develop a sense of precautionary action. We could consider the full, integrated consequences of our actions, instead of taking such pleasure in linear juvenile racing about.

It would take no trouble at all, for example, to institute a serious system of precautionary harvesting when dealing with commodities. To realize that we are not serious, you have only to track the almost-disappearance of the Atlantic cod over the last decade, as country after country has denied, prevaricated, protested, worried about employment, until their inaction meant there would be no jobs at all.

Precautionary action and precautionary harvesting, as well as considering the full consequences of our actions, do not cost money. They actually ensure a longer-lived, more stable income and produce a variety of new money-making opportunities.

Unlike ethics, both imagination and intuition, properly combined, do pay. Intuition pays for generals or businessmen, for the environment or for society as a whole. It is a profoundly practical quality. It pays in both the short and the long run. It is not about self-interest, but self-interest benefits. It links us to the structures of inner beauty.

What I'm saying here should not be mistaken for environmental determination or even a suggestion that animism is particularly a function of nature. Nature is simply the most obvious skeletal indication we have of an inner structure. But the collective unconscious is another. And our cultural expressions are another. Indeed, the ultimate goal of architecture and urbanization is to create man-made places which reach beyond the particular maker and become part of the inner structure. Elias Canetti on Vienna: "I found out something that I didn't know and that wasn't written in any of my books, the idea that a city can love a human being."[23] The city as a living being is something experienced by most of us. It can love or hate its inhabitants.

Equally, a single building can, from time to time, become part of the inner structure of the universe and so express something which reaches well beyond its builders and its users. We cannot even explain technically how the three Greek temples at Paestum, south of Naples, have their most basic visual effect on us. "The shadows are almost as important as the building. . . ."[24] Not just the shadow the Doric temple throws, but every tiny shadow evolving with the day and the season. The fluting in the columns. Not just that there is fluting, but the particular orientations and size and angles of that fluting still throw shadows in such a way that what the building isn't is as important as what it is. This concept of architecture by indirection has been so lost that, in some Western cities with particularly unsophisticated building codes, the very right to natural light has been legally removed.

The Pantheon in Rome is for me the essential example of a building integrated into the universe, perhaps because it reaches back into a world where what we call paganism contained a strong element of matriarchy. Whenever I am in Rome I go inside every morning for a few moments just after it opens. Each time it is different. What is different? The light, the shadow, the shape, the size, of what is essentially an enormous dome set on the ground without any vertical walls. The seasons change and the world flowing over that great circular hole in the centre of the dome transforms the space.

Once I was there on Corpus Christi and sat in the centre beneath the opening. There was a mass with Gregorian chant and an orchestra from Augsburg. I stared up as if into the eye of god. What god? That is another question. Up into the inner structure of the universe. The sensation was that you could be sucked up through the hole into that timelessness of heavens blowing by.

The chanting and the music rolled literally around and around the dome, around itself, again as if it were being sucked up into the heavens. The effect was to produce a wave of unexpected emotion in all of us seated there. I felt it rushing through me. You could sense it in the stillness of the crowd. The priest raised the dish containing the host to bless it, as priests have done a million times around the world over the last two thousand years. He looked up, as they do, but here he looked up through this also two-thousand-year-old eye, into the universe. White, billowing clouds blew by. How many ceremonies of how many cults had slipped into that same gulf-stream swirl over the two millennia?

What was I expecting? The truth of beauty, the beauty of truth, in an inexplicable manner. Such beauty can be an expression of nature or war or creativity or of even more amorphous forces. When writing earlier of ethics and the corporatist trap into which NGOs are falling, I described the early-twentieth-century European reformers and how their apparent strength had evaporated with the declaration of war in October 1914.

Look at this phenomenon in another way. While these millions of workers, activists and politicians were building a web of solidarity against war, a parallel web of "industrialists, general staffs and diplomats" was deep in "discreet" but equally "intensive preparations for war".[25] That was how the historian François Fetjö put it.

Something else more profound was going on. There had been a "destruction of organic culture" in the nineteenth century — at least of any formalized, conscious organic culture. Such a profound change in the formal culture can't help but change the way we act.

The organic reality remains. The inner structure is still there. Rivers will continue to rise or fall beyond our measurements. Fish will disappear or not. Cows will or will not become carriers of poison. The sign of a possible impending catastrophe in all of this is that the efforts of those working to prevent the various organic problems are matched or more than matched by those working to provoke them.

They often feign not to see each other or, naively, to see each other as mere opponents when, like the music wrapping around itself in the Pantheon, they are themselves part of an organic whole, a synchronistic unfolding of the universe's inner structure.

The whirling of this terrible beauty can only be made human by the two sides consciously realizing they are part of a single movement. The experience is the same, the expression of it is some aspect of a single beauty, profoundly passive, yet capable of constructive or destructive application.

SCIENCE

Animism is the ultimate defender of science and science of animism. After all, the scientific world more easily than any other can identify with the idea of a universal inner structure. And most scientists would agree that the profound unity of that structure is an essential beauty.

I described earlier the two centuries during which an aesthetic or artistic world of autopsies and anatomy drove the scientific world of medicine — both medical research and applied medicine. That was not an accident or an exception. It was a normal expression of the inseparable link between the arts and the sciences. Ernst Cassirer, in 1932, just before corporatism and materialism drove a catastrophic wedge between these two worlds, wrote that "Both art and science substitute for objects symbols of objects, and they differ only in the use which they make of their symbols."[26]

It's hard for us to hear these words today, deep as we are in a life of utilitarian determinism which attaches most science to something called the knowledge economy. This seems to cut it off from its sources, which like those of art, are buried deep in non-linear thinking about the context in which we exist. The two are linked — the linear and the non-linear, the utilitarian and the symbol — but there is an essential difference. Bertrand Russell skirted along the edge of this difference when he wrote that intuition "is what first leads to the beliefs which subsequent reason confirms or confutes.... Reason is a harmonizing, controlling force rather than a creative one."[27] But here he was looking for a linear progress from one to the other, as if with each intuitive breakthrough we must dash into rational safety.

His approach resembled that of Henri Poincaré: "intuition is the instrument of invention". Neither really sees intuition as a truly normal part of life or science, only a slightly embarrassing tool of progress.

Henri Bergson was the one who argued most forcefully and successfully for a natural marriage between intuition and science. His explanation for the marginality of intuition in spite of its role at the core of scientific discovery is that intuition, in order to express itself, must use "a mode of expression and of application which conforms to the habits of our thought". This includes "exactitude and precision". Gradually we mistake "the logical equipment of science for science itself".

What is feasible here is to admit that intuition exists. Is used. That being the case, we need to build in space for it. How? As I said at the beginning of the chapter, by developing questions which are not designed to reward essentially rational or linear answers.

Of course, at various moments in science, all propositions meet the wall of demonstrable results. But if you squeeze out intuition, you remove its existential force from the evolution of scientific progress. You isolate and marginalize the imagination. The strongest minds or personalities may find ways around this. But those with less self-confidence will slip away from more original thinking towards respectable predictability.

It was E.B. Tylor, in his major work on animism in 1871, who put it most accurately when he said that the difference in question was between a spiritualistic and a materialistic philosophy. *Spiritualistic* is another one of those words which are difficult to use today. It has been tarred by a confusion with spiritism; and subjected to severe rejection by what some writers were already calling, over a century ago, "the mechanistic dogma".

Yet if you see *spiritualistic* in the context of environmentalism or the arts or an integrated approach towards medicine or pure science, you realize that "the essence of science over the last two centuries [of] scientific progress has [been to] continually undermine the abstract intellectual form of the western religions that set man apart." In other words, the essence of scientific progress has reinforced an animistic, holistic view in which man cannot be set apart. Why then the knowledge economy? Why the astonishing rise of materialism? You could argue that it is just a nervous tic; a superstitious emanation. Of what? Of our latest desperate attempt at an abstract religion that will set us apart.

Scientists around the world today will tell you about the materialistic attack on scientific questioning. About the knowledge economy. About the attempts to marginalize pure science. About universities, in a virtual delirium, renaming pure science as novelty science; that is, as marginal as the arts. They face daily attempts to deflect their work into short-term, quickly commercializeable responses which will temporarily pass for answers.

The point is that dominant materialism is the essential enemy of passive intuition. And that is what makes it so difficult for us to examine even such easy questions as whether a particular tailings pond is sensible or an affront to shared knowledge. Materialism, as the lowest, most superstitious form of romanticism, is a constant barrier to scientific progress.

Think of materialism in its mediaeval forms. Imagination and intuition allowed us to progress beyond where self-interest and materialism and the managers of the day were only too happy to stay. Had we remained at that level of narrow self-interest, the sun would still be moving around the earth. In fact, the earth would probably be flat.

●

SUPERSTITION

None of which is to deny the existence of superstition, cheap hunches and fear hiding behind intuition. This is the fear which is itself frightening for any civilization. It lies coddled just below the surface of normal life, waiting to burst forth as prejudice or racism or mythologies so false that they amount to a self-delusion which prevents us from acting in a sensible manner. This falsely intuitive sense that we are right allows us to dress delusions up in fantasy-like innocence and purity. The more evil, the more childlike.

A German minor aristocrat — a conservative opponent of the Nazis — kept a remarkable diary of the events from 1936 to his execution in 1944. Friedrich Reck-Malleczewen had an unerring ability to understand what people and events really meant. His descriptions of the early Hitler are eerie — as if they were being written today, with full hindsight. In August 1936, he wondered:

> how much we really know about the vaults and caverns
> which lie somewhere under the structure of a great nation
> — about these psychic catacombs in which all our con-
> cealed desires, our fearful dreams and evil spirits, our vices
> and our forgotten and unexpiated sins, have been buried for
> generations? In healthy times, these emerge as the spectres
> in our dreams.... But suppose, now, that all of these things
> generally kept buried in our subconscious were to push
> their way to the surface, as in the blood-cleansing function
> of a boil? Suppose that this underworld now and again lib-
> erated by Satan bursts forth, and the evil spirits escape
> the Pandora's box?[28]

No fact-based political analysis could be as accurate as these words. They describe passive intuition gone wrong, deprived of the counter-balancing effects of other human qualities.

As for the active sort of intuition, we are surrounded by all sorts of false manifestations. Think of the nonsense written about money-making over the last quarter-century. It all sounds so enthusiastically new. Brand new methodology. New machines and new markets.

Yet Charles Mackay's *Extraordinary Popular Delusions and the Madness of Crowds*, now 160 years old, Zola's *Money* and Conrad's *Chance*, both a century old, seem to accurately describe today's junk-bond kings, new market prophets, advocates of economic natural balance and global integration. Conrad created a great business leader who has drawn thousands of individual investors and millions of pounds into a movement for *Thrift* investing. Abruptly, his *Thrift* bank collapsed, deeply in debt.

> "But tell me, Marlow, he must have been a personality in a sense — in some one sense surely. You don't work the greatest material havoc of a decade at least, in a commercial community, without having something in you."
>
> Marlow shook his head.
>
> "He was a mere sign, a portent. There was nothing in him.... We pass through periods dominated by this or that word — it may be development, or it may be competition, or efficiency or even sanctity. It is the word of the time."[29]

And that is enough for falsely intuitive mass hysteria to drive investment. Conrad could draw upon a modern history which began with the Dutch tulip frenzy of the 1630s. The South Sea Bubble burst in 1720, the same year as John Law's paper speculation. But our contemporary techno-worship matched with unregulated markets still lay ahead. He could only intuitively describe what would turn into our myriad mass hysterias, all claiming to be the product of modernity and true knowledge.

What are these hysterical moments missing to make them real intuitive choices? For one thing, a common-sense use of shared knowledge. Any rigorous use of memory, for another. And the sustained uncertainty of active imagination. When imagination is used, a flawed intuitive choice tends to reveal itself almost instantaneously.

I'm not denying that there are real hunches of an intuitive sort. And these hunches make subconscious use of our different qualities and so help an individual to survive or even progress. I met a successful young man recently who had been homeless and alone for most of his teens, sleeping in cars and in the woods, eating out of garbage cans. He said "the first thing you do is rely on your instincts. If it feels dangerous, you run." You intuitively judge people, out of necessity at a distance.

What is this? A few intelligent management theoreticians like Henry Mintzberg are trying to make sense of the intuitive 'skill'. There was an element in that teenager of falling back on unconscious instincts we share with the other animals. But there was also a strong element of the conscious human imagination, caught for years in a sort of institutionalized, sustained uncertainty, and forced to choose intuitively again and again, several times a day, just to eat, to sleep, to keep warm, to avoid danger.

On the other hand, if we are not careful this sort of argument can become comic, almost macabre. Your run-of-the-mill Business School professors are now starting to advance intuition as the latest management gimmick. They are defining it in the way they defined reason and efficiency — like a freeze-frame instrumental truth.

The other element missing from false intuition is any reflection of ethics. After all, ethics plays a large role in the sustained uncertainty of imagination. The French army, for example, combined a number of our qualities when they dealt with the Algerian nationalist uprising in the 1950s. However, they marginalized ethics and concentrated on a highly intuitive approach, which did indeed destroy the FLN, their guerilla opponents.

From January 1957 to October 1958 they deconstructed the enemy, individual by individual. Effective torture, with all of its intuitive characteristics, was a key in their success. Four decades later, in 2000, the chief of security during that campaign revealed that he had caused three thousand bodies of the tortured to disappear. There were apparently many more. The result was a clear tactical success. However, the combination of sustained unlimited arrests of civilians with institutionalized torture and death meant that France lost any hope of an ethical mandate to govern. In a dictatorship this might not have mattered. In a democracy the means of the apparent victory guaranteed the real defeat. And whether their opponents used equivalent methods is beside the ethical point.[30]

What of false intuition in its passive form? I began with an example of real intuition — Friedrich Reck-Malleczewen's anti-Nazi diary. It is part of the inexplicable phenomenon of communication or understanding through creativity. T.S. Eliot said that "poetry communicates before it is understood. It is a matter of words which appear to make up language communicating something, while we are actually experiencing it at a completely different level."

As for the false sort, it does not strengthen us in our understanding of ourselves or of our language. False intuition releases peculiar obsessions. It makes us believe we have understood ourselves in ways which make no sense at all.

I wrote earlier of our 'liberation' from souls and ancestor worship. But in the century following the announced death of God, of ancestor worship, of saints, spirits and a great deal more, we have replaced these with Hero worship. You could even say that "western dependence on Hero worship far outstrips in importance that of ancestor worship elsewhere."[31] To all intents and purposes this has become a religion, and one far more superstitious than what came before. The old souls and saints had some influence, but for the most part left us alone except in the most backward parts of society. Today we are barraged daily, hourly, by false Heroic images and Heroic acts unrelated to heroism. The result is mythology which is more bedtime-story-like than any child's story. What could be more childlike than a devotion to father figures at every corner?

Think of the phenomenon of racial violence in the United States. Between 1882 and 1968, 4,742 Black Americans were lynched. Approximately the same number were 'legally' lynched.[32] These murders were typically presented in public debate as the work of Ku Klux Klan-type organizations and the dregs of society.

Recent research has revealed that these lynchings in fact tended to draw out much of the town's population. Families came as to picnics. The entertainment included an elaborate process of degradation, torture, hanging then shooting, often castration. And finally burning. Pieces of charred skin and clothes were sold as mementos. Postcards showing the mutilated corpses were very successful.

Why put this phenomenon under superstition and the passive side of false intuition? Because it was dependent on society maintaining a view of itself which would normalize such behaviour. And the key to this normalization is, as it was, a strong sense of the Heroic unrelated to the reality lived in.

Torture and murder do not resemble what we think of as bedtime stories. Yet in a grotesque way, what could be more childlike than picnics, straw hats, torture, dreams of liberty, pieces of skin, the pursuit of happiness, Heroic leaders?

Let me put this in a larger context. The Romans are still famous for the bloodbaths they organized in coliseums all over the empire. These were not just massacres. They were highly ritualized. And they were financed by the élite of the day: the emperor, ambitious aristocrats and generals, as well as social-climbing businessmen. The richer the man, the bigger the battles to the death would be. Julius Caesar ran three gladiator training schools. Much of the ritual and fame and commercial endorsements so common today in sports were present in these games and attached to famous gladiators.

Unlike a basketball player, they died by the sword. So the question is: why such a curious mixture of gore, ritual and fame?

Not because Rome was a rough place. It was actually rather genteel. Romans disapproved of Greek sports because the athletes competed nude. That was shocking. On the other hand, people dripping with blood and dying for entertainment was fine. This is strangely similar to the moral standards of today's commercial television and family movies.

Of course, the Roman coliseums were not offering mere entertainment. But then neither is our television. The Roman sports related directly to their fear of uncertainty, in particular of mortality. Tertullian, a Christian writing around AD 200, explained it clearly:

> For of old, in the belief that the souls of the dead are propitiated with human blood, they used at funerals to sacrifice captives or slaves of poor value whom they bought.
> Afterwards, it seemed a good idea to obscure their impiety by making it a pleasure. So they found comfort for death in murder.[33]

It is interesting to think of these surprising stories from Rome, the United States and France in the context of Reck-Malleczewen's "vaults and caverns which lie somewhere under the structure of a great nation. Those psychic catacombs in which all our concealed desires, our fearful dreams and evil spirits, our vices and our forgotten and unexpiated sins, have been buried for generations."

These vaults and caverns are just under the surface, because they are part of the architectural foundations of our psychology, both personal and societal. And what do these fearful dreams and unexpiated sins produce? Inexplicable contradictions between a society's idea of itself and what it actually does. Of course not all intuition twisted into superstition is so horrifying. Sometimes it's more comic than anything else. Go to Uluru, once known as Ayer's Rock, in central Australia. This is perhaps the most famous animistic site in the world. An astonishing rock, 3 kilometres long, rising abruptly 350 metres out of the flat desert like a great spent missile, half buried in the sand. The aboriginal relationship to it is extremely complex and draws in a whole world along expanding song-lines.

Today at sunset, thousands of pilgrims from around the world are lined up behind a wooden fence, waiting to take the perfect frozen image of Uluru at sunset. The fence cuts in a surrealistic manner across the desert. It demarcates the exact distance needed to capture the entire rock by wide angle and the perfect angle for the setting sun, which is an odd concept because the relationship between earth and sun constantly changes. Like the still photograph, the fence suggests a flat earth frozen in the universe. The implications are a crude parody of paganism.

It takes a good hour and yet contains nothing more than the clicking of machines. The beauty of the scene, instead of being expanded into the organic whole, is reduced into a calculable image. Guides give advance advice on how to shoot the rock and when. There is chat involving exposures and wide angles. You might say that this is the lowest form of idolatry, rather like the incident of the golden calf.

The aborigines have been remarkably understanding about this deformation of the meaning of the site into low superstition and have tried to be helpful by providing an interpretation centre. Uluru is the centre of something. It is a source and a destination. You are to walk around it or be in its shadow.

The dream of the idolator is instead to climb to the top. To dominate? To look at the view? Who knows. It is a linear conclusion. Travel to a destination. Conquer the highest spot. Then climb down in order to freeze an image of the golden calf upon which you have just mounted.

FEAR OF UNCERTAINTY

So intuition gone wrong can be slightly embarrassing, but also as deadly as ethics gone wrong. This isn't surprising. A human quality can't be controlled absolutely or defined absolutely. In fact, applying the concept of control or the fantasy of complete understanding is among the factors which can make it go wrong. I keep coming back to our fear of sustained uncertainty, because that is what repeatedly pushes us into absolute arguments; some tragic, some comic.

Descartes seemed to think that intuition was all right in practice, but not in theory; so long, I suppose, as it didn't get in the way of his theories of absolute knowledge. Henri Bergson, the greatest advocate of intuition, couldn't help but try to build the human world around his favourite intellectual pillar.

He might have avoided the absolutist trap if he had proceeded from Adam Smith's *Theory of Moral Sentiments*. He came close: "By intuition is meant the kind *of intellectual sympathy* by which we place ourselves within an object in order to coincide with what is unique in it and consequently inexpressible." He introduced the concept of constant movement, but then clouded it by presenting a choice between the analytically relative and the intuitively "absolute".[34]

Even if Bergson was unable to avoid the classic thesis-antithesis approach, he was still radically understated in comparison to Hegel with his insistence on Absolute Knowing and Absolute Spirit. His *Phenomenology of Spirit* reads a bit like Californian Buddhism. Romantic escapism. Normal Buddhism handles the idea of the organic or intellectual whole in a realistic manner. Nirvana is not Absolute. It is not an escape from the Turning Wheel of existence, but is the Wheel itself, the certainty of permanent uncertainty. And so we do not escape from existence. The innermost heart of the one who achieves Nirvana is one with the universe.

In the Western tradition, even someone as self-declared common-sensical as G.E. Moore seems to insist on absolutes. He announces the self-evidence of moral principles through Intuitionism. But nothing is self-evident. Certainly not moral principles or ethics. If moral principles were self-evident in any way, I would not have been able to mention three very different human disasters in Nazi Germany, colonial France and the American South — three societies which self-evidently 'knew' better. And there are other examples in every country which self-evidently knows better.

The ethical use of intuition depends upon context. Context is not relativism. It is the context shaped by the tension of ethics, imagination, memory and other qualities playing off each other.

As for our obsession with certainty, it is aimed not at proving absolute knowledge, but at convincing ourselves that we are capable of absolute knowledge. In other words, it is the fantasy of a bastion against mortality. It is an admission of personal insecurity, not of philosophical conviction. Our fear of sustained uncertainty does not protect us from intuition. It marginalizes our imagination and so turns intuition into a potential wild card.

Take Joseph Conrad's ironic observation about human relationships. "Even to the dullest of men, marrying is for the most part an imaginative act." It might be better to say that a belief in the possibility of couples — you could even say in the possibility of love — is the imaginative act.

Choosing each other from out of the sea of humans is surely an act of active intuition, perhaps the most common of uncertain, intuitive choices. Deciding to marry is a continuation of that intuition and a reintroduction of imagination. After all, the decision itself will have continual unknown consequences within the limits of mortality. Finally comes the actual legal structure of marriage — the social structure. Conrad called this "the irrational institution". You could also call it the romantic structure, because it attempts to freeze-frame certainty and control into that most fluid of things —

a human relationship. This legal institution is our admission of fear.

Of course the legal structure needs to exist. Societies require structures, as does each human. But if there is a real force, it is in the relationship.

Elias Canetti lived as a child in Ruschuk, Bulgaria. Once, when his father was travelling in England, the boy fell into a vat of boiling water. He was retrieved only to lie dying from his burns. His mother and the doctor were powerless. For weeks he slowly declined. Enfolded deep in his pain, the boy's need or love or animistic force gradually fixated on the father's return. When at last the father arrived, the child's pains immediately ceased and his decline reversed. The doctor, who had delivered the child years before, called this rebirth "the hardest of all the children he had delivered".[35]

There is no certainty in this story. Nor does its happy ending replace science, medicine, progress in the treatment of burns or any other professional aid. It simply demonstrates that there are other forces at work and we neither understand nor control them. I'd call this applied animism. We are more than our bodies. The question worth asking is whether, as our specialist tools grow, we might not be forgetting or denying these other uncontrollable forces. In our fear of uncertainty, are we trading one for the other, instead of building our strength on the basis of both?

●

THE INTUITIVE CREATION

Why are we so determined to erect barriers between fiction and fact or between images and documentary? Is this part of an attempt to destroy any inclusive idea of civilization? After all, these barriers in turn destroy the idea of civilization as an integral part of the physical world. Are they not a manifestation of our desire to set ourselves apart from the earth in the first place, and from each other in the second?

You could describe this as a famous battle against the very idea of the matriarchal whole. Our method is to break down our knowledge and our professional skills into narrow, exclusive categories. And then we feel ourselves empowered to act as if there are no other factors.

I'm not suggesting we have no need of professions and categories and didactic argument and even what we call facts. I'm pointing out that our approach to these elements implicitly marginalizes most of our qualities.

Think of the two words: fiction and non-fiction. Or fiction and fact. By opposing these two categories, we tell ourselves that fiction is not factual and is therefore not true, but is 'imagined' and is thus somehow cut off from reality. The provable, measurable kind of reality is used to organize real lives. Accept the word fiction in this context and you demean imagination while denying intuition.

'Non-fiction', on the other hand, declares itself to be the carrier of fact, an expression of reality, and thus of truth.

Why then does most fact-based work have a remarkably short shelf life? The reply might be that additional facts come along. That we are learning all the time. In that case, it was never an expression of reality or truth. And even if the facts are overtaken, the arguments built upon them should not date with such terrifying rapidity. Decade-old serious 'non-fiction' often seems arcane, irrelevant. The written style itself seems to become old-fashioned.

Two-centuries-old decent 'fiction' on the other hand can easily remain fresh. It often becomes our principal source of understanding for its period and place. And it often reveals to us a greater understanding of our own society as it functions today. In other words, great fiction can be true for its time, as well as somehow timeless, and true for our time. And each of these fictions can function at all three levels.

Why did I quote Tolstoy on military strategy? He was no general, didn't even pretend to be a strategist. Yet he, along with Dostoevski, Gogol, Turgenev and Chekhov, have become our main sources for understanding Russia over the hundred-odd years leading up to the

Revolution. In fact they tell us a great deal about Russia today, to say nothing of the human character in general. On the other hand, few people rush out to read the various nineteenth-century factual — 'non-fiction' — descriptions or analyses of Napoleon and Kutuzov.

How can 'fiction' be capable of delivering truth in a timeless manner? It is an expression of intuition. And why does 'non-fiction' seem to fall so easily victim to fashionable points of view? It generally denies intuition.

We still happily read Balzac and Baudelaire, yet can hardly stay awake for Thiers or Michelet. Yes, Macaulay is in print. But compare the quantity and variety of his readers to those of Jane Austen or Dickens.

Now, through linear analysis, we can see the flaws in Thiers's historical method and that of Macaulay. We have new facts. But does this mean we have today eliminated the problem of fashionable facts which make non-fiction so time-sensitive?

If so, whether we are American or not, our image of the United States throughout the twentieth century should be embedded in non-fiction. Certainly some biographies have survived at least a quarter-century. One or two analytical works from the sixties are still central to our consciousness. Almost nothing from the first half of the century remains.

But if I say Fitzgerald, Hemingway, Faulkner, Tennessee Williams, even Mark Twain or Saul Bellow, the United States comes alive before our eyes. These writers provide us with a truth which not only trumps the theoretical difference between fact and fiction, but does so with a quite different form of truth; one which is neither absolute, nor linear.

These novels and plays belong to the inner structure of the universe. They are expressions of intuition — the passive equivalent of Napoleon or Gretzky seizing a moment of truth out of his swirling imagination. The difference is that the writers have not seized a moment. They have expressed a broad, profound range of truths through a story which animates reality. A timeless, not a factual, reality. They have simply bypassed the clunky mechanisms of linear argument and fact.

I think it could be argued that our growing obsession with specialization has made our non-fiction more literal than ever before. This is the old 'literalism'; what Northrop Frye described as "a literal projection into the external world".[36] Curiously enough, what has produced idolatry versus what hasn't seems largely to be a matter of the literal versus the imaginative. Frye pointed out that a literal assertion was often idolatrous. In other words, idolatry is as romantic as it is literal. Think of today's absolute, demonstrable truths. These truths and facts are more instantaneous, and their shelf life therefore shorter, than in the nineteenth century. The more we dive into narrow fact-based truth, the more we become the victims of fashion and idolatry.

Non-fiction, as our society has conceived it, is a prisoner of the linear. Yet reality is in constant non-linear movement. That which we demonstrate to be clear remains so for a moment, then mutates into a different shape. What is left behind is the incomprehensibility of a linear snapshot cruelly frozen in time.

Jung asked what his dreams were, if not art. What then is art, if not intuition — an expression of the inner structure of the universe? The artist seizes the swirling uncertainty of our imaginations in order to express its meaning. And is art not then our continuing expression of the matriarchal synchronicity which underpins our civilization? We deny its existence, insist that it has been fractured, yet our art is there to prove this is not so.

Let me put this yet another way. You can't have great art without the sacred, even if that art is devoted to profaning the sacred. Without the sacred — call it a purpose — we end up worrying about the details out of context.

What is the sacred? That's more a question to ask than to answer.

Our mythological conundrums have remained pretty stable over the last five millennia. Not much has been solved, straightened out or eliminated. Which suggests that specific answers may not matter.

The point is that the sacred seems to lie at the core of art, and so makes it function. Without it, all you have is the equivalent of art for art's sake, which is not art but atrophied memory — formalized and isolated from reality. Curiously enough, the other essential in art seems to be an element of humour.

The sacred provides purpose and shape for the content. The humour provides distance; the creative distance necessary to avoid slipping into linear reporting or propaganda.

Bergson spoke of intuition as metaphysics. The place you can see these metaphysics at work every day is in the arts. Images, words, sounds, are presented as a representation of reality, when they are really a projection or shadow of reality.

No, this is not Plato.

The greater the artist, the more her creations — the words, the lines drawn, the sounds — appear simple to us. The greater the artist the more there have been reverberations off invisible walls. This may begin in a vast reality, but it is projected from wall to wall until only a tiny gesture is left to become visible. If Tolstoy can still hold us, it is because his words have ricocheted up from some impenetrable, invisible, uncontrollable universe. The result is deceiving simplicity. We read a few apparently innocent lines and find ourselves mortified, exhilarated, crying, stopping to think, when we had no knowledge that these forces would be unleashed in us. That is metaphysics or passive intuition at work.

Sometimes this metaphysical trick almost reveals itself. Pre-twentieth-century artists quite often put their visible magic in their drawings, not in their paintings. The difference between the two images may even be shocking. While the drawings are filled with energy and force, the paintings have highly professional but conventional formality. You might say that the drawings are the artists' dreams, their imagination, their expression of the uncertain. Not surprisingly they come alive with ease.

> To be able to grasp something with our thought, to be able
> like Dürer to seize a hare.[37]

Souren Melikian recently analyzed this phenomenon, describing a drawing of Correggio's which led to his *Adoration of the Magi*: "A breath of life ran through [it]." The painting on the other hand is "almost frozen in its formality". This is so common in art from the Renaissance through the nineteenth century that professional explanations are abundant. The personal pleasure of the artist, versus his desire to sell, is often the interpretation.

But more than that is involved. The drawings are indeed the expression of imagination and intuition. The painting must retain traces of both to be successful. The problem is that craft tends to occupy the foreground, obscuring the art — the seized imagination, the intuition, the synchronicity. The result is a repetition of the memory of images, which is no bad thing in and of itself. That memory, after all, is the history of art. The problem comes when professionalism overwhelms intuitive vigor.

Picasso said that he often bought paintings for the resale value and drawings for his admiration of the art. Even with Cézanne he preferred the watercolours "hardly painted". He complained that Braque had damaged their modernizing campaign with his paintings "bien faits". You could say, with his 'painterly paintings'.

As I said when discussing Imagination, one of the keys to Picasso's domination of the twentieth-century Western image was his ability to bring the intuitional energy and life of his drawing right into his finished work. He was able to paint and sculpt as if our organic society had not been shattered, not even on the most superficial level. Thousands have since tried to imitate his formula — "I don't search. I find! — Je ne cherche pas. Je trouve." But intuition is not a system.

Picasso had been able to transport himself into the core of the synchronistic arts outside the West; those whose organic nature has not been separated from the sacred.

The *sotto voce* reaction of official art criticism tends to be that these objects are emotionally moving, but they lack the distance necessary for real art. They are therefore ethnographic rather than artistic.

It seems to me that on average there is a great deal more professional distance in these organic arts than in most contemporary Western installation art. And the more overwhelming the subject, the more likely there will be irony. This is not the courtier-painter's scepticism. Not the insider's wink. Rather it is a powerful humour, necessary to distance the artist from the direct effects of the force he is releasing. Look, for example, at nineteenth-century Third World assemblage art. As became common a century later in New York, the artists picked up household, industrial and agriculture bric-a-brac or refuse and made an object or an image with. This was a normal part of artistic life in West Africa and on the Pacific Coast. But it was also an ironic expression of the forces thought to be at play in their world; an inner world view of the detritus of the exterior.

Conscious skill or craft is essential in any art. But the result is mediocre without the force of intuitive expression, like a great riptide carrying us out into a world beyond the page or the canvas.

Thomas Mann wrote of Goethe's last great book — *Wilhelm Meisters Wanderjahre*:

> What most astonishes us is the intuition, the keenness and
> breadth of vision — they seem positively occult, but are
> simply the expression of a finer organism, the fruit of the
> most sensitive penetration.

Note the words. They synthesize every author I have quoted. Mann went on to say that Goethe had

anticipated the whole social and economic development of
the nineteenth century: the industrialization of the old cultural and agrarian countries, the triumph of the machine,
the rise of the organized labouring classes, the class conflict,
democracy, socialism, Americanism itself, with the intellectual and educational consequences of all these. [38]

Goethe died in 1832, an old man. This was only eleven years after
Napoleon. Victoria had not yet come to the British throne. Goethe
had been brought up in the middle of the eighteenth century in
Frankfurt in a large burgher's house, where the atmosphere was pre
Enlightenment, not even eighteenth century. The furniture, the
paintings, the library, the kitchen and heating system, all of these were
anchored in the habits of the old trading cities of Northern Europe,
which stretched back into the Middle Ages.

Yes, his life did stretch on into the upheavals of the early nineteenth century. He became the chief administrator of a German
Prince. And he was Voltaire's successor as the most famous Western
writer of his time.

But all the same, where did this ancient writer-cum-provincial
official find the intuitive airstreams which would lead him into a
world not yet born and so far from his own? It was as if he could
lower himself onto the tectonic plates shifting all the way from
Frederick the Great through Napoleon to Lenin and Hitler. And this
he did through 'fiction', while 'non-fiction', then as now, ignored
advice such as that of Wayne Gretzky — to skate to where the puck is
going, not to where it is. Ignored or was unable to understand what
such advice might mean.

The answer to the question is not an answer at all, but an
approach. Uncertainty is taken as normal, and the ability to embrace
it is a sign of human consciousness as intelligence not fear. As for the
synchronistic relationship between our lives and the myths, if it is
real enough to affect our personal lives, it is real enough to affect the

life of our civilization. None of which denies the role of facts — fragile though they may be in comparison to the eternal solidity of mythology. Nor is there any denial of the utility, even necessity, of didactic argument and demonstration. But there it is — intuition in its active and passive forms. Only in a superstition-driven society would it become a threatening force. In a society which accepts the existence of multiple human qualities, intuition occupies its central place. It helps us to act by seizing the swirl of uncertainty of which imagination and civilization are made. It allows us to express the organic nature of our world and our existence in it.

CHAPTER SIX

MEMORY

SHAPE AND CONTEXT

Memory is not the past. It is the water you swim through, the words you speak, your gestures, your expectations.

This suggests that memory has a shape. We use it every day. From it we grasp a context — for our thoughts, our questions, our actions. For our lives.

Without a context there is no civilization, no society, no profound relationships with other individuals or our families or within our communities.

Common sense is shapeless, as is imagination and rationality. And intuition is a function of choice. It cuts across shape. Alasdair MacIntyre, writing of the intersection between ethics and memory, says that today all "[w]e possess... are the fragments of a conceptual scheme, parts which now lack those contexts from which their significance derives".[1]

Only memory gives us the ability to shape our thinking and our actions in a balanced way. What is at stake here is not some complete or, in Aristotles's word, "whole" memory. Think of memory instead as the platform from which we initiate thought or, in Vico's approach, "the power of beginning to think, the power of origin...."

Every breakthrough in science seems to confirm Vico's interpretation. The recent discovery that empathy is concentrated in the frontal lobe, or that memory is installed as sorting stations throughout the brain, all take us back to Socrates, Plato and Aristotle, with their metaphor of memory as a block of wax in the head which we are constantly stamping with a seal. And the idea of genetics — that our transgenerational memory is installed everywhere in our body — disproves the reductionist and linear arguments which came out of rationality. What replaces them? A scientific argument which resembles, of all things, the mediaeval concept of *humours*. Memory, it appears after all, is everywhere in our body. And this memory is shared in a manner which confirms both our original idea of societies and our century-old concept of the collective unconscious.

It seems that the more we learn of how our bodies function — the technical details, the fragments — the more the inclusive, overarching arguments of humanism are reaffirmed, while those of utilitarianism are disproved. The problem is that the technocratic structures we have gradually put in place over the last century, and increasingly over the last fifty years, artificially prop up a utilitarian view. In particular they prop up the intellectual assumptions of methodology, while obstructing a more inclusive approach.

Take, for example, the various utilitarian forces — the shapeless fragments — which are bundled together as an inevitability called globalization. Because they are vaunted as inevitable forces free of social constraints, they are perceived to be free of memory. In that sense they resemble pure religious doctrine, rather than an internationalization of civil concepts. "By brooding over the future," the Buddha said, "and repenting the past, fools dry up like green reeds cut down in the sun." Unfortunately, most great religions require texts which fix the past in place but do not want a functioning memory. They are fixed on a solution which arises out of the spectrum of a rigid memory. So whatever their founders' intent, they cannot help but become an ideology.

Without memory there is a vacuum. Propaganda thrives in a vacuum, as does ideology. As does public relations. All three replace context with scrambled fragments of memory. False memory. Artificial shape.

How is this done? The vacuum permits a sceptical alignment of fragments — call it an endless realignment of memory for whatever purpose, as if it had no shape. This can produce anything from illusions of devotion to delusions of absolute freedom. The careful belonging of a society, for example, can be suddenly deformed into cheap patriotism and jingoism.

The odd thing about this scrambling of memory is that we are the civilization that knows more about most things than any other ever has. There should be no contradiction between knowledge and memory. New knowledge should clarify and enrich our sense of context.

Yet somehow this knowledge does not help us to remember as it should. Of course it helps us in many ways. From plumbing to medication. A continuing flurry of technical miracles is constantly changing our way of life. We know more. Our instrumental memory grows. Our context is enriched.

But we are surrounded by a general feeling of shapelessness. We have difficulty placing ourselves; identifying our direction. It is as if we have no functioning memory, in the sense that memory is the context of our community.

Instead, we are caught up in successive tidal waves of fragments. We're often told that this is the normal disordered shape of progress. And that radical progress probably should imply confusion. But why would that mean a loss of memory; a sense of loss which applies to popular as much as élite culture?

Think of rap music in its early manifestations. It began as an ironic play on our anxiety. Carefully manufactured pieces of music — formal, artificial shapes — were fragmented into a parody of themselves. These fragments floated about us, meaninglessly repeating as they flashed by, leaving no recollection. Showers of facts. Scraps.

The scraps were pulled from the proper little parables of commercial music, the narrow fixed discourse of news broadcasts, the strict biblic moralism of sitcoms and police dramas. Rap played about with all of this false populism and mocked its empty but formal ideologies. After all, this formality didn't — doesn't — seem to have any ethical direction or to fit into any context. The loss of the shape of memory is in effect the loss of memory itself.

Erasmus, writing in 1515, on the edge of a precipice over which humanism would plunge into rational ideology and modern generalized wars, joked that he "hate[d] an audience which won't forget".[2] It was a deeply ironic joke; an intuition of the audience which would believe itself unable to remember.

Both of these — rap and Erasmus — relate to the paradox that the more we know, the more confused we seem to feel. I'm not referring to the very positive confusion of uncertainty, but to a multiplicity of certainties which don't add up to a shape or a context.

Perhaps we are confusing talents or skills with memory. Or as Bergson put it, confusing "motor mechanisms" or "habit memory" with the real thing. After all, every animal has skills. I talked earlier of the intergenerational memory of the Monarch butterfly. If that's all it is — which is already quite a lot — then memory isn't a human quality. It's just an animal characteristic.

But it is a quality. Why? Again because functioning individuals and functioning societies require the context of memory in order to shape their thinking and their action.

In later life, Thomas Paine came to see this civic memory as the key to controlling unaccountable power.[3] What he described is precisely the problem we face two centuries later. Even most of those who support the fragmented elements of globalization as it is presented today do not want the liquidation of the functioning civil memories of democracies, with all their social standards and standards of justice painfully put in place over time. What most of us are struggling with is how our civic memories can be activated precisely in order to shape these unaccountable powers. Again, Vico laid it all out with great clarity:

> There must in the nature of human institutions be a mental
> language common to all nations, which uniformly grasps
> the substance of things feasible in human social life and
> expresses it with as many diverse modifications as these
> same things may have diverse aspects. A proof of this is
> afforded by proverbs or maxims of vulgar wisdom, in which
> substantially the same meanings find as many diverse
> expressions as there are nations ancient and modern.[4]

These shared understandings and experiences remain with us. They are the fundamentals of a sensible approach towards the internationalization of both individual and civic memories.

How are we to release the forces of that memory? Five thousand years ago Gilgamesh wept over the body of his friend Enkidu, attempting with his emotive force to break the skin of memory so that he would live again.

> I have wept for him day and night. I would not give up his
> body for burial, I thought my friend would come back
> because of my weeping.[5]

Achilles did the same over the body of his friend, Patroclus, 1,500 years later. A hundred years ago, Alessandro Manzoni began his masterpiece, *The Betrothed*:

> History may truly be defined as a famous war against time;
> for history takes back from time the years he has empris-
> oned, or rather utterly slain, history calls them back to life
> and passes them in review and sets them up again in
> Order of Battle.

History for Manzoni is time. And he is right. We do wage a constant famous war against time. Sometimes the struggle is easy. Gilgamesh is more alive today than his dead friend was then. Why? Because creativity is the greatest weapon of memory. You might say that memory enfranchises the dead. Having this vote constitutes neither domination nor control. It gives a mechanism to our context as individual humans and as ongoing societies.

And we are these things — individual humans and ongoing societies — and will continue to be. Contracts die as they pay out. Tolstoy remains alive, as do ethical standards and a thousand other remembered social realities.

Fear of context

Many of us, when we hear *memory, shape, context*, understand this as an attempt to curtail our freedom. More precisely, we understand memory as an attempt to remove our right to act as individuals. Memory is seen as a prison, a weapon of received wisdom or established power.

But I spoke of shape and context — the shape and context of civilization — not the prison walls of some tyrannical social or political control. A rigid or a dominant memory would be an ideology. It would deform our other qualities by forcing them through a single spectrum. A selective spectrum. A rigid memory pretends to guarantee the shape of the future by freezing that of the past. Life — the world — viewed from a single perspective is like sex through a keyhole: one-dimensional, abstract, with participation reduced to voyeurism.

Memory as a quality lives in tension with our other qualities. It does have a shape — not tyrannical, but a shape all the same.

To imagine that we have no need of such a context would be the ultimate form of false individualism. On the pretext that we are free, absolutely free, we would impose upon ourselves an anarchistic void of constantly recurring ignorance. Not doubt. Not questioning. But shapeless ignorance in which nothing can be imagined or analyzed, let alone judged. Without context, ethics is powerless and the shared knowledge of common sense slips into meaninglessness.

Such a state of being is neither freedom, nor an expression of individualism. It is a psychosis. Of course, every society needs a psychosis in order to express both its anxieties and its problems. The trick is to use that state of mind in order to uncover our anxieties — to reveal them to ourselves — not to become its victim.

WHAT IT MIGHT BE

For even while I live in darkness and silence,
I can bring out colours in memory....
And though my tongue be at rest,
and my throat silent,
Yet I can sing as much as I will.

Saint Augustine[6]

What might the shape of memory be? It is often presented as a linear line of experience trailing behind us, one event after another, until it catches up or — seen the other way around — recedes into an invisible past. But why would memory be linear when little in our lives happens in order, let alone in an orderly fashion?

Many things happen in our lives at once, often as if part of a single movement, full of contradictions. Every historical event, like every event in our personal lives, is constructed of competing elements. This is why memory cannot be ideological. A shape is a tension of contradictions. Memory is the shape of contradictions.

Every attempt at understanding memory brings the questioner back to its spatial nature. The spatial reigns over mere experience. Bergson believed this, as did Saint Augustine, who was trying to express its timeless, inclusive sense of shape when he said that, "without being joyous, I remember myself to have had joy; and without being sad, I call to mind my past sadness."[7]

That we should want to reduce memory to experience isn't surprising. We try so hard to see memory in a narrow way, as if it were a technical, quantifiable substance. Alternately, we treat it as something unfathomable; something for which psychiatrists treat patients. Or, in a combination of experience and the unfathomable, we deform memory into a romantic vision through gauze with soft lighting — a world of grandmother's cookies and sparkling clean farmhouses and perfect love with sparkling white wine. This romantic version can be spun effortlessly into group characteristics and from there into the perfect love of a group or a race or a nation. This is the deformation of memory which is now used more to sell goods than to sell negative nationalism.

But the key to such romanticism is the belief in quantification. An obsession with quantifying and ordering experience reveals an obsession with stability. And an obsession with stability suggests a terror, not of instability, but of uncertainty and the unknown.

There is a paradox in all of this. Memory actually is filled with stability. This comes from the way we express our experience, not the experience itself. If frightened, we will insist upon a linear, concrete accounting of events, then often dress it up in romantic garb to make it more appealing, and so fall victim to some form of ideology. But if we have more confidence in ourselves, we will see events as spatial and necessarily contradictory.

Octavio Paz described memory as a "knowledge situated between science properly so-called and poetry". Here is a relaxed, self-confident view, open to uncertainty and contradiction.[8]

The "themes, situations and character types" stay with us.

Northrop Frye was describing literature, but the same is true of life in general. They stay with us over thousands of years. That is why we must constantly work so hard to reanimate the stories we write or the way we read them or the stories we live. What we live, read, write begins with Gilgamesh, Homer and religious texts, yet the elements they contain are still dominant and alive today.

That's why seeing our history in technical or linear terms is the first step towards the psychosis of a dysfunctional memory; a false, rigid memory which shatters beneath the violence of great, unstructured waves. In fact, what we think of as experience, whether it be personal or social, fits into some collective experience, whether it be conscious or unconscious. "Nothing disappears," the Swedish novelist Kerstin Ekman writes. "It is all still there. Deep down it is all still there."

Take a simple local example which has come to have international implications. More than two hundred years ago, the French Revolution shattered the idea of society. Various fragments spun off in different directions: the revolutionary one way, Bonapartism another, classic republicanism a third, and Orleanism a fourth.[9] In a spinning uncertainty they have succeeded each other over the years. Just when you think one has disappeared, it reappears and takes power. And while other Western societies have contributed elements to our choice of social models, the sharp violence of the original French event did create a scatter-gun effect. And so Bonaparte and Bonapartism, for example, became the active memory for both international fascism and the primary version of authoritarian corporate leadership.

Patrick Hutton argues that 170 years after it first rose to power, Orleanism is now back in office, this time throughout much of the West. What is Orleanism? A style of governing named after the minor branch of the French royal family. The Orleans, whenever they held power, served themselves liberally while mouthing vaguely democratic, relatively benign policies. So Orleanism is the self-indulgent rule of self-interest characterized by soft profiteering. In such a context, the wishes of larger rather than smaller interested parties are taken to be the natural indicators of public policy. Who would have thought that such a messy, short-sighted, low-level view of power could re-emerge from deep within our modern memory and reinstall itself?

I'm not suggesting that nothing new appears. But newness is deceptive. The Revolution was in many ways new. But then so was the nuclear bomb. I turn to the only masterpiece directly produced by the explosion. Toyofumi Ogura, in his *Letters from the End of the World*, describes his macabre yet picaresque progress across the ruins of Hiroshima in the hours, days and weeks after the explosion — the incomprehensible explosion, in the sense that no one in the city could actually comprehend what had happened. And the Japanese authorities were careful not to enlighten them.

What did Ogura see? "[R]ain reminiscent of the Flood of Noah's time". His observations were filled with such traditional apocalyptic events. He didn't know about Noah's predecessor in Babylonia. But he concentrated on the arrival of the biggest typhoon in a dozen years — an after-effect — and made references to Sodom and Gomorrah, since the city had made much of its fortune as a military centre. Then the blast turned the area into a "primeval ice field".[10]

This may not seem an attractive, seductive way to sell the idea of memory as a timeless, spatial quality. But think of it as a shape which is both stable and in constant movement. It was memory which gave Ogura the context to survive. There was no physical shape around him. All had been obliterated. He found his context in a memory which stretched across centuries and borders.

Because it is timeless and in constant movement, this shape can constantly bring us back to ourselves. Think of it as a field of essential reinvention, for each of us and for those who tell us our stories. Memory reminds us of what we know in a way which focuses us because it seems new.

●

SHAPE AS LAYERING

Another way to say that memory is spatial is to talk of layering. Look at a dictionary. Most are based on a dubious proposition: they tell us what a word means. A few thicker dictionaries give us etymology and history, with representative sentences for each period. That comes closer to the idea of context.

The next step would be to question what a word actually felt like when said at a particular time. How was it heard? What was its impact? And a word is rarely heard alone. What did the surrounding words, each with its own history, feel like? And what effect did each word or phrase have on the others? After all, the sense of each word or phrase is heard or written in the context of the others.

So the single truth of the meaning of a word on a given day, heard alone or even in context, is only a thin layer laid upon the complexity of memory.

In many ways, memory is the opposite of truth. Whatever current fashion says that a word means, that same word will also carry in some invisible way the reverberations of its other, earlier senses. You may believe that you do not know what they are. You may be convinced that you are only hearing that first level of contemporary meaning. But the greater the context of sentences, images, meanings, emotions, the more these other levels are revealed, consciously for those who seek, unconsciously for the rest of us. The process of the words and phrases knocking against each other loosens the hidden meanings. And so with every earnest word of contemporary truth uttered, an observant listener can sense whole texts running off in various directions, unveiling the memory of how we've thought and what we've done.

Aboriginal rock paintings in the Australian outback were commonly painted on the overhanging surface of small refuges in a cliff-face. There was no careful, painterly separating of images. Each person painted on top of the previous painter's work. Is this texture or confusion? In either case, no one can work out how old or new any particular section is. Whatever story is being told, the versions blend one into the other. The art history or anthropological meaning is unclear. But the sense of memory as a layering of timelessness is perfectly clear.

There are a thousand Western equivalents of this aboriginal phenomenon. Wagner built his operas on *motifs of memory* — "recurrent fragments of music". T.S. Eliot so admired Wagner's method that he wrote — or built — *The Wasteland* on the same model.[11] Eliot also constructed his poetry from, at first glance, unrelated scraps and fragments, somehow revealing apparently new sounds and senses which echo up to us as if from our deepest past.

With Eliot you feel the layers heaving up beneath you. This is not so very different from what a Muslim might feel. After all, Mohammed reasserted the timeless context of desert religions over the then-dominant idolatrous influences of Greek culture, particularly in Christianity.

In David Malouf's words, "a country can bear any number of cultures laid one above the other."[12] Layering can come in very different ways. Canada, for example, more or less rejected the European monolithic view of the nation-state 150 years ago and began inventing a new, complex approach in which memory would always be at work, layering and reshaping at the same time, so that the effect would be an ongoing combination of difference and agreement.

In Aachen in Germany you can see an almost overly concrete vision of this sort of layering. It was there that Charlemagne began to reconstruct the Western Roman Empire. The culmination came on Christmas Day 800, when Pope Leo III crowned him Augustus in Rome. The Empire appeared to have been reborn.

And in a sense it was. In a sense also he launched the positive aspects of modern European civilization. The manner in which he conceived it is more or less what Europe came back to in the second half of the twentieth century — a continent of regions, a permanent tension of difference and agreement, not a battlefield of sacred, monolithic nation-states.

In Aachen he built his church as an octagon. His model was San Vitalle in Ravenna, the cathedral of the late Roman Empire. The beauty of Charlemagne's building lies in its simplicity. And perhaps in the significance of the octagon. What in the overly civilized world of Ravenna may have been close to a pure aesthetic, in the newer, rawer world of Europe had a spatial, philosophical importance. Somehow the equal eight sides evoked the idea of a single continent containing many regions and differences.

The thirty-three interior columns, as well as the throne constructed of marble tablets, were brought from Rome. It was not enough to be anointed by the pope. He required the visual confirmation of his reincarnation as Augustus. And so the layering came also in ancient marble. The psychological strength and weakness this represented can be seen in the architecture. The octagon is built to stand without the internal columns. They are aesthetic mythical add-ons. The real memory is in the octagon itself. The columns were both a tip of the hat to his inheritance and an admission of superficial insecurity.

When Napoleon conquered Aachen he immediately carried off all thirty-three to give legitimacy to his own pretensions as the inheritor of both the Roman Empire and Charlemagne. It's worth noting that because Charlemagne's vision of Europe as an octagon could stand in and of itself, the removal of the columns was only a superficial blow to memory — a loss of theatrics. A few years later, Napoleon vanished and the aesthetic decor was put back in its place.

What are we to make of this? What did they share, the poet, Eliot, with the emperor, Charlemagne? The obvious thing is an aesthetic sense of memory and the power of those aesthetics to shape our uncertainty. They shared a sense of memory as a creativity made up of layering.

THE FABRIC OF OUR OWN LIFE

Part of this layering is that the memory we develop is our own. Ours because of experience; because it is spatial and so includes us even in what we have not personally experienced; because it moves as we move.

It is said of G.M. Trevelyan that he saw history not as something lost in an inaccessible past or involving distant, inaccessible mythological figures, but as something "his forbears had made, which his family was still making, and which was thus an integral part of the fabric of his own life." The result in his work was "an astonishing sense of intimacy with past figures, whom he treated not as historical characters, but as personal acquaintances, as social equals and as close contemporaries".[13]

Social conscience and talent in a class-structured democracy allowed Trevelyan to bring this intimacy to the public. The challenge for public memory in our theoretically more open societies lies in extending that sense of intimacy with leading figures and key events out into the citizenry in general. It is their history. Their memory.

The whole approach of Heroes and grandiose triumphs and tragedies is a false popularization of history. Yes, it does capture our attention. But then so did Roman triumphs. This approach banishes our memory into Arthurian mists and inaccessible mountain-tops. Where we can have no useful relationship with it. Our attention is captured, but we are held in passivity. That is why the self-declared popular entertainers — such as Disney, indeed Hollywood in general — are false populists. They entertain in the old class-shaped mould, exciting and moving us with dreams of Heroes beyond our grasp. This is memory stolen from the citizenry and then preached back at them.

I'm not arguing for kitchen-sink history. But these great figures and events can be treated as our intimates. We can deal with the apparently grandiose triumphs or tragedies or anything else as part of a real world we inhabit.

J U V E N I L I A

At the same time, we have to be careful of brilliant men playing intellectual games with memory. Bertrand Russell proposed a question which became famous in scholastic circles:

> It is not logically necessary... that the past should have
> existed at all. There is no logical impossibility in the
> hypothesis that the world sprang into being five
> minutes ago....[14]

Except perhaps for the lady next door whose family died in a death camp more than five minutes ago. Or, put in professional terms: "If someone admitted that nothing could serve as evidence for the five-minute hypothesis, but still maintained that it is a 'logical possibility,' what would he mean?"

That, by using the debating-club techniques of his youth, he was having us on. Thomas Reid, a hundred years earlier, both put it clearly and missed the point. "Perhaps in infancy, or in a disorder of mind, things remembered may be confounded with those which are merely imagined, but in mature years..."

Do things really become so clear? It could as easily be demonstrated that children remember more accurately than parents, because they suffer less from the fear of mortality.

Let's go back to four events already discussed. Who remembers that British democracy invented the modern concentration camp at the end of the nineteenth century? Of 200,000 Boers penned up — men, women and children — 50,000 died of neglect. Or that, only forty years ago, France through its army tortured to death 3,000 Algerians and caused their bodies to disappear. Or that 4,742 American blacks were lynched between 1882 and 1968. Why are these realities not remembered? Probably because the remembrance is so disturbing. So difficult to live with.

The difference in the fourth example — the Nazi Reich — is that the effect of the Nazi experience and the Holocaust was so over-whelming that the memory cannot be escaped. Unlike the other three experiences, that of the Germans brought their society down in rubble. There was no room left standing for effective amnesia. Today many younger Germans — two generations removed from the actual events — are so scarred that they consider themselves freed of any attachment to the nation-state.

The point of repeating these examples is simply to show how complex memory is. It is not about blame. That's the job of the law. And to say that memory exists to avoid repetition is too simplistic. To say it is there to help us understand what we have done comes closer to reality. Yet the common reaction to being reminded of anything troublesome is at first denial, and if that doesn't work, anger — anger at having one's self-confidence undermined. The one who reminds is usually accused of disloyalty.

We know that memory exists in part to give us some sense of con-text, of what happened, good or bad. But we don't want to know. And we can convince ourselves that we didn't do what we can't remember. This amnesia allows us to believe that we are absolutely free; benefi-ciaries of pure individualism.

Pretending not to remember was given deep intellectual roots by Descartes. He saw memory as an obstacle, as "weak and unstable".[15] Thought could strengthen it, but the answer was to free our intellect by marginalizing our memory. And so he conceived that we could will ourselves to forget in order to be free to marshal our arguments for the future. By consigning much of what we remembered to the writ-ten page, memory would lose its power over us and we would, more or less, free up space in our minds for independent thought. A *tabula rasa* to achieve individual freedom. I would call this an attempt at thought without context, which presents certain problems.

First, it doesn't work. Leibniz in the seventeenth century: "[S]uppose that some poor wretch suddenly became king of China, but only on condition that he forgot what he had been. [A]s if he had to be annihilated and a king of China created at the same instant...."[16] Of course he would not be able to forget, nor would it make him a better king. In fact, if he could forget, he would be incapable of reigning. If he could forget he would be, as an emperor, certifiably insane.

Second, we're lucky it doesn't work. There is no such thing as engaging in a completely free argument or action. Everything we do is somehow preconditioned. The questions we need to ask are: Is it consciously preconditioned? To what extent? Can we alter the conditions?

In all three cases, the answer is: It depends. On what? On the degree of the answer to each question and the relationship between the three. The more we ask, the more we understand whether we are thinking or merely reacting. Our ability to improve conditions depends upon how sensibly we identify our memories and therefore work with them.

Third, Descartes's idea of a written society freeing our minds was wrong. The authority of orally transmitted memory was simply replaced by the authority of text. This is both better and worse. It laid the foundations for a profoundly scholastic society in which the power of the written can overwhelm serious, reasonably independent thought. Think of how dependent our society is on references to justify even the slightest attempt at originality. Here is the core of what drives the division between fiction and non-fiction.

Descartes's argument seems to be that only in the imaginary domains — those deemed to be outside written knowledge — is there any encouragement to think independently from memory. At first glance this seems a wonderful idea: a structure which encourages free thought and imagination. But what it really means is that thought — context — is pushed aside by form and method. As for declaring pure imagination to be free, that is nonsense. Fiction is shaped by the context of real memory.

Fourth, only memory, positive or negative, allows us to continue as if we relate to each other. Let me go back to the Truth and Reconciliation Committee in South Africa, or indeed to equivalent problems in Chile and Argentina. You can't detour around these disasters. You have to face the memory straight on, not in order to resolve or structure or punish or to engage in measurements of guilt, or even to seek apologies in and of themselves. But the clear acknowledgement of what happened "creates a communal starting point".[17] You need the context to be able to pick up and continue. José Zalaguett, who served on the Chilean Truth Commission, puts it this way — "Identity is memory. Identities forged out of half-remembered things or false memories easily commit transgressions."

And fifth, well, it involves the logical understanding of memory in its largest sense; that which Jung drew out of our long experience — "[W]ithout history there can be no psychology, and certainly no psychology of the unconscious."

🍎

RESTRAINT VERSUS CATHARSIS

Many see memory as an accumulation of violence or of evil. The past, for them, is a catalogue of human failure. Each new day is an opportunity for happy amnesia as they push forward.

That history is full of violence and failure is obvious. The twentieth century is there to remind us. That we remember those failures is as it should be. Our error lies in thinking that what bothers us about the past is the past itself.

Memory is not about weighing successes against failures. Again, that would be linear. A fixation on quantification. Both of which lead us into an extreme view of experience, in which there is a constant choice between good and evil, between light and darkness. This is not applied ethics, but a fairy-tale version of memory.

Most of our past consists neither of success nor of failure, but of restraint. Or rather, it consists of calm waters thanks to our restraint. Those who see history as an exciting tableau of Heroes, Heroic events, clashes, triumphs, tragedies have simply passed over the still waters. They believe that blood spilt is the ransom of freedom. That our characters — individual and national — are built through the blood of battle, whether individual or in organized groups.

This is the romanticism I mentioned a moment ago. It is directly linked to perfect love and sparkling teeth. Blood is not the ink of history. It is not true that "the dead cannot speak until they have drunk blood."[18]

The courage of those who spill their blood in a good cause is, of course, courage. Even those who die in good faith for a bad cause have died in good faith and may well have died with courage. What's more, there is a periodic need to defend a cause.

The point here is simply that restraint is one of the great strengths of memory. And, in the midst of recurrent hysteria over the ransom of blood, the still waters of restraint tend to be crossed over as if nonexistent. I should add that the commercial manifestations of romantic memory are even less interested in restraint than the political. Restraint doesn't sell. Hysteria does.

Yet these still waters represent the human at its most civilized. Restraint suggests that we are acting in a reasonably conscious manner; a manner conscious of the implications of our actions. We have restrained ourselves.

As for those who speak of the weight of history, they usually mean the weight of failure or the weight of inevitability. This suggests that the lighter the weight, the less the memory. Again, this is not true. The less the weight, the more complex and successful the society. The lighter the weight, the freer we are therefore to deal with problems, to imagine solutions.

Think of memory as our skin. Each violent act is a wound, usually self-inflicted. It is a slash across society or between societies. These wounds never entirely heal. They suppurate. One violent act tends to provoke another. No sooner does a scab form or a scar thicken, than it is ripped open again.

With each recurring scratch or blow, the suppuration, scars, deformations worsen and the cathartic experience is intensified. The tissue continues to build up, layer upon layer, until the adversaries are divided by a mountain of infertile, hard and shiny flesh.

Gradually the pain is overwhelmed by our fascination for the monstrous wound. We are drawn to it, hypnotized by it, addicted to the pleasure of inflicting more pain upon ourselves and upon the *other*. This is memory, but memory raging with self-importance; memory gone wrong.

Compared to such excitement, smooth, unscarred skin does indeed seem innocent. To go back to Sun Tzu, it is as if the battle won in the mind of a general is not a battle. It seems as if there is no memory because there is no disastrous evidence. No bodies, craters, ruins, scars. No triumph.

The scar tissue of memory gone wrong, never quite healing, is not in and of itself violence. Rather it is the deep infection of violence. Distrust. Preconceived ideas. Facile prejudice. Predictable formulae. Ventings of emotion. Verbiage in place of language.

We all have wounds. We are all struggling to heal them. Consider the Cromwellian and William of Orange massacres in Ireland. Or the suppurating wound of American slavery. Think of France and Germany in the 1950s penetrating deep under most of their modern history — deep beneath their terrible scars — in order to free themselves from the suppurating wound which kept them killing each other.

In their case it was not enough to turn away from three wars over a hundred years, not enough to abjure conflict. Their destructive reactions go back as far as the Napoleonic wars and the plundering and atrocities in East Prussia between 1806 and 1812. And so the two countries had to reach deeper into their memories, right down to their mediaeval pre-Reformation relationships. Those which died with Erasmus. In a sense, in order to imagine what seem to be the entirely new relationships of the European Union, they had to get down to the Charlemagnian concepts of Europe as a continent with non-contradictory differences holding it together.

I spoke earlier of memory as layering. When it comes to public affairs, cathartic memory is, more often than not, the negative side of layering. The non-cathartic memory is far more subtle, more interesting. It has all the complexity of restraint. It understands that each action creates a new layer of skin, which will grow upon our individual or societal bodies in a sound or diseased way.

A healthy memory is not based upon inaction. It requires the conscious understanding of our acts. The cathartic gesture, on the other hand, is driven by reaction, which is a passive, unconscious form of action.

I'm not suggesting that there is no room for the cathartic experience. We have it in our personal lives, in births and deaths, in our friendships. Creativity is a catharsis for the artist and the public. Sports, adventure; there are endless opportunities for catharsis. But once it moves into the ordering of societies, memory becomes dysfunctional and the scarring begins.

I quoted earlier Alasdair MacIntyre's argument that we struggle today to make sense of "the fragments of a conceptual scheme, parts which now lack those contexts from which their significance derives." What we have, he says, is the "simulacra of morality" studded with "key expressions", but the context escapes us.[19]

From a very different political position, the French philosopher Jacques Ellul said exactly the same thing:

> Modern society is, in fact, conducted on the basis of purely
> technical considerations. But when men found themselves
> going counter to the human factor, they reintroduced —

and in an absurd way — all manner of moral theories
related to the rights of man, the League of Nations, liberty,
justice. But when these moral flourishes overly encumber
technical progress they are discarded — more or less speed-
ily, with more or less ceremony, but with determination
nonetheless.

These two statements may seem a little over the top when viewed from the comfort of middle-class democratic life. And certainly the efforts by thousands of citizens to establish a new ethical framework have been remarkable over the last few years. But consider those efforts in the context of what I said earlier about the frustrations and profound contradictions tied to long-term NGO efforts. Or think of the examples I've already used.

After all, there really was a genocide in Rwanda. Nothing has been done to the relevant international mechanisms to prevent another elsewhere. Mad cow disease continues to be treated — if you follow the slow progress of the question — as an annoying impediment to commercial activity. International overfishing, with its long-term implications, sails on from denial to denial and defensive half-measure to defensive half-measure. As for international structures, in an age of falling borders, they continue to be imagined first in the framework of commerce, and only in a marginal way according to any framework of the public good. And all of that in the last decade.

When you strip away the rhetoric obscuring our actions, you find what does appear to be fragmentary behaviour. And utilitarian self-interest — itself profoundly fragmentary — does seem to advance with heavy footsteps through the flying dust of ethics.

What might have been is an abstraction
Remaining a perpetual possibility
Only in the world of speculation.[20]

In such an atmosphere the very idea of restraint as the context for memory is hard to put forward. Why did Ellul and others fix on technology as part of the problem? Not because they were or are against the use and advance of technology. But because they thought it preposterous that humans should be led by objects which they themselves invented and constructed; because they thought this was an abandonment of conscious human action.

Take our astonishing new mechanisms of communications. These contain no human qualities — no common sense, no ethics, no intuition, no imagination, no memory and, indeed, not even instrumental reason. Yet these mechanisms flash and turn, like a hungry beast with an unquenchable appetite for material produced by humans. The machinery is so much more voracious than our ability to feed it, that what it most requires in the place of a shape, which might be called memory, is cathartic expression.

Think of it. The enemy of healthy memory is the cathartic, or at least the gratuitously cathartic. And the principal requirement of our technology is not facts, not memory, but gratuitous catharsis — something which moves so fast that content is irrelevant, repetition a strength and identifiable shape a weakness.

Harold Innis, who gave birth to much of modern communications theory, once said that "most forward-looking people have their heads turned sideways."[21] To see the shape of things, I would say. To avoid the blinkers of fleeing forward.

But the marriage of technology and catharsis is a perfect recipe for such forward flight. Where would restraint fit in? "If you have a society in which there are forms of communication that will not allow for the cultivation of remembrance, then you will not gain the necessary continuity to hold out against the forces of power." In such an atmosphere the non-cathartic, to the extent that it is visible, is presented as emotionally mediocre. Indeed, restraint is treated as weakness, an excuse not to take the exciting ride.

But if we step back from the race, the fashion, the excitement of the present slipping constantly away, we find we have a solid attachment not only to that present, but to the past and the future. It is the strength of memory used consciously and with restraint to avoid self-inflicted wounds. Memory seen this way is the enemy of arbitrary power, whether it be in our personal lives or a political phenomenon or an utilitarian outcome of technological changes.

THE USE OF MEMORY

Is this an argument to suggest that memory could be utilitarian if carefully used? Not exactly.

It is almost in reach of the practical. But if you push this idea of concrete utility too far, memory is deformed into a rigid, romantic, linear fixation. The past is then turned into something which appears to justify whatever we want to do; a cover for arbitrary action. But memory is useful precisely because it protects us from the arbitrary.

How then do we use it?

I remember hearing Le Clézio, the great French writer, who is one of Conrad's spiritual children, say that the decisive moments of literature — those of Shakespeare, Cervantes, Conrad — are created "through memory not travel". Conrad, with a magician's cape, seemed to be travelling his stories across the seas. They were actually moving over "the mirror of the sea"; the reflection being our memory. "Art consists in bringing the memory of things past to the surface. But the author is not a *passéiste*. He is linked to history; to memory; which is linked to the common dream."[22]

And so memory brings us back to the shared knowledge of common sense and the prolonged, shared uncertainty of imagination, and the shared expression of intuition.

Of all these, memory relates perhaps most intimately to the passive half of intuition — to the expression of what we might be. You can see in creativity, in the novel for example, the writer struggling constantly to reanimate our memories. They are "working against this loss of self", as Saul Bellow puts it, binding us to the great river of creativity which, through our deepest memory, ties us to our experience.

What does this mean?

Listen to Günter Grass accepting his Nobel Prize. Victorious capitalism, he says, is now "…megalomaniacally replaying the errors of the supposedly extinct brother (socialism and communism). Why? Because both share the same memory. They are born of the same intellectual and technological events. And so we are trying to repair the damage [of socialism] with [the same] Enlightenment tools." This is not, as Grass says, because we have no others, but because we have not yet remembered that we have others.

The difficulty is to remember our way out of unnecessarily blinkered patterns. This is Cicero's cliché — those who don't know history remain children. It is Edmund Burke speaking in Parliament to defend the demands of the American colonists. He called for an inclusive use of memory "… in order to correct our errors…*or at least to avoid a dull uniformity in mischief* and the unpitied calamity of being repeatedly caught in the same snare." Remember Grass: "Megalomaniacally replaying the errors". Memory is there not to imprison us in the past, but to free us from the traps of habit.

Context. Non-rigid shape. Careful layering. These three elements allow us to rediscover ourselves and our ability to act differently in a stagnating or suppurating continuity. They are as applicable to marriages and families as they are to international relations.

This may seem an odd approach to usefulness, given the constant technological explosions which we are repeatedly told have imposed a technical — utilitarian — imperative not just on our lives, but on our civilization. There is a sense that these recurrent explosions have also shattered our memories or swept them away in fragments of shapeless information.

But is there really a technological imperative? If so, that would mean an utilitarian imperative. Has our ability to use our memory as a central quality really been negated by a change in our practical way of doing things and by waves of shapeless information?

Not really. We have been cowed by these machines. By their ability to both consume and shower material. We have been so sucked into their fascinating mechanisms that we have forgotten about the difference between detailed utility and fundamental usefulness. Once we have been hypnotized by the details of use and operation, it is but one more step to expect that the shaping of our lives and our society will flow from these mechanisms, as if they and the machinery and their programs existed in and of themselves, by their own right.

But utility is not a force in and of itself. It has no roots in the particularity of humans. There is nothing magic about methodology and mechanisms. There is perhaps some magic in the source of this utility. After all, our memory is one of the forces which allow us to imagine and invent the utilitarian.

And the actual process of utility does indeed require most of us to be intimately involved in a particular activity. Some of us design software programs, just as some once designed printing mechanisms or wrote instruction manuals for various uses. Some of us sit at keyboards and screens, just as some used to type or set type.

But the extent to which we have been cowed can be seen in how many of us sit before screens, when this is not directly related to our job or expertise. This is pretend utilitarianism. Utility as romanticism. And so, in the name of modernism and efficiency, senior civil servants around the world, who are paid to think and lead, now spend a third or so of their time typing and doing clerical tasks. We have forgotten that, while utility is necessary, utility itself is of no real interest to unfolding civilizations. Nor is the complexity of mechanisms. With most things we use, we are more likely to be passengers than pilots or mechanics. The whole point of the utilitarian is the cool, distanced relationship of exploitation. We should make the most of it. In other words, we must take our distance from the vortex of technology in order to fully benefit from it and feel independent enough from these mechanisms to shape them to our own purposes.

There is only a technological imperative if we believe that we have a personal relationship with technology. It is curious how much difficulty we have with the idea of animism — that we live in a context with what exists on the planet and must therefore deal with that relationship. On the other hand, we are eager to pretend that we have an animated relationship with inanimate machinery of our own fabrication. What's more, we pretend that we are the subservient half of this relationship. This is a bit like having an emotional and sexual relationship with an inflatable doll.

These are mere objects. They are our slaves in a way that a rock or a tree can never be. Machinery cannot shatter our memory. Nor, despite our contemporary impression, can technology sweep away our memory in fragments of shapeless information. Technology has no will, no memory, no purpose and no direction. It is not a force in and of itself. It can be an expression of our specific needs if we assert ourselves. The utilitarian can be made to serve us in the context of memory, whether we are seeking to remember or seeking to change our patterns of life.

Memory lost

For some reason we don't seem to be asserting our authority over circuit boards. We're still wandering in an aimless manner, hypnotized into false innocence before the promise of wonderful new worlds to be brought to us by new means of communications.

We blame our innocence on the permanent technological disorder. We cannot keep up. Much of what we call intellectual activity is just frenetic involvement with the details of these new mechanisms — frenetic, incessant activity devoid of context.

What is true of computers is true of pills. The disorder of new medications gives us the impression of constant movement. Yet over the last fifteen years we have gone from the demonstrable certainty that malaria was conquered — which it was, for about two decades — to an unfocused, passive, societal acceptance that it is back, and in a stronger killing form than during the nineteenth century.

What happened? We had no context for the parallel tracks on which disease and the idea of cure move. We actually provoked the return of the disease with our misunderstanding of the cure.

A recent study of those antibiotics used to treat meningitis and pneumonia found that between 1995 and 1998 the percentage of drug-resistant bacteria had grown from nine to fourteen per cent.[23] The rate is exponential. Almost all experts agree that the cause is the over-prescription of antibiotics.

Countries with strong public-medicine systems are beginning to react by pushing doctors to cut back on their prescriptions. Where private medicine dominates, the bad habits are worse. Many would blame the drug companies, who are busy addicting the doctors to the use of medications by handing out free samples and inviting them to education conferences which are usually commercial indoctrination sessions in holiday settings.

But the problem needs a more distanced approach if we are to understand the context. There is an excitement attached to prescribing these drugs. Like magic, the doctor reaches out and slays the dragon of death. It is the power of false individualism over that of disease. The memory of death is erased.

Yet for decades sensible doctors have been warning that we could be thrown back to where we were fifty years ago, when people died of ear infections. Disease resistance to the treatments for syphilis, gonorrhea, typhoid and tuberculosis are growing. The World Health Organization says North American doctors over-prescribe antibiotics by about fifty per cent. Many rush on, kicking up the dust of utilitarian progress, tossing their pills at the diseases like confetti at a bride.

All of this is about a loss of context. More than technical progress is in question here. Thomas Bernhard, the great Austrian novelist, wrote of a character described as Wittgenstein's nephew — "[H]e despised the society of today, which resolutely denies its own history and which consequently has *neither a past nor a future.*"[24]

You might think at first that this is shame or denial, given Austria's role in support of Nazi ideas. But in 1936, in the *Diary of a Man in Despair*, an almost identical vacuum is identified by Friedrich Reck-Malleczewen. "I wrack my brains over the perpetual riddle of how this same people which so jealously watched over its rights a few years ago can have sunk into this stupor, in which it not only allows itself to be dominated by the street-corner idlers of yesterday, but actually, height of shame, is incapable *any longer of perceiving its shame for the shame that it is.*"

Why take these two examples from a subject we believe we know well? Because our ability to remember the meaning of our own period is, if anything, worse than that despised by Bernhard and Reck-Malleczewen.

The latter writes of seeing Hitler driven by in pomp — armour plating, bodyguards and so on. "A jellylike sky-gray face, a moonface into which two melancholy jet-black eyes have been set like raisins. So sad, so unutterably insignificant, so basically misbegotten is this countenance that only thirty years ago, in the darkest days of Wilhelmism, such a face on an official would have been impossible... [D]isobeyed as soon as its mouth spoke an order — and not merely by the higher officials in the ministry; no, by the doorman, by the cleaning women!"

What he is getting at is MacIntyre's idea of shattered context. What he is describing is not the loss of standards or intentions, but that of the mirrors which give us the strength of irony.

●

FALSE MEMORY

Yet we believe we remember a great deal. And since no argument need be apocalyptic, I would agree: we do remember a great deal. What's more, we certainly wish to. Sometimes, of course, we are carried off into dead ends of false recollection. False memory comes in many forms.

There is laziness. Sōseki Natsume, the Japanese novelist, had a cat as a recurrent hero. What, the animal asks himself, is *usual*? It's "merely a word expressing the square of *often*. What one does once, one wants to do again, and things tried twice invite a third experience." This is the most simplistic level of experience as memory. "Once we've done a thing more than three times over, the act becomes a habit and its performance a necessity of our daily life."[25]

This is not tradition. It has no significance. If 'laziness' seems unduly unkind, perhaps 'fashion' is the right word. I would call *habit* the false memory of familiarity. This is the bane of thought and creativity; the ally of collaboration versus ethical action.

Bertrand Russell was particularly feeble when the question of familiarity arose. He seemed to see it as a key to trust. "The characteristic by which we distinguish the images we trust is the feeling of *familiarity* that accompanies them." He then added "feeling" as the other element of trust. Memory is to be identified through familiarity and feeling.

But this is also the classic justification for prejudice and racism, both claiming in this way memory as their witness. And feeling as part of familiarity can mean anything — good or bad — about anything. Russell then went on to create a measurement of memory as some sort of "correspondence between beliefs and facts". Which facts? All racism is based on 'facts', particularly when there is an atmosphere of shattered ethics. Skin colour is a fact. Accents are facts, as are languages. The Nazis measured noses. Measured, calculated, tabulated, averaged out, concluded.

Surely familiarity, feeling, beliefs and many facts are products of memory not characteristics of it. Russell is arguing that dust or a clean floor is the characteristic of a mop. They aren't. It would be far better to see memory through ethics, for example, or common sense.

What of transient memory? "Beware the vividness of transient events." That was the advice Clausewitz gave. The then General Colin Powell, at the time of the obsessional silliness of the O.J. Simpson trial and verdict, said "This is a very vivid event, but it is a transient event. So I would say let's all take a deep breath and relax." Shared for a brief moment, it is the sort of memory which slips away quickly because it is not really a memory of any shared reality.

If you don't take that deep breath, a transient event can be implanted artificially as a memory, and then you are stuck with it. It will not function as memory because it is false. If you try to make it function, the result will be a wound which, with application, may turn into a particularly unpleasant suppurating sore.

Another sort of false memory is the tidy sort. "Symmetry, in any narrative, always means that historical content is being subordinated to mythical demands of design and form."[26] That was Northrop Frye's demolition. Tidy mythology is at best bus-station fantasy. This is quite different from fiction which, being real, is asymmetrical. It is untidy by nature.

A more disturbing version of this false memory is our need to clean up places or stories of real importance. I don't mean simply to edit or physically sweep, wash and paint what was in reality dirty and messy. What I'm talking about is our need to restructure memory so that it suits our most utilitarian habits.

At Auschwitz, for example, the Prisoner Reception Centre, where Jews were registered, stripped, shaved and tattooed, is now the Visitor Reception Centre: an information kiosk, a cafeteria, a ticket office. "When my head was shaved," a new woman prisoner later said, "and

I had striped clothing and my arm was tattooed, and they took my clothes and shoes away, I just did not feel like living." She tried to commit suicide. It is true that today's visitors need an entrance and services. Not surprisingly, the old entrance was in the right place and was therefore made to serve.[27]

I'm not suggesting that those visitors are not disturbed, moved, overwhelmed by what they see. I'm not making an obsessional, purist argument. And I am not suggesting that Auschwitz has been robbed of meaning. But there is a problem here. Under the Nazis the utilitarian need for their particular idea of order took on a terrible form. Now, that same utilitarian need for order has taken on an innocuous form.

In other words, the purpose and consequences are quite different. But the underlying methodologies are the same. Historians of sites look at this in confusion and wonder what to do or say. What is the reality of memory in such a place? How can you remember it? Is tidying of this sort too great a risk to take with, if not the most important, one of the most important physical memories of our time? Why take the chance of rewriting — re-forming — such a reality?

The novelist Caryl Phillips, with his West African, West Indian and British background, found himself asking the same questions as he wandered through the old Elmina Castle — a Portuguese slaving fort on the coast of Ghana. The dungeon for females, where over time tens of thousands of women had been shackled while they waited to be shipped to the Americas, is now the gift shop.

And what of pathological and punitive memory? "Justice fails to be done," Archbishop Tutu said, "if the concept we entertain of justice is retributive justice whose chief goal is to be punitive." Why does it fail? In part because memory can have no meaning in such a case if it cannot link with ethics or even intuition or common sense.

Justice Louise Arbour, as the prosecutor of the International Criminal Tribunal for Yugoslavia and Rwanda, was constantly faced with exactly this type of false memory. She was rarely dealing with victims who operated simply from factual accuracy. They also dealt in allegories and metaphors. How is anyone to combine and make sense of these facts, allegories and metaphors? For example, the accuracy of the chronology of events as recounted may be less important than the state of the person who has experienced the atrocity; or indeed, the memory of the one to whom an impression of this state has been passed. The need here is to work to re-establish what Arbour calls "the integrity of the memory".

The voice of order might say that the best way to prevent these events from contributing to a pathological state of mind is to maintain a certain public silence. In reality, the only way to keep the allegories and metaphors under control is to recount the events as publicly as possible.

There is a curious link here to the South African situation. Only by recounting the events could the victims reassert their dignity. In the Yugoslavian case, a clear public airing could help the society escape from the hysteria of an experience mythologized right out of any livable orbit. In the case of South Africa the aim of speaking out is to escape the hysteria of reality denied.

The difficulty with such allegories — with nationalisms of hatred, for example — is that you cannot simply remove them. That would leave a vacuum which would accentuate the self-destructive tendencies. That which exists — even if false or deformed — must be replaced with something which is livable. Prosperity is not the answer to that particular need. What is required is an appropriate memory or mythology.

🍎

WHAT IT ISN'T

Paul Ricoeur, the French philosopher, says there are three false memories: blocked, manipulated, obligatory. Mémoire empêchée, manipulée, obligée.[28] To this he adds the obvious: history does not have a particular or formal method — "n'a pas de méthode propre." Neither memory nor history is the child of the social sciences.

Ricoeur mentions Freud and the unconscious when he talks of blocked memory. But it is much more than that. The Cartesian argument that we must forget in order to be free to think has grown over the last two centuries in every direction. A whole 'common sense' school — often utilitarians or apologists for established power — has insisted that to get past the worst in our past we must forget. The late-nineteenth-century French thinker Ernest Renan shaped this public debate with his arguments about our need to forget. [29]

In many ways manipulated memory is a product of blocked memory. The desire to forget opens the door to fantasy. It is this manipulated form which has made many people feel that memory cannot be trusted.

Here is the tool of classic racism, of false pure roots, of past tragedies or wrongs being isolated from context and turned into running sores, of rather passive, harmless pride being turned into xenophobia.

And the last fifty years have produced new, intensive varieties of manipulated memory: Propaganda deconstructs and reassembles sounds, images and words in a profoundly meaningless manner, which makes it easy for information to be not misrepresented, but actually represented however wished. Public relations does the same indiscriminately with politics and commerce and sports; in fact, with just about anything. Even the documentary approach — the visual form of non-fiction — can easily fall into this category, as useful fragments are chosen from the tidal wave of facts and matched with propaganda or public relations. The outcome depends on the intent, not the facts.

As for obligatory memory — mémoire obligée — it speaks for itself as the ultimate form of memory blocked and manipulated. Ricoeur says that treating memory as an obligation or a duty is a trap — "le piège du devoir de mémoire". You cannot project remembering into the future, which the idea of duty implies you can.

Memory as a duty — un devoir — is usually used "with the intent of short-circuiting the work of history as an auto-critique".

How can something so open to misuse be a human quality?

The answer is: just as easily as any of the other qualities. They are equally open to being blocked, manipulated and treated as obligations. Why do the flaws of memory seem more obvious? Because in the twentieth century, reason used as an ideology has found memory a particularly useful mechanism to either denigrate or exploit. Each era has its fashions and particularities.

How do we remember?

With great difficulty. In the ruins from which the archaeologists retrieved the first tablets which brought Gilgamesh back to life, there were also tens of thousands of tablets recording commercial transactions. These have not reunited us with an ongoing reflection of ourselves which we find useful or intriguing or surprising. They lay there dead under the sand for thousands of years, were discovered and remained dead. There was nothing wrong with that market activity. Quite simply, it was then, and remains, eternally locked into our present. Gilgamesh, on the other hand, was released as vigorous as ever and he sprang back to his place at the core of our vision of ourselves as humans.

Why insist on these very different fates? Because our highly sophisticated and educated society asserts a great truth: that human self-interest through commercial transactions constructs human society.

History is the story of memory quickly sorting itself out. Events and people are retained or dropped. As time moves on, these cards of memory may be reshuffled several times. What is dropped may be picked back up and vice-versa. This reflects the spatial, cyclical nature of remembrance.

Almost invariably, the first items to be dropped, and rarely to reappear, are commercial. Along with them go those individuals who were famous in their time as captains of industry, wizards of finance and masters of trade. One moment they are everywhere, knighted, ennobled, honoured, at the tables of power, at the side of artists. The next moment, they have vanished.

Commerce itself only keeps its records as long as the public authorities oblige it to. It is eager to discard its own memory. Why should history do any more?

On November 27 or so, 2000, Mr. Jack Welch announced his successor as chairman of General Electric. His moving on made front pages around the world. "Big Shoes to Fill." "Calling it Quits." "Highly Regarded Leader." Over twenty years he had led his company to become the largest, when measured by market capitalization — an astonishing definition of success by free-market standards.

After all, his success was not the printing press or the steam engine or the computer. He did not even bring about a transformation of our utilitarian mechanisms. He succeeded at management and capitalization. I could describe this as empty bureaucratic accomplishments. To put it more abstractly: a victory of form over content. He was a legend in the market and no doubt in business schools.

Who knew of him? A few thousand. Who remembers now? In five years who will remember?

Who were the last five chairs of any major corporation anywhere? The industrial revolution, we are told, changed everything and brought us democracy and individualism. Who were the philosopher-princes we ought to be thanking?

We remember Robert Owen because he wrote against them while successfully running his model factories. We remember some engineers and inventors such as Brunel and Edison. Of the great nineteenth-century robber-barons — less than two centuries ago — whom do we remember? Only those who built libraries, theatres and museums or who created and donated great collections or funded disinterested enterprises. As in Buddhism, they *earned merit* by acting outside their interest-directed world.

I'm not suggesting that people should be criticized for their involvement in commerce. To the contrary. Self-interest is a key utilitarian characteristic of our society. Commerce is a key utilitarian mechanism of that characteristic.

But neither self-interest nor, more specifically, commerce is a foundation of society or civilization. Why? Because neither has an inherent memory. Those involved in commerce are not troubled by this. If they want to find a place in society's continuity, they can reach outside of their business activities to family life or participation in the public good. Or they use the money at their disposition to draw elements of society's continuity into their world.

Either way, commerce remains commerce, a child of the present.

How can self-interest have held on to the myth of its leadership when it has such an incapacity to fulfil the function of memory? Part of the answer is that MacIntyre must be correct when he writes of the splintering of our context.

Without that context, there is a vacuum. And the result is a new kind of timelessness. Not a spatial kind, which includes past and future. But rather a linear sort in which there is only the present.

There is another indication of this fracturing. If you follow the obsessions of the creative world, you discover the intuitive anxieties of a civilization. And increasingly the creative forces of Western democracies are obsessed by the malfunctioning of time. By speed, yes, the speed of change. But also by the problems of memory, the tidal waves of shapeless fragments, the information which drowns us rather than informing. Can it be captured? Controlled? Shaped? We feel this is more problematic than ever and so we become more anxious.

Our frustration carries us back to Gilgamesh, weeping to break the skin of time. You could argue that the underlying theme of the modern novel was first laid out by Manzoni as a "famous war against time" in which memory and history are the weapons of civilization.

Think of the great novels of Conrad creating metaphysical, timeless stories behind the innocent façade of tales from the sea. Kafka using administrative nightmares to illustrate our incapacity to pass from past to future, in what we might accept as a normal manner. Proust picking up the Wagnerian method of trying to reattach us to our passing time and memory. Ford Madox Ford and James Joyce doing the same in a still more complex way.

And all of that before we had fully digested the extent to which the First World War — the ultimate war of time — had shattered our sense of shaped memory. Samuel Beckett was the natural expression of what followed. *Waiting for Godot* seems every day to be more clearly the essential description of our time. As for Conrad's inheritors, such as Gabriel García Márquez, they have sought in every direction for a way to imagine our shape inside a new sense of time. The magic realism of Márquez and others is an attempt at creating an imaginative mechanism which will help us to remember in the world we have built.

MEMORY VERSUS REPERCUSSIONS

Let's go back to a key example. How are we to remember the Holocaust? All the survivors will be dead in a few years; their children, not so very long after that.

Here is the event which most clearly told us we were functioning in a shapeless manner. The normal signposts of evil and institutionalized lunacy seemed to have disappeared along with any mechanism of balance. In other words, people were functioning with "the fragments of a conceptual scheme, parts which now lack those contexts from which their significance derives".

When we say *remember the Holocaust*, there are multiple implications — are we to remember the deaths as a memorial; to remember the horror, a condemnation of our failure; to remember the senseless freedom of action, that anyone could do anything because there was no agreed shape or context for even minimum human behaviour; to remember the ease with which it happened.

We have ample evidence of the power of catastrophic events. Their repercussions tumble on through history, creating victims centuries later.

I've spoken of Ireland, South Africa and American slavery. There are dozens of other examples. Latin America still spins and tumbles from the terrible violence and errors of the Spanish conquest. The Congo has never recovered from the Belgian genocide more than a century ago.

Each of these examples gives us a hint of how, by attempting to destroy the context of others in the name of our particular inevitable linear progress, we undermine our own sense of context. That is the meaning of Conrad's *Heart of Darkness*. The self-destructing victim — Kurtz — stands for all of us. The death of his victims is a tragedy tied to a genocide. His own death is symbolic of a civilization which has lost all sense of context and therefore of memory. Writing of the conquest of Mexico, Le Clézio said — "It is the extermination of an ancient dream by the furor of a modern dream, the destruction of myths by a desire for power. Gold, modern weaponry and rational thought against magic and the gods."[30]

I'm not making an argument in favour of magic and the gods. I'm pointing out that we kept our own magic and our gods — witness the role of Homer — but removed those of others. The question is: how often can you righteously undermine others without losing your own sense of context? That was the tragedy of Kurtz.

The culmination of this shapeless floating seemed to come with two events. First, the war of 1914–18, when Western civilization combined modern technology and management methods, so that form completely overwhelmed the context to produce the first organized slaughter of our own citizenry.

T.E. Lawrence wrote to the great strategist Basil Liddell Hart: "With 2,000 years of examples behind us we have no excuse when fighting for not fighting well." Which the soldiers did, however badly they were generaled. We try, with a certain desperation, to remember those soldiers each year, but otherwise stumble on in denial.

There are a dozen explanations for what happened next. First, having settled into self-denial, we simply blinked as the massacres continued. There were the Soviet liquidations in the cause of socialist purity. Later, the gays and gypsies were killed by the Nazis with a pretence of moral respectability.

But it is the murder of those six million Jews for no reason at all which brought the other massacres into perspective. The Holocaust stands as the clear sign of a civilization out of control. Not Nazi civilization, but Western civilization, bereft of memory and ethics and of any link between the two. In many ways it was reason spun into a purposeless furor: scientific, delusionary murder.

What is the meaning of memory in such a context?

We have been struggling with this for half a century now. The most obvious use of memory would be to fix our experience in place, to warn us the next time we begin slipping off the rails.

There we have already failed. Since 1945, there have been a dozen or so genocides. An estimated million Chinese in Indonesia in the 1960s. An estimated million in Cambodia, under the Khmer Rouge. Iran, Iraq, The Congo, Rwanda, Uganda, Yugoslavia. And the unprecedented number of refugees demonstrates that the last half-century, so widely seen as peaceful within a handful of Western democracies, has been one of the most unstable and violent for the rest of the world.

We cannot disassociate ourselves from actions which are largely carried out with weapons we manufacture and sell. Nor from actions carried out in the context of political differences which we invent and encourage. And even when we have not directly encouraged these conflicts, they are often the outcome of an approach towards the nation-state which we invented, which made its way through the West with positive and negative results, and which we have now more or less dropped. But before doing so, we did everything we could to spread this approach to the colonies. It is that time-lag in national politics which has made the developing world such a gold mine for Western exports, military and other.

The early vehicles of this Western proselytizing were piracy, religion and trade — yes, trade. This was from the fifteenth to the eighteenth century. By the nineteenth century we had formalized everything into Empires. Our culture — deified by our empires — had become the cover for our interests. And in the twentieth century we went back to trade and a new sort of rolling religion. Thus we proselytized as truth whatever old and new fashions we had fallen in love with for a short period of time — urbanization, measurable incomes, management methods, large engineering projects. These were all truths in their time and therefore the actual requirements of the receiving society didn't need to be examined seriously.

As we continue to leap from one of these fashions to another, we erase our memory of the effect of the one that came before. These are the religions of Western modernity.

And so the genocides and massacres go on. With Rwanda — certainly a smaller genocide than the Holocaust, but still much more than a massacre — the West sat very still, as if frozen in place. My point is precise: we found we were unable to use the still living memory of the Holocaust to motivate ourselves into action. General Dallaire has put this down to racism, which may partly be true. But it was only with great creaking and delay that we moved into action in Yugoslavia, a part of Europe. The effort was so painfully reluctant that we allowed the worst to be done before engaging.

'That is what happens,' many would say. 'Time softens the impact of memory.' We do not have the emotional strength to retain the horror or, indeed, in a different sort of case, the love.

> And we forget because we must
> And not because we will.

With these lines, Matthew Arnold took the predictable approach, exactly that of Ernest Renan. He might as easily have written,

> And we remember because we must
> And not because we will.

There are, after all, simple, well-established ways to remember. "Memory must have an object," Thomas Reid wrote in 1785. "Every man can distinguish the thing remembered from the remembrance of it."[31] But to keep alive the thing remembered, the remembrance of it must give us some access to the thing itself. If not, all you have is ritual.

And so, in these last years of living, direct witnesses, we have been doubling our efforts to break the skin of memory in some ongoing way. Remarkable museums or parts of museums have been built. The Holocaust Museum in Washington, by presenting elements of the thing itself in a direct way, seems to provoke remembrance. Elsewhere, sculptures have competed with each other in a search for rawness, out of fear that any traditional hint of beauty or elegance might lock the thing itself in aesthetics. When the severe monument in Vienna was unveiled in 2000, Simon Wiesenthal, ninety-one, insisted "it is important that the art is not beautiful, that it hurts us in some way."

The rebuilt Reichstag in Berlin is a remarkable attempt to deal with the whole unravelling of a great civilization. The core of this living demonstration is the chamber itself. The history of parliaments is that the chambers are some combination of intimate and grand. They are built as invitations to orators to debate; to win over opponents. They are intended to be places where intellect and emotion play with each other. Here the chamber or Bundestag has been reconstructed in the coldest, most dispassionate manner. Any attempt at emotion would die before it reached the members. Pericles himself could make no headway.

What escapes this and the other monuments is the experience of terrifyingly pure evil. Perhaps only that could keep us awake to the reality of violence and the nonsense of fragmented conceptual schemes.

The closest we can come are places such as former death camps. But to function in this way they would have to exist in a radiating vacuum of purity. In which case there would be no ticket sales or cafeterias in the front hall. But the obvious utilitarian limitation of a fixed memory is that it is seen by a few and unseen by those who do not wish to see.

What other tools do we have?

Greek mythology was an oral force with a didactic purpose. Certainly that is the other kind of memory people have tried to create around the Holocaust — a language which breaks the skin of memory. It may not necessarily be embedded in Homeric prose. It may be embedded in our everyday language — what we feel we can say and cannot say.

Some people kick in protest, claiming it is politically correct and artificially imposed. But much of it is looking for ways to refuse the old oral contradictions, which allowed us to slip into organized mass murder. What is interesting is that we are consciously trying to construct new language — oral language — which will keep us away from destructive actions.

There is an urgency and an oddity to all of this. The living witnesses of the Holocaust are already installed in our memories, as if dead.

Odysseus, on his long trip home, sat unidentified in Alcinous's palace in Phalacia, listening to the blind bard Dimodocus singing of the war before Troy.

> Odysseus, clutching his flaring sea-blue cape
> in both powerful hands, drew it over his head
> and buried his handsome face,
> ashamed his hosts might see him shedding tears." [32]

Is he weeping for his friends dead in the wars? Or is it, as George Steiner says, that Odysseus is overwhelmed at hearing himself "emptied into legend". "He had passed already into the insubstantial everlastingness of fiction."

Here is the idea of memory as a timeless — not ritualistic — reality, constantly accessible. This is very different from the comforting oppositions of good and evil laid out in a Hollywood movie. Here memory is aimed instead at permanent uncertainty through the evocation of the imagination.

Imagination and memory together are the best weapons we have against our desire for emotional comfort, forgetting because we tell ourselves we must.

There is another way of coming at such a need for memory. John Locke once called it contemplation.[33] This is not contemplation in the standard religious sense, but concentration on a form of remembrance.

I've noticed that civilizations which are still attached to an animist reality have clearer access to memory as a permanent uncertainty. Their reaction to great suffering is more sophisticated than ours within the Western tradition.

Think of how the aboriginals handle their memory of what was done to them in Canada, the United States and Australasia. Or think again of the South African Truth and Reconciliation Commission. There seems to be a clearer access to reality, which allows people to both retain the memory and yet continue dealing with its repercussions over a longer period of time — what you might call a conceptual scheme within a context. Why is this? Again in both cases the approach resembles that of Vico. In place of the linear — fixed rigidly facing the future — there is a sense of circles and cycles.

> To forgive is not just to be altruistic. It is the best form of
> self-interest. What dehumanizes you inexorably dehuman-
> izes me.

These words of Desmond Tutu might have come from any number of death-camp survivors.

There are cycles of life, of suffering, of survival. The aboriginal view of elements or seasons or song-lines or winds may lack the energy of the linear, but it has shapes which can be tumbled and bruised by any wave and still have meaning. Our rigid frameworks simply shatter and become a helpless part of the fragments which shower down upon us.

And there lies our difficulty with remembrance. If we stick to our rigid, linear approach, we cannot effectively remember the thing itself. We sail on, seemingly leaving our experience behind us.

But memory moves in cycles and circles and so overtakes us when least expected. We are then caught in the repercussions of our actions. Suddenly we recognize the parallels with past acts. We both remember and are powerless to use that remembrance. Only a circular or cyclical approach would allow us to act and remember at the same time.

How then do we keep memory in context? How do we protect against the linear? How do we build in timelessness? How do we develop a circular consciousness of our own acts?

Memory will only respond to these needs if it is enriched by ethics and kept down to earth — by common sense. If our imagination is not engaged, we cannot understand how a past act might relate to one in the future.

How then do we remember the Holocaust in a way which suggests action to prevent another genocide? We build clear ethical lines into remembrance. We listen for the language which we know leads to organized racism. We project our imagination into events not yet fully formulated.

The moment memory is taken seriously, it becomes clear how fragile and complex it is.

●

FLOATING IN A GRAVITY-FREE UNIVERSE

When I say to a German or a Spaniard that the strength of the new Europe lies in its return to the strengths of the mediaeval model, they look quite upset. All they can hear is "mediaeval". And they see themselves as modern.

If I say to Europeans that the reconstruction of the continent is our real memory of the Holocaust, someone will reply that Europe is a rational construction. He would be referring to its all too visible administrative structures. But these structures and those of economic integration are now the elements which most weaken Europe because they alienate the citizenry.

The core intention from the beginning was social and political. Why? Because the rational version of those social and political forces had disconnected the continent from its memory and the relationship of that memory to ethics and common sense. The result in the 1940s was an unprecedented level of sustained violence. This culminated in serial mass murders. So the reconstruction of Europe is our true monument to the Holocaust.

Let me take this a step further. Central Europe is now beginning to enter into the European project. In a sense, this brings the original project full circle. You could say that Middle Europe is the very essence of the mediaeval European idea. After all, Germany, France and Britain were profoundly nineteenth-century nation-states. Britain and France built the altar to national centralization and single myth, single race, single religion, single language nationality. Germany rushed in behind, trying to catch up.

But Middle Europe — or Mitteleuropa — was always the centre of multiracial, multicultural, multilinguistic ideas. Of course this included racism, as was demonstrated by its late embracing of nineteenth-century rational nationalism.

The completion of Europe will mark the return not only of the best of the Middle Ages, but of the positive aspects of the Austro-Hungarian empire. There were many negatives. But the positives were tied precisely to a continental rather than national dream, a decentralized, federal structure and a celebration of multiracial, multicultural and multilinguistic cooperation and creativity.

My point here goes back again to MacIntyre's observation of our fragmentation and loss of context. The reconstruction of the continent in a circular manner, re-establishing inclusive elements from an earlier period of experimentation, could go a long way to reformulating our contemporary context.

Many other democracies — Canada and Australia, for example — were actually constructed upon the mediaeval model from as early as the mid-nineteenth century on and so never attempted to become classic monolithic nation-states. They were conceived as federations with multiple personalities, multiple religions, multiple races and communities and, in Canada's case, multiple languages. In fact, only the United States remains caught inside an Enlightenment nineteenth-century model. Europe is therefore by no means alone in its attempt to take a non-linear conceptual approach.

Whether you see it as circular or cyclical, this approach is complex. You can try to understand it through the arguments of Vico or through animism or indeed other experiences. It requires an acceptance of the idea of constantly readjusting to larger movements, while maintaining the cycle. It is a bit like floating in a gravity-free universe, unafraid of the fragments moving about you. When I speak of re-emergence, it is that of a very old memory which could allow us to find our way through to a context anchored in our history.

THE QUALITY OF CONTEXT

There is no difference between individual and civic memory. You may reply: 'But love is for one or two, while principles of justice may be for millions. If the principles are to last, they must be encased in specific memories and carefully differentiated.'

I would go further. You cannot love a community or a population. You don't even know the people in question. You probably don't even love your whole family. To believe you love a nation is a romantic transferral of something else. Besides, if you can love one nation you can hate another. Such grandiose misuse of a positive emotion invites an equal misuse of a negative.

The alternative is not to say that civic memory is based on abstract argument. Nor is belonging based on calculation or self-interest.

There is personal love and there is civic belonging. Both feed into each other. They are part of the same memory. But you do not love the civic body. You love individuals whom you must first know.

You can see why Vico thought remembrance, not reflection and speculation, was the basis of philosophical thought. But remembrance, in order for the personal to fit with the civic, without becoming confused one with the other, requires shape and context.

So let me begin again. Memory has a great deal to do with various kinds of belonging. We must belong in order to exist as individuals, indeed as humans. That is why inclusivity is a sign of civilization, whether in the individual or the group. That is why every serious religion, without exception, gives priority to those who, because they suffer or are marginalized, do not belong.

Love is one manifestation of belonging. It is something which links us to another and thus to memory, because it is shared. No doubt love is remembered differently by each individual, but it is none the less based on a sharing. And it provides us with a way to live in our communities. It is the first step out of the artificial isolation of one person into those reflective relationships which make us individuals. From there it is several steps to fulfilling ourselves as responsible individuals in a civic structure.

Belonging then to a place, community, nation, state, is part of the same process, but the result of different roles. If through belonging we were to convince ourselves that the driving force in our relationships was love, we would have consigned ourselves to the rigid prison of ideology. We would have slipped into an absolute delusion; what Louise Arbour called a pathology of belonging. Call it a pathological form of memory.

The hint that this sort of memory is false is that any of us can belong to more than one memory at once. We have multiple ways of belonging. And they often seem to contradict each other. Why shouldn't they, given our complexity and the complexity of levels at which we exist and the curiously non-linear way in which we progress from past to future? Remember Saint Augustine's simple explanation for this complexity: "Without being joyous, I remember myself to have had joy... that of which I was once afraid, I remember without fear."

There is a curious shape to all of this, a curious form of context. It is a oneness which revels in flexibility. There is a great investment of time and a profound understanding of time implicit in memory. And yet the core of its functioning turns on timelessness.

Think of memory yet another way. What is the purpose of context? Not, surely, to lock us in place. We are mortals. We die. What would the purpose be of immobilizing us, except to gratify the ego of frightened people?

Context, like responsible individualism, is a way of laying out our freedoms. These freedoms must begin somewhere. In our personal lives, in our relationships, eventually in our society at level after level in more and more complex forms of belonging. These forms of belonging are complex because they involve matching the freedoms of ever-greater numbers of people. That is in part Desmond Tutu's meaning when he explains that, for any agreement to work in a society, it must be fundamentally acceptable to both sides — not that each memory must be the same, but that each of us must be willing to accept — indeed to live with — our own memory. That is one way to avoid fragmenting further the way we remember ourselves.

And so each level of established freedoms becomes a context for making ethics work. Not ethics as a great and impossible mountain for Heroes to cross or die. But ethics as multiple intersections wound into our ongoing lives. A living memory of freedom as obligation; as real, accomplishable ethics. Why in intersections? Because there we can most naturally "look the beast in the eye" as Tutu says we must. Because otherwise "it has an uncanny habit of returning to hold us hostage."[34]

Just as we must begin by being free somewhere, vis-à-vis someone, so we must begin by sharing justice somewhere, with someone, with others, with real people not theoretical, ideal people. As always with memory, all of this is founded in reality and devoid of abstraction.

Yet, you might say, memory by my own argument is best expressed through our creativity — our stories, the conundrums of our imaginations. Even there memory comes out of solid, but rarely grand, foundations. Think how much of our shared memory is built out of small stories about small people.

Think of Alice Munro's stories, of Mme Bovary, of the tiny people in *The Cherry Orchard*, of the real ordinariness of the apparently mystical people in *One Hundred Years of Solitude*, of Antonio Skármeta's *Postman*. Somehow, if properly imagined onto the page, these individuals' universality multiplies as they reside closer to the apparently ordinary individual.

There is no denying that there are other manifestations of memory: belonging as fear, backed into defensiveness, denying the other; belonging which feeds on self-pity, the propaganda of ills suffered, real or otherwise; delusions of abstract love, which must necessarily turn on pure emotion unrelated to reality, but thus felt all the more strongly.

And these deformed memories become the justification for a world which denies memory itself as a quality. We are to be saved from it by utilitarian methodology and inevitable forces. These will subsume reasonable belonging in self-interest and in an artificial form of freedom devoid of belonging and responsibility.

That is why there is such discomfort around concepts of globalization which are not complex internationalism, but merely simplistic linear logic, with one gear and one direction. Call it childish futurism.

In this comic-book world, context is as old-fashioned as the very idea of functioning memory. But memory is indeed an expression of context. And as such it is the key to our ability to act in a conscious manner, in a responsible manner, in an awareness of the other.

What was it Harold Innis said? "Most forward-looking people have their heads turned sideways." That is the essence of a conceptual scheme in which the context of memory can function.

CHAPTER SEVEN

REASON

*Reason, gentlemen, is a fine thing, this is unquestionable,
but reason is only reason and satisfies only man's reasoning capacity, while wanting is a manifestation of the
whole of life — that is, the whole of human life, including
reason and various little itches.*

Dostoevski[1]

If reason were only reason, would that not be a good thing? Why per-
sist in insisting that it is an all-purpose, all-seeing, all-doing force,
innately ethical, virtuous because progress is a virtue and reason the
engine of progress? Why should any quality have to be both the ideal
expression of our humanness and the instrumental mechanism by
which we should act? After all, any honest glance at our own experience tells us that none of this is so.

I would argue that this opposing of two forms — Pure Reason
and Instrumental Reason — is just old-fashioned religious
dogma. The godhead versus the functioning church. I'd argue that
neither pure reason nor instrumental reason exists. They are a
classic fantasy.

If our worst fear is the unleashing of irrationality, then the most
dangerous position we could take would be that of naive expectation.
What could be more naive than to expect too much from a single

quality? To live in denial of our reality is to open the doors wide to the worst of irrationality.

Suppose that reason is thought and argument. That is already a great deal. And that makes it the least utilitarian of our qualities.

Then reason would be only reason, which is no bad thing. Why shouldn't we settle for a more modest sense of it? One which corresponds to what we have seen work rationally over the last two millennia. Perhaps then what we believe to be rational consideration will actually relate to rationality.

There are, of course, thousands of definitions of reason. Why not just put them aside for the moment in order to ask what our options are in the real world of thought and action and effect? If we continue to take reason as our godhead, then we do indeed set ourselves up for a Manichean game. For every positive claim, someone can match it with a negative. This is the conundrum I've already mentioned — a century of unprecedented physical progress and unprecedented violence. Even progress is a conundrum. It has been used willy-nilly to save lives and to take them, to process information efficiently and to limit citizens' freedom, to run hospitals and to run death camps.

Is there another option? Perhaps it is merely to take a more modest, a less ideological approach to what reason might be.

REASON AS THOUGHT

Eliminate the godhead of pure reason and the jumped-up utilitarianism of instrumental reason. What is then revealed is the quality itself.

Reason is thought. Argument is an adjunct of thought. Both are unrelated to purity, certainty and instrumentalism. This least utilitarian of qualities is simply waiting to be rescued from those who have kidnapped it as a cover for their directionless obsession with form, methodology, technology and managerialism.

Let me come at this in a more roundabout way. As with common sense or ethics, reason requires a relationship of tension with our other qualities in order to function. Irrationality shows itself in a taste for absolute answers or truths, in self-referentialism or in a belief that specialization implies a privileged access to truth. Our central protection from irrationality is the tension between reason and the other qualities.

This approach may be frightening to some people. If our qualities are of equal value and the equilibrium we seek is never complete, then it would be normal for reason to be absent from our lives much of the time. Or, even if present, only in a marginal way. So neither the intent nor the approach may be rational. The quality itself may actually be absent or marginal. And yet the result will most probably not be irrational.

You could say that the outcome may be NON-rational behaviour, and that may be no bad thing.

Let me repeat this argument: Reason, unlimited by other qualities of equal value, will become irrational. Like any other quality, it *is* because it is a limited phenomenon. The grandiose concept of reason as all-inclusive, both pure and instrumental, is standard religious doctrine or, in modern terms, ideology. If reason is thought and argument, then instrumentalism is not a rational phenomenon. If reason is a limited phenomenon, then its absence may often be a good thing. And that absence may lead not to irrational behaviour, but to something positive called non-rational behaviour.

That we may have trouble with such a non-Manichean argument isn't surprising. From Athens on, attempts have been made to present reason as a form of universalism. The Greeks saw the human mind as rational and the universe as a rational order. They saw a correspondence between the two. On the other hand, while humans might be superior to other forms of life, the Greeks didn't consider themselves apart from these other forms or their planet. We should therefore live, they believed, in accordance with nature.

There is a problematic assumption now — that, just because nature and the universe make a certain sense, therefore they are rational. But something could just as easily make sense because it is ethical. Or because it is in the context of our functioning memory.

One thing is fairly clear: if you accept that reason is thought, then neither the universe nor nature is rational. They do not think or argue. Nor are they irrational, since they make sense. Rather, they are non-rational. A better word might be that they are animist.

THE MONARCHIST DILEMMA

Let me go back for a moment to the problem of overstating the importance of any one quality.

A self-declared absolute monarch is gradually seen more for his very real and ever-increasing faults than for his strengths. This is a characteristic of power. The more absolute, the more strengths turn themselves into weaknesses, faults and eventually destructive tendencies.

And the more absolute the monarch, the more he defines reality in either/or terms. Are you for him or against him? To declare yourself against — since he has the power — is to marginalize yourself, to turn yourself into an oddity, to become the one who does not believe what must be believed in order to be normal. By that I mean, in order to conform.

This brings us back to the Manichean outcome of absolutism. And to the basic question — why would anyone accept an either/or description of reality? This is indeed the road to extremism. There are "two excesses," Pascal said, "reason excluded, only reason allowed."[2]

And yet there it is: reason presented to us every day as civilization's only option; reason pumped up as a strength which can make us more than monarchs.

> Stride into the world joyfully,
> Against all wind and weather
> If there is no God on earth,
> We ourselves are gods.

THE FALLACY OF THE UNATTRIBUTED END

What could make you or me into a god? The clichéd summary is — "I think therefore I am."

Really? I think therefore I am what? It is odd that of all sentences this one should become the *in-a-nutshell* basis of rational individualism. After all, it didn't conquer the world in its original Latin. Instead it was in French that it became the cliché of that idea of rationalism. Yet it doesn't even meet the basic criteria of the French language, which is that you should finish your sentence.

Why wasn't it finished? Think of it as the equivalent of one of those fast Parisian quips — just the sort Montesquieu made fun of in the *Persian Letters*. If you finish the sentence, it reveals itself as meaningless.

"I think therefore I am" a human being. Therefore I am one among other human beings. Therefore, if I am, it is not because I think but because two other humans had sex, I was born, grew up and went on to live in a society with other human beings. To summarize: I am because of copulation plus the conscious and unconscious continuation of the society in which I think.

Alternately, "I think therefore I am" an individual. Individual in comparison to what? Without comparison, the very idea of individuality is impossible. Therefore "I am" in comparison to other individuals; thanks to my reflection in the mirror of others.

Or if reason is thought: "I think therefore I am" because I think in the context of others who have thought before me, now think all around me, and will go on thinking after me.

We may well be the only creatures capable of thought. But that can be said of all our qualities. And thought only takes on significance because "we are" part of something which exists beyond us. Call it society. It is our ability to extend our considerations beyond ourselves which makes them thought. Otherwise, what we are engaged in is just something more sophisticated than normal animal activity — a quantitative not a qualitative difference. I would call this self-interest, not thought.

Put another way: What is the implication of believing that there is an underlying rational truth, a rational godhead? Well, since we have never come up with such a truth, in spite of having tried over the centuries, what we are left with is the ultimate meaning of ideology. That is, we insist upon treating speculation as a statement of the absolute. Note: the term here is speculation, not uncertainty. This is not imagination, which flourishes through the maintenance of uncertainty. This is logical speculation as certainty; and therefore speculation as a decision-making mechanism. This is not imagination seized by intuition to produce action. Instead, we are to leap from the delusion of certainty to instrumental action; from deluding ourselves about what we know to action. Neither thought nor argument has a role here.

This is false reason or reason as irrationality. What is speculation masquerading as certainty? "I think therefore I am."

ANIMISM AND REASON

And if nature and the universe make sense why wouldn't it be more accurate to call this state of being animism? First, as I argued in Intuition, the term indicates both life and sense. It is close to what the Greeks must have meant when they said the world was rational.

After all, the Greeks' rational universe included a complex family of active gods and the regular consulting of oracles. Socrates, the father of our rationality, made particularly interesting use of the Oracle at Delphi. The point of these gods and oracles was not to justify a decline into superstition. Rather, they were a way to embrace the complexity of the world.

This same view of reason exists in most sophisticated animist texts. The West Coast North American nations — for example, the Haida, north of Vancouver Island on their separate archipelago called Haida Gwa'ai — have always had oral poetic sagas as complex as those of Homer. In the discussion of Imagination, I quoted these lines from a long poem by Skaay. They portray the mythological raven as flying until

> something brightened toward the north.
> It caught his eye, they say,
> And he flew right up against it.
>
> He pushed his mind through
> and pulled his body after.[3]

This is animism. You'll notice that thought leads the corporeal. On the other hand, the conceptualization is remarkably non-linear. In the twentieth century, Europeans would have called this surrealism. These epics are filled with non-linear conceptualizations which have the advantage over surrealism of being integrated into society.

Here thought may lead the corporeal, but it is also presented as a natural phenomenon within the whole. Not as something which invents us.

What does that mean in concrete terms? Well, I remember walking in a rain forest on that same West Coast. It was south of Haida Gwa'ai on Vancouver Island. The boardwalk divided an uncut or selectively cut forest from one cleared decades before and replanted.

What grew on the left was rational in the contemporary sense —

it was both pure and instrumental. The lines were relatively straight. There was one species of trees. They were all of the same age. Very little else grew. There seemed to be neither sound nor movement. The ground was relatively bare. It was a form of truth. Call it applied ideology.

On the right side of the walk was a jumble of tree species of all ages. The undergrowth was a complex mess of bushes and plants. Above and below there was movement and sound.

On the left, a purist irrationality disconnected from reality. On the right, a jumble, but one which seemed to approximate the sensible confusion of reality; the balance of reality; the full force and intelligence — not thought — of animism.

What does this difference mean, let alone matter, if the rational trees grow, can be reharvested and no measurable damage is done? That is the classic falsely rational question. The actual rational response would be that things just don't seem to work that way.

The world is not a series of free-standing, single-purpose feed-lots. Everything is related to everything else. Effect will rarely be a measurable spin-off of cause. And so, rice production in China has always mixed varieties because the resulting complexity makes each strain more resistant to fungal disease than a monospecies approach.

The instrumental logic — it is not reason — of the feed-lot forest is identical to that which produced mad cow disease. As it is to the factory-ship logic of vacuuming up one species of fish at a time.

What makes instrumental reason so profoundly irrational is its devotion to mechanistic solutions conceived in a limited time and space, as if the matter at hand were free-standing. Instrumental reason IS only because we believe it to be a form of thought, when all we are dealing with is a narrow logic built from within.

These days we would say that the complex forest is an example of biodiversity, like the complex ocean or myriad other elements. There is a growing understanding that this is central to our physical reality and our civilization. But because common sense and ethics are so marginalized, this progress is rarely tied to our actions, except with defensive reluctance, as if a sacrifice were being made. The contrast is between the complexity of reality and the naive, childlike self-confidence of our false rationality.

This contrast produces the argument which always begins from the point of view of what is declared to be utilitarian need. It is a very convincing approach because it seems to be about feeding our children, feeding the hungry, and other essentials. The trick is that it begins from a short-term close-up position. This is justified as the foundation of the argument because it is said to be rational. That the short-term, logical, linear, instrumental nature of this central argument may actually be the root cause of the problems is never dealt with. That would be romantic. Instead, the claim of rationality keeps us focused in close-up onto symptoms and far away from causes.

Many will therefore have difficulty with the idea that our larger reality is animist; that it is not rational and does not have an instrumental rational purpose; that the feed-lot approach has its place, but not as the generator of actions. Why? Well, for a start, because we have no idea how the non-rational reality in which we live will respond.

To make those who have difficulty with these ideas happy — or at least happier — we could simply say that such complexity makes sense; that we are dealing with a natural phenomenon or circular phenomenon close to the ideas of Giambattista Vico; or that the complexities of reality have more to do with active memory than with reason.

Another way of putting this is that just because a relationship works doesn't mean that it is rational. After all, we don't expect human relationships to be rational. Why then would those of tides or fish or forests be? Or indeed, why would economic patterns be either rational or natural?

To protect us from the forces of darkness

Many of us hold desperately to what we want to believe reason to be. At that point it becomes fantasy. Or a fear of reality. We see reason as our only protection against the dark forces into whose arms we are only too capable of sinking.

And so we desperately close our eyes and minds to the role which unlimited reason has played, both in unleashing those dark forces, through the unrefutable truth of Pure Reason, and in directing them, through the mechanisms of Instrumental Reason.

It's worth pointing out in passing that, if you coolly focus on the essential irrationality of the Pure and the Instrumental, it will be far easier to accept that they do not exist; far easier to understand reason as thought, and non-rational behaviour as a good thing.

Besides, we have a clear memory over two and a half millennia of being threatened with an either/or scenario — Reason at any cost or sink into anarchy. "[T]he soul consists of two elements, one irrational and one rational."[4]

Aristotle himself knew this wasn't so when he wrote it. Or rather he happily and repeatedly contradicted himself elsewhere. When writing of theatre: reasoning is "the speech" used "to argue a case or put forward an opinion". So we're talking about thought and argument, not the soul. Or again, in *The Politics*: " [S]peech serves to reveal the advantageous and the harmful...." Speech is *logos* or reason. We alone among animals have it. But it is neither content nor soul. It aids us to "reveal". It is our particular tool, but only makes sense as an intellectual — not utilitarian — tool.

Our history is full of attempts to expand reason beyond thought and argument. Thomas Aquinas set out "...a permanent peace treaty between faith and reason", a well-intentioned optimistic idea.

Immanuel Kant ambitiously multiplied the role of reason in several directions.

The point is that these and dozens of other 'expansions' created an all-encompassing rational artifice. And that in turn almost required — the artifice was so grand — the adoption of the two-level religious or ideological approach. Purity plus application. Abstraction plus action. God plus Son of God or indeed apostles and church structures. Absolute monarchs with Divine Right plus an administrative structure of officials. Absolute economic truth and inevitabilities plus microeconomics. All of which could be summarized as pure reason plus instrumental or utilitarian reason.

This isn't what philosophers such as Kant intended. His complex arguments were aimed at removing the idea of purity from philosophy. Strangely enough, the effect of his arguments was the exact opposite. It was as if his all-inclusive parcelling up into detailed categories of the rational argument created the modern idea of reason as a godhead.

Or, to put this in an earlier context: If everything that makes sense is rational, then what we are talking about is a new version of predestination. And we know from past experience that predestination, whatever form it comes in, has a contradictory effect. It makes us feel as if we are closed up inside a large prison of inevitabilities. And thus relieved of responsibility. And so we feel free to act however we wish within its walls. If things must be, then whatever we do will be part of that inevitability.

And so to believe in economic rationality — as part of an inevitable, naturally balanced force — is to create a cover for irresponsible, anti-social behaviour. To say that humans and the world are rational is to say — perhaps unintentionally — that we can cut, catch, heat however we wish, with no real side effects.

To claim the rationality of the whole is to remove all meaning from the particular; worse still, from the complexity of the particular.

The very idea that both the world and we are rational is to set nature up as our enemy and our slave. "The world is made for man, not man for the world," was how Francis Bacon put it. If we're both rational, then we get to decide what rationality is. After all, we alone are doing the thinking. And if nature doesn't respond clearly to our self-interest and our ego, well then, we must train it like a domesticated animal, treat it as it deserves to be treated for showing a disappointingly low level of rationality.

If you try to squeeze reality or individualism inside reason, they simply won't function.

●

THE STRENGTH OF IT

In 1846 the French astronomer Urbain le Verrier, working at the Paris Observatory, discovered the planet Neptune. He didn't do it by looking through the telescope. There were elements of common sense in his process, as there were of imagination and intuition. But the central point is that he thought out the necessity of its existence; or rather, the necessity of the existence of another planet in our solar system. He reasoned and calculated its exact position. This remarkable piece of thought-cum-argument-cum-calculation was then sent off to a state-of-the-art observatory in Germany to be confirmed by actual observation. We could say: to be confirmed by instrumentalism; a mechanical act clearly separated from reason.

Neptune was discovered through thought. You may wish to focus on the abstract nature of that thought or on the mathematical calculations involved. It really doesn't matter. Either way you have a hint of how remarkable our reason can be.

Were it not so strong, yet so unpredictable, we would not be so tempted to mistake reason for god. After all, thought has no instrumental limits. That is why we continue to uncover layer upon layer of knowledge. As each curtain of obscuring ignorance is removed, yet another layer of possibilities is revealed.

While our understanding of ethics, indeed of human relationships, has moved remarkably little over thousands of years, what we think might be true in myriad more specific areas has continually changed. You might say: what we think has progressed. We may not have worked out how to apply this thought. We may even have slipped backwards, as the violence of the twentieth century demonstrates. But the thought exists in its rational, non-utilitarian form.

You can find this same approach towards thought and understanding in most civilizations. At the very heart of Buddhism you may ask, "What is absolute truth?" And the reply comes — "There is nothing absolute in the world."[5] But the process of thought and argument is central to our continued existence, if for no other reason than its role in making us conscious of that existence.

Take Robert Owen's idea, early in the industrial revolution, of the Model Factory. His underlying argument was that a corporation does not have the right to maximize its profits; more specifically, that the legal ownership of technology does not confer either unlimited ownership of the profits or unlimited rights to follow the instrumental logic unleashed by this technology. In other words, the apparently irrational demands of society should trump the apparently rational logic of technological progress and ownership rights. The reason, of course, was that the demands were actually rational and the logic was not. It was just lowly logic.

Owen both thought about all of this and owned a factory. He thought that his theoretically irrational actions — shorter workdays, no children under ten employed, schools — would cost him money. He was wrong. It turned out that by investing in social development the profits would be greater. As for his competitors, who took their rights to be absolute, along with the logic of technological progress, they mistook their logic for thought. They earned less in the long run and slipped more easily into boom-and-bust cycles.

The key point here is that Owen developed his approach very early in the industrial revolution. His father-in-law had been a bit of a reformer, but Owen couldn't really draw on any solid warnings or hints or lessons from others' experiences. How then did he get it right?

He used elements of common sense and ethics. But these played only a supporting role to his ability to think his way through the situation. He was able to understand in the first quarter of the nineteenth century what most capitalists didn't really understand until the late 1930s: that ownership is never absolute — not over technology, not over ideas, not over employees.

Of course, understanding doesn't mean accepting. By the early twentieth century all the relevant elements were clearly visible for those who wished to think about them. Many chose not to. They concentrated instead on their self-interests and pretended that nothing else mattered.

Not all of them, of course. In 1906, the German industrialist Robert Bosch introduced an eight-hour workday and paid vacations for his workers. He did very well. His fellow industrialists ignored the implications by categorizing him as marginal. They called him a *Red*.[6] The company is still highly successful.

There are enough examples to demonstrate that economic success is not necessarily the product of instrumentalism. More surprisingly, success is not even necessarily the central force driving self-interest. Self-interest is more often driven by the desire to maintain social delusions in order to cover up our personal insecurity. That is one of the explanations for the permanent instability in the marketplace.

I mentioned that many capitalists didn't understand what Robert Owen was thinking until the 1930s. By then their own economic failure and the threat of massive social change as a direct result forced them to think about his thoughts — or rather, the then current version of his thoughts.

Of course, memory is difficult to maintain, while self-interest and personal insecurity are permanent characteristics. And so, from the 1980s on, when the relaxing of economic borders opened up the possibility of reestablishing nineteenth-century standards, this time in the developing world, many rushed ahead. They claimed that in the process they were helping these countries to develop.

Today's theoretically rational justifications for absolute ownership rights are as unapologetic as they were two hundred years ago. The phrases we are hearing about economic determinism, technological inevitability and the ownership of intellectual property are just revised versions of the phrases of the early nineteenth century.

But we are so caught up within instrumental logic that we rarely use our strength of thought to alter our focus on reality. Rather, like the NGO's tendency to present its view as a positive reflection of a negative original, so the intellectual opposition to current economic practices tends to treat the utilitarian as central. At some level it is assumed that responsible action will involve a sacrifice, probably a financial sacrifice.

Even concepts such as *sustainable development* seem to begin from a reluctant admission that the purpose of our existence and that of the planet is development. Development may indeed be worthwhile in many circumstances. It may also be counter-productive in others. It is development, after all, which has produced agricultural catastrophe over the last fifty years in Africa, to say nothing of brand-new and unprecedented urban poverty on the same continent. The point is that even when we want development, that does not mean it belongs at the core of our thinking. It may be a specific outcome, the more consciously chosen the better.

In our current context, sustainable agriculture ends up sounding like a costly approach. And it always sounds as if the effective method would be industrialized agriculture. A moment's use of our reason can destroy this logic. After all, sustainability is tied to long-established, proven methods. Coffee-growers in many places have always planted lower-yielding and mixed varieties.[7] In the short term this produces less, but in the medium to long term, more coffee and steady financial gain. Just as Robert Owen's approach enriched his workers and thus society, so the careful coffee-planter enriches his soil and thus his long-term production.

But Owen was not primarily thinking about production. He was asking questions about the nature of society. Whether in industry or in agriculture, the underlying questions have to do with our relationship to the whole. If you don't ask those questions, you end up acting irrationally.

Why were Owen's competitors and their successors unable to understand his idea? In part because they were fixated on their misconception of reason. They were attempting to reason in isolation, separate from their other qualities. And so they slipped, just as they do today, into the delusion that a linear, instrumental, utilitarian, rational logic was an absolute rational truth. They couldn't help — just as today they can't help — but slip into an obsession with self-interest, even if self-destructive. They could not see reason as thought because thought frightened them, just as it does today. And so they pretended they were thinking, when they were actually using logic.

In other words, they were acting irrationally. It was Owen's carefully thought-through rational model which would be adopted — all too slowly — by middle-class democratic societies. And the result would be an unprecedented creation of wealth.

The resulting taxes and public-good regulation of middle-class democracy would bring social services, education and stability. The destructive boom-and-bust cycles of free markets were thus moderated. That stability, the sharing of wealth and higher shared social standards combined to produce unprecedented overall growth.

You could call this a rationally inspired approach. But it was neither pure nor instrumental. And it was neither conceived nor implemented as a result of economics or economic prosperity. Instead, a view of society prevailed and gradually won us over. The humanist view has been with us for millennia. Periodically it must be rethought to fit its time. The debate over its modern shape had begun in the ninth century, gone into a higher gear in the twelfth, and been gradually put in place from then on, as idea after idea was put forward, debated and won support.

Two centuries after Owen, we are in the midst of a new industrial revolution and the utilitarian declarations of the early nineteenth century are being repeated in an irrational manner. This time around the irrationalists are being comforted by an army of equally irrational, linear micro-specialists — economists and management technicians first among them. These are often dressed up as consultants and private think-tank researchers. They tend to use phrases such as *technological determinism, inevitable economic forces* and *rational methodology* — a reheated Holy Trinity which is presented as the new truth.

Each time the movement for unlimited economic rights reappears, it has a new set of pseudo-rational arguments. For example, the last decade brought a growing obsession with 'intellectual property'. The terminology is terrifyingly clear about how reason is thought of. It is to be essentially utilitarian. Thought — of which the intellect is an element — is merely property. The concept of unlimited ownership once attached to property and to machines is now attached increasingly to ideas. Pozzo, in Beckett's *Waiting for Godot*, orders his slave, Lucky — "Think, pig!" And then stops him four times to be sure he is correctly placed and that his opening words are appropriate.[8]

And so our civilization, which says it glories in free speech, is busy tying down for exclusive use or royalty income, every idea which contains any possibility of economic exploitation. But ideas lie at the core of argument and thought. They are the tools of free speech and so of democracy. And the essence of democracy and free speech is not royalty income.

The curious sidebar to all of this is that those who say they are in favour of free trade are busy protecting their ideas — that is, getting economic control of ideas; that is, setting up highly protectionist private-sector structures. We seem to be exchanging the moderate, balanced protectionism of the public good for the heavy, inflexible protectionism of the private sector. Put another way, we seem to be exchanging the disinterested regulation of the public sector for the self-interested regulation of the private.

For a civilization to attempt to live off licensed knowledge is the intellectual re-creation of the old absentee landlord problem. Abruptly it is to be believed that owning knowledge — that is, controlling rather than spreading the use of our imaginations — will make societies and their citizens rich. This argument is apparently meant to justify reducing much of our imagination to mere utilitarian commerce.

It assumes as normal an enormous sacrifice for democracy and for the academic imagination; a normal and natural outcome of what is meant to be modernism. This is an astonishingly corporatist point of view.

Perhaps it is the ultimate deformation of the old industrial-revolution idea that the corporation is a 'legal person'. Two hundred years ago this was a highly imaginative idea to facilitate financing. Today the 'legal person' pretence has become a grotesque parody of itself. You can see this in the delusionary notion that the rights of a corporation over knowledge should be given general precedence over those of individuals. Worse still, because that 'human right' of ownership is on paper an abstract legal fiction, it somehow seems to trump normal human rights which involve concrete realities. The obvious example is the extended and broadened intellectual property rights surrounding new drugs. The instrumental position is that the human right of a corporation to protect its intellectual property trumps the medical need of a sick person.

How does this happen? The force of real reason is buried today beneath the equivalent of religious rhetoric and mountains of computer print-outs. This makes thought and argument very difficult. It isolates reason from ethics and imagination and from the careful measure of memory.

And so, you can end up in the apparently reasoned exercise of indifference to the *other*, of obsessive self-interest, even, as Camus put it, in the reasoned exercise of hatred. "Men like you and me, who pat children on the head in the Métro in the morning, transform themselves into meticulous executioners in the evening. They become the managers of hatred and of torture."[9]

What then is the strength of thought? Surely it is an expression of consciousness. And surely consciousness is dependent on being conscious of the *other*. Camus also said, "There is no freedom without both intelligence and reciprocal comprehension."

The strength of reason is its ability to free us precisely from ourselves, from thinking we *are* because we think. Rather it is that marriage between thought and *the other* which makes reason both conscious and intelligent.

Because that consciousness has so often been abandoned for absolute truths and methodology, reason has often rightly been criticized from the left and the right for having failed. Sometimes these criticisms will themselves be so ideological as to confuse what reason has become versus what it can be.

The English conservative Michael Oakeshott tried to use what reason had become to eliminate the very idea of conscious thought. He ridiculed Robert Owen as an Utopian and claimed that men like Voltaire knew no doubt and denied the past. In fact, their whole approach was a celebration of doubt and a revival of memory.[10] They saw reason clearly in a context with other human qualities from memory to ethics and imagination.

Looked at another way, Oakeshott was also in part right. The distinction between the single quality of reason and the balanced concept of the Enlightenment has been largely lost. As a result, we have both glorified reason as a godhead and reduced it to a matter of perfecting systems, that is, of inward-turned methodology in search of simple truths.

Again, the real strength of reason lies in the opposite direction. You could call it the shapelessness of thought. Pericles said to the Athenians that thought, argument, even doubt, would make them bold. Certainty would be the boldness of the enemies and it would come from ignorance, from a fear of conscious debate.

Yet if the twentieth century proved anything, it was that the certainty of utilitarian reason could as easily be the ally of evil as of good. In fact, it raised the question of what linear progress actually meant.

The reasonable position after our experience would be that the human race does not progress. We may slowly evolve in scientific terms. But in terms of our own qualities we don't change.

We all know that we know more. And our technical progress has been revolutionary. But what we do with this knowledge and machinery remains as open a question as it has always been. "Ignorance made you happy," the Chorus said to Oedipus. "The truth has made you blind."[11]

You could argue that this inability to progress is the human disease. We may design the most noble of laws and yet twenty or fifty years later discover that they are being used to accomplish the opposite. Social theories which rid us of state violence — the death penalty, for example — reverse themselves effortlessly and bring it back.

And there lies the essential strength of reason. Our ability to think is our ability to illuminate our disease. What maintains our understanding of our laws and safely directs our use of knowledge, methodology and machinery is our ability to consider it. And to expose all of this to the cross-tensions of ethics and memory and common sense. And to make intellectual use of the swirling uncertainties of imagination.

It is imagination which allows us to drag our intellect out of its self-referential tendencies, just as it is ethics which helps us to stay away from logical truths which are profoundly destructive. And it is the shared knowledge of common sense which protects us against intellectual nonsense. And the context and shape of memory which can help to steer us away from that ideological certainty which convinces us we can cut free from all that exists and do something else. These qualities drag our reason onto fertile ground and keep it away from the isolating delusions of purity and instrumentalism.

In practical terms our laws do not protect us, nor our systems and certainly not our gadgets. All of these can be used to protect us. But the use is entirely dependent on our ability to continually think our way through the situation. We protect ourselves against our dark side by controlling ourselves. We can use argument or shame or a multitude of other tools of comparison. But again, these are tools of a process led by thought. And that thought is certainly not about locking in truth. If anything, it is a constant struggle to remain conscious of our acts.

If you attempt to tie reason to progress then you will limit thought by basing it on a delusion. And from there it will slip effortlessly into a tool of self-interest and ideology.

Take a rather common human experience, which negates the idea of progress. Death. We all do it. The only question is when. It renders self-interest meaningless. Technology can play a peripheral delaying role. But the outcome remains the same.

This is perhaps the most interesting moment to think about reason. What can thought do when we need nothing more? You could argue that this is a moment of non-reason. I would prefer to treat it as one of disinterested thought, liberated at last from truth and method and delusions of utilitarianism.

I remember, the first time I went into a palliative-care centre, being amazed to find a relaxed, cheerful atmosphere. I'm not saying there was no tragedy, no sadness. But there was none of the grim, earnest battle against death which you find in a regular hospital.

The director, Dr. Claude MacDonald, said — "We have a different purpose. Other hospitals must fight death. We are about life. About making the best of life, given the circumstances." Their two practical concerns are bodily pain and clarity of mind. They want to reduce the pain in a way which allows people to think. The third element — not so practical — is to help people deal with their thoughts. They — we — suffer, Dr. MacDonald said, from great "pain of the mind". How are we to think — to reason — when the delusions of progress and methodology and self-interest have been ripped away. And only thought itself remains. The strength of reason can then be felt precisely in the atmosphere of these palliative-care centres: thinking in order to normalize what is normal.

Why does everyone say there are not enough of them? Why do we not build more? Because they undermine the narrow falsely rational obsession with the battle against disease and death. I'm not suggesting that we don't all wish to live longer. But much of what holds us back is an approach towards health built entirely around reacting to sickness. The palliative-care centres remind us of our reality. And they remind us that death is not a disease; that the end of life is part of life, not a lost battle against death. They offer a healthy rational approach towards a system based on wellness and on life. This is much more sophisticated than the typical linear idea of progress.

●

THE WEAKNESS

The weakness of thought is obvious. It tends to think itself into isolation, and from this self-referential world, into delusion.

This weakness is the characteristic which caught Plato's attention, and Descartes's. Of our six qualities, reason has the greatest difficulty working with the others. What seem to be missing are the mechanisms to reach out easily to find what other qualities have to offer. Plato and Descartes misinterpreted this weakness as a strength — a splendid isolation of superiority. They therefore set about interpreting delusions as reality.

The more we are driven by our fears, the happier we are about this weakness. It offers us the illusion of certainty. "[I]t is established beyond all doubt," Beckett's Lucky said. "[T]he facts are there...."[12] And since reality — our physical existence — can only undermine that certainty, we define reason and thought as something above the corporeal.

Plato is probably the father figure of the arguments which normalize this weakness. "When [the soul] tries to investigate anything with the help of the body, it is obviously led astray." When does "the soul get a clear view of facts"? "[W]hen it ignores the body."

Here you can see how totally Plato misunderstood the meaning of Socrates' death, how profound is their disagreement about reason and human nature. You can see the straight line from Plato to Descartes and on into the twentieth century. This is the argument of fear in which reason is withdrawn from the context of our other qualities. On the positive side you can also see the straight line from Socrates on his deathbed, thinking his way to his own end, through countless other humanist propositions to something as personal as our approach to palliative care today.

And so it is thinking, not knowing, which makes us rational. The chorus in *The Bacchae*:

> To know much is not to be wise
> Pride more than mortal hastens life to its end.

Pride is another form of fear. And again, reason is kidnapped to provide the underlying certainty, to protect us from those fears. This is most obvious in places of power, where the stark terror brought on by the demands of leadership is swept under the carpet by the posturing of the leader-Hero. They know but cannot deal with the reality of power — the reality, as Cervantes put it, that "offices and great responsibilities are nothing more than deep gulfs of confusion."

Don Quixote has become a reminder that little is what it appears to be and we must live with complexity. Deformed rationality has become a life-preserver for those afraid of reality and complexity. They crave a certain simplicity.

For two centuries modern reason has been clearly established as the alibi for each successive Utopian project, whether it originates on the right or the left. The Utopian inevitability of these projects will be rational. The inevitable failure of each of them, on the other hand, will be explained away a centimetre at a time until it has evaporated.

The only remaining great rational Utopian project of the eighteenth and nineteenth centuries is the United States itself. Everyone else has moved on, for better and worse. But the United States was frozen in place by its constitution early in the new rational movement. Its inherent wealth and constant growth have helped it avoid those moments of true rational reality when the whole edifice collapses. And so the structure of the benevolent, rational monarch remains, as does the late-mediaeval concept of balanced estates held together by rational structure, as do all the terrifying contradictions of a foundation constructed on the one hand of class and slavery, while on the other of equality and freedom.

The obvious observation is: it works. The counter-observation would be that with such wealth and power anything works. The point, however, is not one of judgement. It is merely to show how a rational ideology locks a society into a logic so ferocious that it becomes impossible to think your way out of the contradictions.

Take, for example, the projection beyond the borders of this slavery/freedom conundrum. The Australian David Malouf remembers the arrival during the Second World War of the American garrison in his hometown of Brisbane. In order to maintain the race divisions of the United States, Malouf's side of town, the South Side, "was declared black".[13]

Rational/irrational contradictions of this sort can be found in all the democracies. Malouf's own family were Christian Lebanese from what was then Syria. Before the Maloufs emigrated, the Australian authorities had declared immigrants from greater Syria (not Egypt or Turkey) to be white, providing they were Christian. Malouf, with wonderful irony, calls this a notional view of race. You could describe all of these instrumental views of race as notions of rational truth.

If the first rational weakness is thinking ourselves into isolation, the second is the instrumental logic which comes out of the resulting ideologies. "Reason is a universal instrument which can be used in all kinds of situations."[14] Descartes makes it sound like a magical screwdriver. Of course it isn't an instrument at all. That's why our technocracies hold so hysterically to the idea that it is. They say they fear the dark side if we let our rational guard down. In fact they fear the uncontrollable requirements of thought and uncertainty if reason is properly embraced. Or rather, they fear the loss of the illusion of exact measurement. Each time I am struck by yet another wave of statistics — which will be forgotten before the night is over — my mind slips to Juan Ginés de Sepúlveda, the Spanish scholar who measured the rational capacities of the Europeans versus those of their aboriginal subjects in the Americas. The conclusion was certain. The natives were inferior, therefore the Spanish right to their land was an inevitable consequence and the aboriginals were lucky to be allowed to become vassals of their new masters.

I use this example because it highlights the surreal aspect of utilitarianism pretending to be instrumental reason. Or rather, it highlights how easily reason in isolation can slip into parody and from there into straight self-interest and violence.

It would insult the value of both conservative and social democratic values to suggest that these parodies belonged to one side or the other. A conservative like Michael Oakeshott is right when he says that "[W]ith every step it has taken away from the true sources of its inspiration, the Rationalist character has become cruder and more vulgar."[15] He was in total agreement with the Marxist and anti-rational Frankfurt School or more recently with Günter Grass. On receiving his Nobel Prize, Grass talked of "the light of cold reason, limited to the technically doable, to economic and social progress, a reason that claimed to be enlightened but that merely drummed a reason-based jargon into its offspring, capitalism and socialism.... We look on in horror as capitalism — now that his brother, socialism, has been declared dead — rages unimpeded, megalomaniacally replaying the errors of the supposedly extinct brother." In Oakeshott's words, "the aim is certainty." The underlying weakness is not one of left or right any more than are the bogus claims of strength.

In fact the most obvious comment one could make about the "extroverted rational type", to use Carl Jung's typology, is that "the life of this type is never dependent upon reasoning judgement alone; it is influenced in almost equal degree by unconscious irrationality." In fact, his behaviour is dominated by irrationality. Jung says of the rational type that "there is nothing of which he is less informed than his own unconscious." In that sense he is "irrational".

The combination of rationality misused both as religion and as cold methodology makes it flee human reality, into the promised land of the future common to all Utopias. And so what presents itself as supreme because useful, in reality skitters off into irrational unfulfilled claims.

"The supreme value is not the future," Octavio Paz wrote, "but the present. The future is a deceitful time that always says to us, 'Not yet,' and thus denies us.... Whoever builds a house for future happiness builds a prison for the present."

🍎

FALSE FREEDOM

Flight into the future. Certainty. Truth. Inevitability.

All of these reiterate a state of fear. How do we escape fear? By escaping reality. And how do we escape reality? By discovering the truth. By proclaiming a future Utopia. By revealing uncontrollable forces. By limiting our interventions to managing the consequences of these certainties. We are the happy instrumental slaves of great rational truths.

And so we are free. Free of responsibility. Free of doubt. Free to act as we please.

Dour though he was, Pascal understood what was happening.

"The last step that reason takes is to recognize that there is an infinity of things lying beyond it."[16] And so our history is filled with declarations of rational superiority designed to free us.

Kant:	"All our knowledge begins with the senses, proceeds then to the understanding, and ends with reason. There is nothing higher than reason."
Jefferson:	"Reason and free inquiry are the only effectual agents against error."
Hegel:	"To comprehend what is, this is the task of philosophy, because what is, is reason."
	"Reason is the law of the world and...therefore, in world history, things have come about rationally."

Except things have not come about rationally, unless you have a view of what reason is which is so vast that it has no meaning. And what is, is not as Hegel claims, reason. Or rather, if it is, then a rock is rational, in which case reason is the same as animism, in which case we should begin the whole question of rationality over again.

What about reason as our only real protection against error? Jefferson takes care to add in free enquiry as a buffer. But even then, history tells us it isn't so. And why state that free enquiry is a separate phenomenon? What then is reason?

And why should there be nothing higher than reason? Why should Kant put reason higher than ethics or imagination? What is this desperate need for a Platonist, pyramidal structure? It is, of course, the need to be freed of uncertainty and fear.

All of these declarations and literally thousands more have been built up from the rather simple and limited base of a Greek idea. *Logos, logike*: to say, to state, to explain, to explain why, to give reasons.[17] The sensible evolution would have led us to thought and argument. Our fears caused us to exaggerate the case in order to create a protective ideology and so to turn reasons into certainty, truth and inevitability. The resulting false freedom could be called a "total conception of life". This was the phrase of Mussolini's early Minister of Education, Giovanni Gentile, a Hegelian philosopher. Indeed, his central inspiration came from the "bleak rationality and coherence" of Alfredo Rocco, who, as Minister of Justice, created the legal fascist state. We forget now that 'Totalitarianism' was Mussolini's term for this rational state. It was a positive term. After all, there was nothing higher than reason. Nothing truer. It was effective against error. After all, what is, is reason.

Necessarily divisive

There is one more weakness, which belongs more to reason as now conceived than to the quality itself. As generally conceived, reason now makes it impossible for us to stand back in order to look upon the shape and meaning of the whole. Instead, we are trapped into a building-block view of the world.

There are the great truths and there are the piecemeal systemic illustrations of them. Most of us are limited to participating in a single block. At that level, on that scale, we may pass for specialists and even have an opinion. Particularly if it is for internal use — inside the building block. How curious that a quality presented as all things to all people should be so divisive.

It is hardly surprising that we are jealous of our personal territory. Our mission is to hold our own fort, each of us excluding the other. This is our 'capital'. Our 'human capital', to use one of the more recent clichés of managerialism.

Notice how ridiculous these little fashionable phrases are when heard on their own. *Human capital.* Human is the adjective, capital is the noun. What is meant to be a strength is actually a demeaning insult.

The trick with the rational system now in place is to see the link between the great truths and the building-block illustrations. We need the link in order to justify ourselves. This can only be done if we have faith in the system to which our personal territory belongs. The system is our rational backbone. It, not we, is the concrete manifestation of the rational godhead. We are rational because the system is rational.

But reality suggests that what the system actually does is divide us up into our small, defensive building blocks. Think of the bombing of the Chinese Embassy in Belgrade during the Kosovo campaign. That particular mission was the outcome of a perfectly rational system. The map used by the pilots had been prepared by the Pentagon's National Imagery and Mapping Agency. Someone there made a basic mistake. But the building-block atmosphere of specialization meant that no one else really looked at the map with a critical eye. The expert had already done his job. He or she or they were responsible for the maps.

Think of how many checkpoints it then went through afterwards. Surely someone should have picked up the mistake? Some of those who looked at the map as the program made its way up through the system to final approval actually knew Belgrade well. They had served there. Some of them had even been to the Chinese Embassy.

But that isn't the way it works. Each checkpoint actually reinforces the original expert's decision. The more people checking, the less they check. The original source comes with an illusion of truth — that is, of expertise and responsibility. From there on, layer after layer of assumptions are laid down.

Rational management in fact reinforces error and discourages questions. To use your intuition, your common sense, your imagination, even your memory at its most practical, would be to show that you do not have confidence in your colleagues. To check and question would be professionally insulting. To show initiative beyond your responsibility would be pushy.

What happens in a bombing campaign, with a risk of losing lives on all sides, happens effortlessly in all management structures. They divide us one from the other.

And the more our education is concentrated on training rather than thinking, the more those divisions are formalized. Utilitarianism and specialization both have their roles, but as an organizing principle they undermine lateral thought and questioning.

Is this division necessary? Not at all. It is not an outcome of rationality, but of an ideological approach towards reason. Counterbalanced by other qualities, reason is saved from this weakness and is drawn towards its strength.

The most obvious instrumental source of this divisiveness today is higher education. There a destructive idea of the multiversity has emerged. Both students and professors are rewarded for their insularity. It is true that in some places a countermove is afoot. Interdisciplinary work and lateral thinking are encouraged. But so far this is the response of a tiny minority. The very idea of knitting sectors together remains a sign of weakness, even of unprofessional behaviour; of disloyalty to one's corporation. It is as if rationality in universities has more to do with power than with education.

●

METHOD

Montesquieu's Persian, transposed to contemporary Paris, or today's alien arriving anywhere in the West, would notice, almost immediately upon arrival, that we are obsessed by method; and that we are convinced our obsession with methodology is a proof of our rationality.

Their question would be fairly direct. Why would any method be assumed to be rational? Why today would the most common face of reason be method? Why would reason be expressed more through form than through content?

"Empty rooms when they are lit up are more terrifying than dark rooms."[18] Part of the explanation lies in the creation of the modern nation-state. In place of the absolute monarchs and the mediaeval structures, we needed a system to hold the whole thing together in another way. It was conceived as "a rational universally applicable code". And the laws which have followed have built upon that logic, that idea of a centralized administration.

What was missed was the real role of reason. It related to the programs being proposed and had nothing to do with methodology. So long as the purpose of a program was — is — clear, the method would make sense. Public policy must be led by ideas or it fails. The same is true of most organisms. Talking of music, the composer Philip Glass put it clearly — "In a certain way, until a composer finds his own voice, it doesn't much matter what he does."

You could see this obsession with methodology at work throughout much of the developing world over the last few years, as the International Monetary Fund attempted to force economic theories, which have worked nowhere else, onto countries already in an economic crisis.

The Chief Economist at the World Bank — Joseph Stiglitz — was constantly lamenting this obsession with form over content. "Quite frankly, a student who turned in the IMF's answer to the test question: 'What should be the fiscal stance of Thailand facing an economic turn down?' would have got an F."

The problem in part, Stiglitz said, was the tendency of everyone to work in secrecy. One could expect it of the troubled government of a developing country. But it was the tendency of the rational method everywhere to encourage secrecy. In banks. In international institutions. In all government bureaucracies. It was that underlying culture which he found particularly difficult.

But then secrecy is merely one aspect of such 'rational' systems. The real point is that these are systems and methods, not thought or argument. Method is not a deformation of reason. It isn't reason at all. It is a requirement of structure. A necessary face of utilitarianism.

FACTS

What then of facts? They are meant to be the building blocks of rationality.

It is a fact that the world is flat. It is a fact that Thalidomide stops morning sickness. It is a fact that feeding dead sheep to cows is an efficient method for raising livestock. That antibiotics do not remain in livestock at the time of human consumption. That cigarettes do not cause cancer. That men are more rational than women. That the Maginot Line will stop the German army. That deregulated money-markets will produce an efficient economy. That large mechanized fishing boats will create a more efficient fishery. That radiation-based foot-measurement machines are helpful in buying the right-sized shoe. That spraying asbestos on our walls and ceilings creates an effective insulation for buildings. That spraying insecticides onto roadsides will reduce governmental mowing costs. That deregulated airways will encourage competition among airlines.

Among all of these, the fact to last the longest as a fact is the one which states that the world is flat. It must therefore be the truest of the group. Indeed, the most rational.

Two thoughts come to mind. One from Northrop Frye: "[T]he more trustworthy the evidence, the more misleading it is."[19] The second is from Jacob Bronowski: "No scientific theory is a collection of facts. It will not even do to call a theory true or false in the simple sense in which every fact is either so or not so.... All science is the search for unity in hidden likenesses."

Frye and Bronowski are engaged in rational argument. They remind us that facts are not rational. While reason may make use of facts, it is not built upon them. Rationality is not based upon proof, but upon thought and argument.

The failure of the idea of instrumental reason

I've stated that Instrumental Reason does not exist.

Why should reason be instrumental? For that matter, why should it be utilitarian? Isn't instrumentalism just a fancy word for utilitarianism? Aren't they two functions unto themselves? Functions are not qualities. And they are certainly not adjuncts or outgrowths of qualities. They are the handmaidens of anyone who wanders by. A quality may well be able to use them to good effect. But attach them artificially to a quality and they will simply drag it down to the level of their directionless competence; in the case of reason, instrumentalism drags it down to process, to shop-floor techniques such as efficiency.

It is this instrumentality which cuts reason off from the other qualities. It was the instrumentalism of a supposedly rational approach towards arms-production which made it so irrational; the instrumentalism of international debt policy which still causes the developed world to screw the poorer nations to the floor while calling upon them to rise up.

No matter how much we're told that Descartes's dictum is old stuff — passé — it remains at the heart of our rational misunderstanding. The source of contemporary false individualism — the idea of the stand-alone human individual — remains that neat little conceptualization in which we think ourselves into existence. This is the heart of Irrational Instrumentalism. This is the key to the notion of an unbroken line from Pure Reason as a godhead to practical reason as the inevitable structure of a responsible life.

What follows is delusion: that we can exist outside the whole. We convince ourselves of this in spite of being begot by others, begetting others, living thanks to the consideration of others, the self-control of others, the bridges built by, bread baked by, words written by others. By the *other*.

The exercise of individualism may indeed include reason, but no more than any other quality. After all, what gives force to each of us is precisely the context created by the permanently shifting equilibrium of our qualities and of our society. Lose the context and you are deep into irrationality.

Think of reason in its full instrumental stance. I mentioned the arms trade. What started out in the 1950s as an apparently sensible economic theory, built upon maximizing the applications of technical progress and balancing trade flows, gradually turned into a catastrophic, self-destructive, gigantic, inflationary flow in weaponry. And what started out in the 1970s as a sensible attempt to lower agriculture produce prices, while both using up waste product and increasing production, gradually turned into mad cow disease. Reason, when deformed into an instrumental dictum, seems quite naturally to slip from complexity into a strangely linear mode.

Why strange? Well, think of the desiccated methodology of a logic which proclaims the supreme virtue of technical innovation, as if this were the true meaning of progress. Note: they assert the *true meaning* the way their grandparents asserted the *true cross*. Such logic becomes self-referential and leads to a dominance of form over content as it becomes increasingly irrational, trampling all over reality in the name of these self-declared truths.

You might think that all of this delusionary believing is new — the fruit of our latest tidal wave of technological breakthroughs. Not at all. Take our worship of technological progress in computers — the virtue of a machine which can improve the state of mankind. We live this progress as if it were the front edge of progress and modernity.

One of the first breakthroughs was the IBM Hollerith punch-card machine, the forerunner of contemporary communications technology. Throughout the 1930s it helped us streamline our aging nineteenth-century administrative methodologies. It helped us organize policies for greater numbers of citizens and could be seen as a handmaiden of egalitarianism.[20]

It was also used throughout the Nazi regime to streamline the identification, listing and deportation of Jews. At Auschwitz, prisoners kept for labour had their forearms tattooed with five-digit, IBM Hollerith-machine identification numbers.

Neither technology nor instrumentalism has any natural or logical or structural relationship to ethics. In fact, neither has a rational relationship to ethics. A Hollerith machine does not have an opinion. It does not have a destiny which relates to good or evil, progress in well-being or progress in destruction. If the word progress means 'something new', or 'an improvement in methodology' or in 'delivery' or 'production', well then, this is indeed progress. What a depressing concept. And to link this sort of progress to reason is to make a mockery of the idea of human thought and argument. Mockery turns into the grotesque if you attempt to link the Greek idea of reason and virtue to technological change.

After all, the Nazis didn't simply use this equipment. They were supplied. Humans living in Allied countries, walking their own streets as highly respected citizens, understood their individual obligations in a context best described as *inevitable progress*; itself defined by Instrumental Rationality. This 'rational' understanding involved technology, the ownership of intellectual property and corporate obligations. Their obligation to their corporation and to maintaining its control over its intellectual properties trumped their obligations as citizens.

And so, throughout the war, IBM's executives — real people, real citizens — used complex corporate structures to continue supplying the Nazis with the necessary paper and parts; and also to continue collecting the monies owed.

Here we see what we think of as today's highly modern overarching concepts of management and efficiency already hard at work sixty years ago. Management. Technical professionalism. Loyalty to the corporation. Primacy of the share-price and short- to medium-term profits. The primacy of intellectual property over freedom of speech. The employment contract as the guarantor of institutional loyalty. Those same contracts as the mechanism for control over the employees' use of their expertise and their related thoughts.

These are the essential 'values' of what we call Instrumental Reason when it is applied to any sort of corporation, public or private. Alternately, you could say that these are the essential 'values' of corporatism.

Does this mean that every corporation would now necessarily act as badly as IBM did during the Nazi regime? There are several ways to reply. First, what is the difference between IBM's values and those of the pharmaceutical companies in the developing world with their intellectual property control over drugs which treat AIDS?

The more fundamental point is that Instrumental Reason, not being rational, has no natural relationship to our other qualities. It does not relate to ethics. What does that mean? Quite simply: corporations are not ethical. That is, they are not meant to be ethical. They are meant to be self-interested. Competition, as they understand it, leaves no room for ethics. And again — since Instrumental Reason is not rational — they have no relationship to memory. They cannot remember — institutionally — the IBM experience. It would therefore be impossible for them to link the actions of IBM to their own.

Individuals use ethics and memory. And they institutionalize their use through society. Corporations use neither and therefore cannot institutionalize them. So corporations are without ethics and memory. I am not referring to the individuals who work for these corporations, and whose ethics and memory will be more or less limited by other individuals for whom they in turn work. In other words, only society can empower these individuals to make their organizations follow the standards set in the context of each society's memory.

The grotesque assertion of the last few years that there is no society, that we are led by machinery and self-interest and economic determinism, has as a direct outcome the practical marginalization of ethics in the name of Instrumental Reason-cum-corporatism.

The third response would be to answer the question with a question: Did IBM act in a normal manner? I would then ask, do you mean in a normalized manner? The essence of Instrumental Reason is that it renders the most improbably or catastrophic action *normal*. And so in the spring of 1945, the last cheque for Hollerith services was transferred from the German Army to the U.S. Army, which delivered it to IBM's representative in Berlin. Yes, instrumentalism can roll like a steamroller in any ridiculously logical straight line right over the complexities of civilization.

The astonishing thing is how surprised — how virginally surprised — so many professional philosophers, managers and specialists are when the consequences of their instrumentalism are pointed out. They cling to the supposition that technical progress is, in and of itself, a force for good. Perhaps one of the elements which drives this conviction is a subconscious leftover of the church's old opposition to new knowledge. And so each failure of instrumentalism does come as a surprise to them. They then interpret it as an exception to the rule — a human failure requiring structural adjustment.

This perpetual surprise is a reminder of just how isolated instrumentalism is from memory. Yet clarity of the situation is there deep in our experience. Francis Bacon, in his novel *New Atlantis* (1627):

> [B]y means of our solitary situation and the laws of
> secrecy... we know well most parts of the habitable world
> and are ourselves unknown.

Pascal in *Pensées*:

> When malice has rationality on its side, it puffs itself up and
> parades reason in all its lustre.[21]

How do we avoid such a delusionary state? Jacob Bronowski put it neatly when he described the truth in science "not as a dogma, but as a process". Thought and argument, not truth and application. Understanding as a point of view, not as knowing and judging. This is the precise opposite of the desperate attempts of managers — both public and private sectors — to reduce pure science in universities to a mere extension of goal-oriented applied science. Their declared intent is to tie scientific education closely to funding sources in large corporations.

The implication is a denial of real uncertainty, indeed of thought. Why? Because if the goal of science is carefully predefined then we are pretending to know what we don't know. This is the ultimate in the ideological fear of the unknown. You might call it a modern purification ritual — purification through instrumentalism.

There are early hints of this tendency in the rational political acts of the eighteenth century. Take the Declaration of Independence of the United States. Jefferson's first draft contained the phrase: "We hold these truths to be sacred and undeniable." This is about as strong a statement as you can rationally make. You declare your theory to be true, which is a form of courage if you then declare that you can demonstrate these truths through thought and argument. They will therefore remain rationally "undeniable". They will win the argument.

But Benjamin Franklin, usually a down-to-earth influence, was on the drafting committee. He deleted "undeniable" and wrote in "self-evident". That is, not requiring argument. Therefore not requiring reason. Quite simply: an absolute truth.

Reason taken on its own will turn into ideology. After all, those truths in the Declaration were not self-evident. How could they be in a society built upon slavery?

Taken in context reason is so much more interesting than in its pumped-up, isolated glory. Think of the intense, conscious rationality which Wagner applied to his music in order to create something which seems devoid of reason and yet is capable of reaching deep into our subconscious. The result is so powerful that we hardly know what is happening to ourselves when we listen.[22]

Or think of the great Doric temples of Greece. These are in part the expression of astonishing rational ideas. They are expressions of thought. You could describe them as an argument for the human relationship to the divine. Yet much of their effect is not part of the building itself but comes from the shadows; not simply the shadows thrown by the building but, for example, the shadows created by the fluting on the columns. You could argue that while those columns hold up the temples, to our eyes their real existence is not physical. You might call them an argument in light and shadow.[23]

Neither of these examples is instrumental. They describe a way of thinking. The result is an argument — an argument in sound and in sight. But there is no rational progress from the thought to the music or the temple. The idea is not applied. It is a way of thinking.

What of the link here to our qualities? It is not linear or rational. If anything, the shape which thought gives to the concrete is the result of its non-rational relationship with our other qualities; a relationship built of tension. Think of the permanent uncertainty of imagination when you think of those columns which live through the ever-moving light and shadow of day and night. Think of the common sense of a shared — uncalculable — knowledge of human relationships to shapes. Think of the context which memory provided. Think of the intuition of choosing which played such a role in the creation of these temples. Surprisingly enough, intuition may be the quality most intimately linked to reason, as it turns upon choice for action and choice for expression. Think of the ethics expressed through the mystery of seeing a building not through its stone but through its relationship to light and shade.

I used the word *mystery*. Like all great creations, the essential impact this music and these buildings make is tied to mystery. Yet within that mystery lies an element of reason. After all, reason is a key element in the magical results of both Wagner and the Doric temples.

Why should we be surprised? These sounds and buildings are central to our imagining of ourselves.

This is quite different from attempting rationally to link the idea to the result. The effect of such a process-minded approach would be to severely limit the very idea. An idea of light and shadow would be reduced to a calculation.

There is nothing linear here. There is nothing which relates to what we now think of as process. There is no suggesting that reason must dominate in order to lead and organize society. There is no suggestion of getting more out of reason than there is in it.

If you remove the requirement for leadership, reason will function happily as one of our six qualities. The result will be the disappearance of our linear hysteria.

Thought and argument, limited by such forces as memory and ethics, are then free of their false obligation to provide solutions. Or rather, they are freed of pretending that they are able to provide linear, self-contained solutions. They are free of the terrifying delusion that we *are* because reason exists.

INSTRUMENTAL REASON DOES NOT EXIST

This brings me back in a full circle to where I began. Instrumental Reason doesn't work because it doesn't exist.

The difficulty is that for most of us it has become the most obvious manifestation of reason. After all, the godhead cannot make many down-to-earth appearances. The instrumental version "...of reason goes so deep into the modern consciousness," George Grant lamented, "that any other account is very difficult for a modern man to understand at all."[24] And there is absolutely no encouragement from within our constituted structures for anyone to try to imagine another account. "[O]ur society increasingly forces on its members this view of reason." In Jürgen Habermas's terminology, we are colonized by functional reason.

Charles Taylor, better than anyone, has described this reduction of reason to mechanics.[25] Because it pretends to deliver rational solutions, it claims primacy of place. Because it claims efficiency and calculable success, it can marginalize not only other views of reason, but any other human quality.

How did it get there? Taylor says it rushed into the vacuum left by the disappearance of any sacred structure. It became the new yardstick. What with claiming facts as its inexhaustible supply of holy wafers and technology as its handmaiden, Instrumental Reason has created "...a widespread unease that [it] not only has enlarged its scope but also threatens to take over our lives".

It is presented as a form of freedom tied to a flowering of the individual. Yet its real effects are employment contracts designed to ensure not only loyalty but control over intelligence and opinion; knowledge treated in exactly the way land once was by absentee landlords; choice reduced more to packaging than contents. Perhaps its most depressing effect is the discouragement of independent citizen-participation. Each of these illustrates the irrationality of instrumentalism. These "institutions and structures of industrial-technological society severely restrict our choices." "[T]hey force societies as well as individuals to give a weight to instrumental reason that in serious moral deliberation we would never do, and which may even be highly destructive."

Taylor has tried to imagine how we could improve the situation by redefining Instrumental Reason. For myself, I see no advantage in making the best of what is fundamentally an illusion. It does not even meet its own self-defined standards as a 'rational efficiency'. And its calculated successes are never measured against its calculable failures.

Take the simple example of the sterilization of troubled women throughout the Western democracies over the last half-century. It was done without their knowledge. The professional, natural cooperation between psychiatrists, mental institutions and operating doctors was a perfect illustration of the reality of Instrumental Reason. Recent reports in France gave a national number of 15,000. "We operate on the instructions of others." "It is not our decision." 'These young women had problems and so the intervention was made for their own good.' As for the calculable aspect, there is a "lack of data".[26]

A friend of mine was recently told that he had advanced cancer of the intestines. He should prepare for the worst. Forty-eight hours later, on the operating table, it was discovered that he had appendicitis. This was no more than an error; a frightening one, but errors are bound to occur. What was revealing was the reaction of the doctors. They denied any error. They described the event as a one-in-a-million medical oddity. They had done everything correctly, followed all the rules. Not only was there no apology, the patient was left to feel somehow responsible. Somehow a troublesome, non-conforming oddity. Instrumentalism, obsessive structuralism, narrow professionalism; all of these force sensible, intelligent people to think, speak and, if necessary, act in an irrational manner.

A cumulation of events such as these is creating a growing discomfort with the assumptions of Instrumental Irrationality. People are beginning to look less compliantly at the range of their powers. Suddenly people are beginning to believe that, if they think something through and decide, it can then be made to happen, with or without the instruments of structure. There are hints here that people wish to recuperate the rational idea.

Thus for decades we were made to feel that although tax havens were not ethical, they were inevitable, given free markets. We were even told they were useful. Suddenly, faced by an explosion in money-laundering, Western governments have begun forcing regulations and some transparency upon them. With the smallest amount of rational consideration — rational thought — in an ethical context, public officials have shown they are able to make these instruments of the market do whatever the public weal wishes. And this at a time when globalization is meant to have weakened the power of democratic governments.

Or look again at the experience of mad cow disease in Britain. For years the attitude was pure instrumentalism — 'professional, rational instrumental loyalty'. Failure was regularly denied. Gradually some experts began to speak out in a non-instrumental manner. In a combination of imagination, ethics and reason, men like the epidemiologist Roy Anderson said that they could have changed the course of events if the process had been open. He might have used Jefferson's term — if there had been 'free enquiry' instead of linear instrumentality.

Finally, look at the breakdown of the 2000 international conference at the Hague on global warming. Extremely interesting things were said in the controversy surrounding its failure. For example, Dominique Voynet, the French Environment Minister:

> What has just happened, even if it is terrible to say it, is the failure of expertise and the triumph of politics. Because the preparatory documents are so complicated, we are forced to go beyond them. For three years, the experts have been struggling among themselves to no effect, over commas and parentheses. We no longer have the right, no matter how good they are, to hide behind their prudence. The politicians must make decisions.[27]

Those, you may say, are merely the words of an angry politician, or a politician trying to blame someone else for her failure. But look at her argument. It is that rare thing: a rational rejection of instrumentalism. And beneath that rejection, there is a more fundamental loss of faith in the ideology which locks reason in behind lowly, unthinking instrumental functions. The next step involves the realization that there is nothing to be feared in such a rejection. After all, reason cannot be related to instrumental reason, as the latter does not exist.

A few months later, in July 2001, the conversations were taken up again, this time in Bonn. The result was a successful agreement. Not a total success, but a success none the less. The practical explanation was that the political players had taken over leadership from the specialists, whether from their civil services or the NGOs. They were able to make the necessary compromises because the argument was suddenly one of ideas and policy rather than a pretence of instrumental rationality.

●

Utilitarianism is not reason

If instrumental reason does not exist, what is it? The short answer is jumped-up utilitarianism.

I'm not suggesting there is anything wrong with the utilitarian, any more than with methodology and systems or management and efficiency. They are all necessary functions. But just because something functions doesn't mean it is rational. A toilet functions, is utilitarian, is based on a method and a system, manages waste and is much more efficient than any business-school generated 'rationalization' initiative. Does that mean the human quality of reason is encapsulated in the toilet?

Waste does need to be processed, and the toilet does it well. So utility and process are just fine, in their place.

Some might argue that the disposal of waste and the distribution of clean water are among the most important areas of solid progress we have made in the last 150 years. They would be right. But that doesn't make process rational. And it would be impossible to prove that this process was a child of reason.

If you examine the sources of the initiatives for waste disposal and clean-water distribution you find individuals and societies driven by a constant mix of human qualities. Thought and argument were of central importance. But so was ethics — a sense of the other and of inclusive responsibility. So was imagination, allowing people to conceive of what was happening to their society. So was intuition, driving people to make decisions. So was the memory of what happened to their society when these elements were not dealt with.

You could argue that there is rationality constantly at work in the conceiving of such systems. And that would probably be so. But that doesn't make the systems rational.

The point is: if utilitarianism is given leadership in a given area, it will set about demeaning, marginalizing and unravelling the non-utilitarian elements at play. Why? Because utility is not thought. Nor is it argument. It does not, in and of itself, have a purpose or a direction. A toilet would just as happily dispose of fresh caviar or unwanted goldfish. It will indifferently send its cargo off through a system of pipes to be deposited in a sewage-treatment plant or directly into your drinking-water supply. That was the point about the IBM Hollerith punch-card machine, indifferently an organizer of death camps and of efficient workplace structures.

Utilitarianism can only lead us if it reduces all else to its own narrow truth of utility. The closest utility can come to a purpose is efficiency and, related to that, self-interest. This can be made into a seductive proposition, thanks to myriad fast, apparently clear, short-term answers and concrete illustrations of those answers.

But what makes a society a society or a civilization is precisely its more complex, less clear, more long-term, non-utilitarian aspects. And so it was a consensus around the 'nature of the other' which solidified the idea of responsible individualism and social inclusion, which drove the movement for egalitarian waste removal and clean-water supplies. This was an illustration of culture in its broadest sense. It included what we have always considered to be culture — ideas, literature, images, music, architecture, the sciences. Why do we think of these as culture? Because they are the repositories and the mechanisms of thought and argument.

I'm not suggesting that utilitarianism's unravelling of reason is the product of malevolence. Rather, it comes from a lack of sophistication — the sophistication of disinterest. Sophistication here includes the ability to step back from mere interest and utility in order to use our qualities. This is the element of conscious distance and consideration which makes us human. This ability to take our distance — to see ourselves — in turn assumes some sophisticated balancing of reason with our other qualities.

None of this is a comment on whether utility is good or bad. Or waste disposal. Or trade. Nor is it a comment on the necessary function of self-interest. I'm simply pointing out that these characteristics and functions are not in and of themselves rational. They are not equipped to lead society.

Why then are we so obsessed by utilitarianism? We have always wanted the comfort of clarity and permanent systems. We remain uncomfortable with our own qualities and strengths — with complexity and uncertainty. You can trace this need in an unbroken line back to Plato. "We'll call the part of the soul with which it *calculates*, the rational part."[28] He was busy trying to reduce reason to self-interest and utility with one hand, while demeaning the voices of uncertainty — the poets — with the other.

But the argument that reason is a thinking — non-calculating — quality has a longer and a firmer tradition. Solon set the tone almost two hundred years before Plato, with warnings that calculation was self-interest and a form of public evil.

> Public evil enters the house of each man, the gates of his
> courtyard and cannot keep it out, it leaps over the high wall;
> let him flee to a corner of his bedchamber, it will certainly
> find him out.

This was the message at the core of Socrates' rational approach towards death. A non-calculating approach. And that idea remains solidly with us. Rousseau: "As soon as public service ceases to be the main concern of the citizens and they come to prefer to serve the state with their purse rather than their person, the state is already close to ruin."[29]

What does that mean today? Think of the facility with which democracies now talk of training youth rather than educating them. Tony Blair is typical of those seduced and excited by the utilitarian solution. Echoing the latest utilitarian fashion, he argues that "human capital" is the key to future prosperity. I'm not suggesting that students shouldn't have training, but a rational citizen is not human capital any more than she is a utilitarian mechanism.

> The past century proclaimed the equality of citizens before
> the law — a conquest carrying formidable weight — Th[is]
> ...century upholds, in fact consolidates, this principle, but
> adds another which is none the less fundamental: the equal-
> ity of men before work, understood as a duty and a right, as
> a creative joy that broadens and ennobles existence rather
> than mortify or depress it.

These are Mussolini's words before the Council of Corporations. The deleted word in this quotation is Fascist. "This Fascist century".[30] My point is not to call anyone a fascist. Rather it is to point out how seductively the utilitarian, interest-based corporatist viewpoint has chased reason from our public imagination and replaced it with mechanistic dogma. It is so omnipresent that we no longer recognize it as such.

You can reply to utilitarianism as Seneca did — "How narrow the mind which is fulfilled by material goods."[31] Or you can mock darkly its pedantic self-assurance as Hemingway did in his "Natural History of the Dead," with a pseudo-rational description of war casualties.

"Can we not hope to furnish the reader with a few rational and interesting facts about the dead? I hope so."

> The surprising thing…is the amount of paper that is scat-
> tered about the dead. Their ultimate position, before there
> is any question of burial, depends on the location of the
> pockets in the uniform. In the Austrian army these pockets
> were in the back of the breeches and the dead, after a short
> time, all consequently lay on their faces, the two hip pockets
> pulled out.…

When I say utilitarianism chases out reason, the impetus is obvious. Reason will press us to be conscious. It will force us to use our
memory, to say nothing of our ethical judgement. The utilitarian,
being mere method and self-interest, is dependent on perpetual virginal naïveté. Its short-term clarity is intended to bring results and
produce a direction. And we must not notice when it doesn't.

So a rational leader like Harry Truman quite naturally points out,
"That people have to keep their eyes and ears open at all times or
they'll be robbed blind by…the big business interests. Every generation seems to have to learn that all over again, and it's a shame." And
indeed, various arguments of inevitability tied to what we now call
globalization have caused us to willingly suspend our disbelief yet
again, even though the evidence of our naïveté continues to pour in.
Think of Nike withdrawing its financial support from American universities such as Michigan, Oregon and Brown. Why? Because these
schools expressed concern over working conditions in Nike's overseas
factories. Universities are supposed to be independent centres of
thought — of rationality — but they were caught in a web of utilitarian logic. They need money. They are an attractive, soft, advertising
centre for sports-equipment manufacturers. And the equipment in
question is produced according to an utilitarian model.

Or think of a current fashion which is presented as utilitarian truth: the new large markets created by globalization require larger corporations. We should therefore be pleased by a frenzy of mergers and acquisitions, leading to many companies larger than nation-states. But the logic simply doesn't work. A decade or so ago we were told to deregulate and open our borders in order to stimulate competition. Today we are told that the return in force of monopolies and oligopolies is a healthy and in any case inevitable outcome of opening up to the world. So the plan to increase competition has done the opposite.

Which is it meant to be? In utilitarianism it really doesn't matter because there is no direction and there are no ideas. Looked at rationally, these big corporations are bad for the global market and for our societies. Anyone who *thinks* he is in favour of the marketplace must be against the trend. Anyone who *believes* in the marketplace may be able to trick himself into naive acceptance.

A DEPENDENT QUALITY

At first glance these arguments as to what reason is not may appear negative, even pessimistic. But this, as I said at the beginning, is the normal, indeed the best, way to deal with an absolute monarch.

The energetic shoving aside of false reason in its various forms actually uncovers or releases the real thing. Having done that, I now risk appearing unnecessarily optimistic. Those addicted to the solutioneering of method and facts and instrumental reason and utilitarianism will find it self-indulgent and wasteful to understand reason as thought and argument. They have problems to solve, things to do. To bring them up with a jolt I could reply: like Mussolini, they have problems to solve, things to do. Or like a dog, they have a bowl of food to empty, a hydrant to pee on, a fire to be slept in front of.

The idea of reason as uncertainty through thought and argument has been with us for 2,500 years. That idea has always included the sense that, of all our qualities, reason most clearly activates the human ability to be disinterested — to distance herself from herself, to see herself, to see the *other*.

And this very moving and noble idea of what we are capable of has been repeatedly relaunched over the centuries. Each time a sense of humanity is reinjected into society.

Yet it is Plato's fear-laden version which repeatedly reasserts itself. Fear of what? Of real danger? Or of the uncertainty which reminds us of all we don't know about our mortality?

> The fanaticism with which all Greek reflection throws itself
> upon rationality betrays a desperate situation; there was
> danger, there was but one choice; either to perish or — to
> be *absurdly rational*.[32]

Nietzsche's analysis is correct, except perhaps the last sentence should read — "either *to know* you will perish or — to be *absurdly rational*."

There was — is — no real danger, only the fear. The fear of danger here is the fear of uncertainty. And because of that fear, reason can swing into deformity perhaps faster than any of our other qualities.

All that is needed is a troubled time or a voice capable of exacerbating our fears, playing upon them, or a critical mass of insecure minds in a critical place. Suddenly we discover that our ability to think and argue has been locked up in methodology, truth and dogma. This is the cheapest, the fastest, way to self-confidence. And in fleeing the dangers of free enquiry, reason is blown immediately into the truly dangerous waters of certainty. Thought, after all, may be our most unusual quality. Perhaps it is also our most delicate, the one most immediately dependent upon the tension created by our other qualities.

That is why the worst thing we can do is to overstate the rational case. Of the six qualities it is the least capable of assuming such hyperbole.

Treat it as mere reason — as thought and argument. Cut loose the sucker-fish — the facts, methodology, instrumentalism, utilitarianism. Stop treating it as the source of truth. Stop pretending that thought is virtue. Remember the advice of the great Japanese novelist Sōseki — "[S]ometimes it is reasonable to act contrary to reason."[33] Remember that life is not a Manichean choice between good and evil. Only a false rationality leads us into that trap. Ethics can deal with the choices of life in a much more complex and interesting way.

Finally, beyond reason there is indeed irrationality. But of greater importance, there is non-rationality.

CHAPTER EIGHT

NORMAL
BEHAVIOUR

What is the expression of our humanness, if not to live our lives, struggling with the dynamic of an impossible balance. This is something which lies within each of us and therefore within our societies. To know, imagine, sense, think, to some extent even to understand, this constant dynamic is to express civilization's essential nature.

What is normal behaviour? Is it not to seek equilibrium?

I don't mean by that the pursuit of the Holy Grail. We are not on a line between a point of departure and one of arrival. No linear concept of progress is suggested.

To seek equilibrium is to engage in a dynamic of constant movement, constant tension, yet also to remain in the same place — the place of our real life and real society.

The tension of seeking is normal. To expect or demand resolution is to slip into ideology — a form of death. Life on a force field of qualities attracted and repulsed by each other is normal. The tension is, in and of itself, a dynamic equilibrium.

I am not describing the privileged domain of an élite which, thanks to more education and more money, has been freed to act normally, freed to use its qualities. Normalcy is not a privilege. The obligation or opportunity to use our qualities is not a reward for utilitarian success.

The many who believe that it is a reward are expressing the persistent inheritance of Plato. What is that? A frightened and self-serving conviction that society is a pyramidal structure, in terms both of power and of our capacity to use our qualities. This is marginalized individualism. False individualism. It reflects a strange combination of highly structured corporatism and self-indulgent individualism. This is the old pessimistic view of us — of each of us and all of us, together in our societies.

Reality is quite different. In scientific terms — to use John Polanyi's phrase — it is equilibrium which makes life possible. We are part of that scientific reality. What is true for an atom or a force field is true for all of us. We express this through our desire for life, for life with others, through our engagement with the non-linear nature of progress.

I was interrupted as I finished those words by the news that a hijacked Boeing 767 had been flown into the World Trade Center. From what at first sounded like a bizarre accident, a wave of explosions and accidents and deaths spread through the day, at the end of which a rather fragile, awkward man appeared on television to read a speech from a teleprompter in order to reassure Americans, indeed the world. He read with his eyes glued to the scrolling words. There had been little time for the speechwriters and you could distinguish quite different styles mixed together, some talented, some not.

The essential was elsewhere, as it had been all day. Thousands of individuals were denied a choice in their destiny as their lives were pulverized. Others, in three airplanes, had not been able to find the elements in their situation to change their reality. On a fourth plane, the passengers were able to sense the swirling uncertainty of events. They seized their moment and, though they died, in effect changed their reality by saving the lives of others. In the buildings struck, thousands more were able to make choices and to act. Some were terrible choices, but acts of human will all the same — to leap to their deaths rather than be consumed by an inferno racing towards them. Moments before, they had been at their desks, calmly settling into a day of predictable behaviour, a day which had begun with the turning of a door-handle and the venturing out across a section of their society.

Many found ways to save themselves or help others. No doubt there were also scenes of panic, of individuals acting for themselves. But what was remarkable was that, like the future leader of the French Resistance, Jean Moulin, isolated in 1940 in Chartres, thousands were acting with an ethical sense of themselves, using their shared knowledge to make the best of impossible situations, imagining and intuiting their way through the rubble of civilization, thinking their way into dealing with the immediate reality of this disorder. They passed in moments from the superficial existential minutiae of an ordinary day to the deepest caverns of suffering. Some passed right through those caverns, others could not, while we, not far away, sat buttering our toast, "eating or opening a window or walking dully along".[1]

All of these events were illustrations of technology as a "double-edged sword".[2] We were reminded that this machinery is not progress in any linear, optimistic sense. It cannot lead. It is mere technology and it can be used by different humans for whatever purposes suit them. Like a paving stone in a nineteenth-century street, it is dumb and inert, waiting to be driven over by someone in a carriage, walked upon by someone grateful to be raised above the mud, or picked up by a rioter and thrown at someone else. A passenger jet may indifferently deliver you to a beach holiday or become a deadly missile. An exacto knife may cut a piece of paper or a throat.

The day was also littered by the incapacity of technology and information-dominated structures to deal with the future in a balanced or effective way. This was true from the security systems at the airports to the enormous mechanisms of national security services. It was a day on which "instrumental reason" showed itself not to be rational, but to be dependent, like all utilitarian activity, on the leadership of complex humanism.

When the news of the Boeing 767 penetrating the World Trade Center interrupted me, as it did people around the globe, I had been about to discount Vico's argument of 1744 that "philosophy considers man as he should be and so can be of service to but very few, those who wish to live in the Republic of Plato and not fall back into the dregs of Romulus".[3] On September 11, 2001, those *few* were unable to use their positions of leadership to prevent what happened.

Once the events had taken place, individuals — among the many and the few — reacted as best they could to the demands of reality. Most acted with great effectiveness, many with courage.

Vico was wrong. Philosophy is a commentary on the nature of our existence and so on the qualities all of us share in some way. How useful is that? Well, that nature and those qualities exist whether we recognize them or not. What remains in our power is how conscious we are willing to be of our humanness. By conscious, I mean how much we wish to exercise our qualities and to do so one in concert with the *other*. To be conscious of them is to be more confident in our use of them.

What was disturbing on that day and in the days that followed was how many of Plato's few concentrated exclusively on a narrow, linear approach towards terrorism. They talked of eradication, punishment, in effect, of revenge.

We have some 130 years of experience with modern terrorism. Concrete action is always necessary. Guilty individuals must be dealt with appropriately. We know that there will always be a minute percentage among us ready to kill others for a variety of reasons. We also know that part of the problem is not so much generated as made possible by instability, disquiet, confusion somewhere. The soft terrain from which terrorism has always operated can range from generalized poverty and suffering to directionless comfort and self-indulgence. Conscious civilizations — those which use their qualities in concert — know that they must deal with the causes of that instability and loss of direction in order to shrink that context from which terrorism feeds.

To use our qualities is to be conscious of our actions. A dynamic equilibrium implies an integrated sense of reality's complexity. For forty years now the West has led a rush to balance its trade figures by aggressively selling its armaments abroad. The world is awash in weaponry. You can trace the parallel rising lines of unstable areas slipping into violence as the quantity of weapons on the market increases. To act as if our actions do not have consequences is to pretend that we are without qualities and are naturally passive factors when faced by the actions of others. It is to reduce ourselves to forms of reaction.

"What about love?" someone asked early in this book. Is not the willingness to kill yourself for your cause — taking others with you who would see themselves as innocent bystanders — a form of love? I personally might call it fanaticism or hatred. But the terrorist would no doubt see it as love — love for his cause or his own group or people. Love is always a limited vision of who the *other* might be.

That's why love is a force or a characteristic, but not a quality. In order for a society to function with a certain tension — a dynamic equilibrium — the states of being it must avoid at all costs are love and hatred, all-consuming and therefore all-destructive.

You might say, love doesn't have to be that way. What way then? A letter to Jane:

> I am Tarzan of the Apes. I want you. I am yours. You are
> mine. We will live together always in my house. I will bring
> you the best fruits, the tenderest deer, the finest meats that
> roam the jungle. I will hunt for you. I am the greatest of the
> jungle hunters. I will fight for you. I am the mightiest of the
> jungle fighters. When you see this you will know that it is
> for you and that Tarzan of the Apes loves you. [4]

This is as good a summary of the love argument as you can get. And it is perhaps irresistible on a personal level. You might want to adjust it slightly for urban couples, two-job families, same-sex couples, and so on, but the elements are there. This is a personal program. It isn't a social program. The related social program is laid out by Tristan and Isolde, consumed by a love potion.

> "From this world, oh set us free!"
> "Extinguished in the twilight's streaming
> all our doubting
> all our dreaming
> all our memories
> all our fancies."

Note that love eliminates social responsibility, doubt, imagination and memory. Common sense, ethics and reason need not even be mentioned in order to be eliminated. Tristan, as he later lies dying, sets the ground rules for his loyal servant Kuvenal:

> Those whom I hate
> thou hatest too
> those whom I love
> thou lovest too.

Saint Francis believed that love might allow you to escape self-interest and hatred. He wanted "to see with the eye of the heart, hear with the ear of the heart". But he never faced the impossibility for any society to function at that level. How could everyone differentiate on a stable, ongoing basis between his high pure love, the pure carnal love of others and the love which is the hatred of others, to take just three varieties? The use of Christian love to hate non-Christians over the centuries is our primary memory of this impossibility. Indeed individuals and groups have used every major religion at different times to engage in this game of love and hate.

Francis was no sooner dead than his formalized movement of

love — the Franciscans — was given responsibility by Rome for elements of the Inquisition and the eradication of heresy. Yet he and they had withdrawn from all involvement with property and ambition. His example had brought other human strengths to the fore as he embraced the world of the poor and of nature. Ethics blossomed, a form of common sense, of intuition. It was a very great revolution which caused the power structures of Europe to tremble for a few decades. And then he died and the whole movement was recuperated overnight by those who had opposed him.

You cannot run society with such hopes if citizens do not have a solid sense of their own equilibrium. The very best intention can swing in a second from unambitious devotion or love to the pursuit of others who do not love in your way.

The great Islamic spiritualist Abd El-Kader explained carefully that love could only be a reflection of God's love for humans. "You say that you love Me?" the Koran relates. "If that is the case, you must know that your love for Me is only a consequence of My love for you."[5]

This, of course, is precisely the Christian position. "Beloved, let us love one another for God is love."

In the Western tradition, love has never belonged to us. It has always been a godly attribute — a force which we cannot shape or control. That is why, when we have it, it overwhelms us for better or worse.

Note: I am not denigrating, minimizing, discounting or attacking love. It may well be the essential within us. After all, why wouldn't our characteristics reflect our essential nature? But if we cannot shape such a force we must in some way be passive before it. Taken beyond our personal lives, it can only become an ideology.

The same could be said of a dozen other human characteristics. To be *happy* in the modern sense: where does it leave us? "We are happy." Beckett mocks, "What do we do now, now that we are happy?" "For God's sake," the great nineteenth-century Italian leader Mazzini wrote to a friend, "do not teach your son any Benthamite theory about happiness either individual or collective. A creed of individual happiness would make him an egotist: a creed of collective happiness will reach the same result soon or late."

It is with our qualities that we make something of ourselves.

I do not mean that we face a choice between the personal and the public, but between two kinds of personal. The one — that of love and happiness and other characteristics — involves a state of being which may be a gift of the gods, whether religious or mythological. Or it may be the expression of amorphous forces within us. In either of these cases, this is the personal self which does not link you to me — to the *other* — the *other* of the world outside our personal self. If we love the *other*, to take a single example, why did we do nothing to stop the murder of the Rwandans?

The second kind of personal life is the expression of ourselves through our qualities. It ties us to a partially conscious sense of ourselves, to others, to society. When we use these qualities, even if we are alone like Jean Moulin, we are part of the humanist reverberation. Vico said in his memoirs that the one thing he feared was "to be the only one to know; a situation which always seemed to me to be the most dangerous, because it exposes us either as a god or someone demented."[6]

With common sense we are neither gods nor demented. We have our shared knowledge. Given our stretching and contracting qualities we have the ability to live with myriad tensions — "a tension of loyalties", as Northrop Frye put it, because "there are no uncritical loyalties."[7] And so we can embrace the idea of criticism as a positive strength; that criticism which, Octavio Paz said, could "unfold the possibility of freedom and is thus an invitation to action."

These are the elements which help us to make our way across our society every day, both in a personal and a civic way. Personal consciousness, civic consciousness; personal virtue, civic virtue. This may sound unrealistic, even boring, in its self-declared goodness.

So think instead of the idea of tension — uncertain, creative tension. This is an uncomfortable pleasure. It runs throughout our celebration of the unresolved. There is a certain eroticism in the idea of a playfully permanent state of uncertainty. There is a certain necessary boring endlessness in the idea that civilization is in permanent construction on the ever-thickening foundation of our memory.

We were taught at school about the heroic nature of Pericles and his demanding, optimistic humanist message. And then the Spartans destroyed Athens and his citizen-based experiment. When I was a student I felt that there was a certain masochistic self-satisfaction in the way this failure was presented. Now I might call it a Platonist or Hobbesian self-satisfaction. What we were rarely taught was that, despite the uncertainty and costs and complexity of this experimental society, Athens's citizens did not abandon it. The Spartans managed to hold on for a few years. Then, under the leadership of Thrasybulus, a moderate and a product of Athenian civic education, the citizens drove the utilitarian dictatorship out. In the days following their victory, they were careful not to slip into revenge. They amnestied most of those who had collaborated with the dictatorship.[8]

What is the point of this story? That the Athenian idea of citizenship — flawed and limited though it was — put public service, civic education, democracy and restraint ahead of wealth, economics, self-interest and emotion. And that this idea had been built up, layer upon layer, from Solon through to Pericles. When the disaster came, individuals had a resilient enough memory of the public good to hold on until they could choose to go back to the inefficient, costly system of citizen-based democracy. To reject that of authoritarian efficiency and profit. They were addicted to the Periclean argument that "words are no barrier to deeds; but rather harm comes from not taking instruction from discussion before the time has come for action."

The Athenian argument always sounds grand. We lay aside our knowledge of how flawed and contradictory it was because it is the clearest example we have in our memory of individuals attempting somehow to live conscious lives. And this attempt was made through an idea of qualities and characteristics which in different ways they attempted to balance.

We use this memory as we should — not as a promise of some Utopia to come, but as a first Western context for struggling with how to live our lives and how to shape our public good.

In 1787, the aged Benjamin Franklin — struggling through all the constraints of a man who knew his history — tried to make up his mind about the proposed American constitution. On September 17, too weak to do it himself, he had his written opinion read to the Convention by someone else. His words were filled with ethical doubts, attempts to imagine the future, rational analysis. "I confess that there are several parts of this Constitution which I do not at present approve, but I am not sure that I shall never approve them...the older I grow, the more apt I am to doubt my own judgement.... I agree to this Constitution with all its faults, if they are such, because I think a general Government necessary.... When you assemble a number of men to have the advantage of their joint wisdom, you inevitably assemble with those men, all their prejudices, their passions, their errors of opinion, their local interests and their selfishness." At last, in an attempt to marry his common sense with an intuitive seizing of reality, he gave "consent to this Constitution because I expect no better, and because I am not sure it is not the best..."

Given his stature, Franklin sealed the course of events, perhaps even set in place the course of modern Western civilization. We know now that he was profoundly right and profoundly wrong. The constitutional system was a good one for the half-continent which would go on to lead the world. It still permits a remarkably complex society to function without losing its necessary internal differences. But it was also catastrophic for the citizenry, because by normalizing slavery it normalized racism in a utilitarian, rational manner unprecedented in world history.

That normalization of the abnormal made it impossible for society to embrace its real intent. These institutionalized contradictions led not only to a massive civil war, but to a great wound which continues to suppurate in ways which we still cannot predict or control, altering realities at home and abroad. This was a flaw which could not work its way out.

All of our societies contain within them the contradictions which may one day incapacitate or destroy us. In this, most schools of philosophy and religions are agreed. In accepting the idea of uncertainty and opposing forces, they assume that of suffering. The great American judge Learned Hand put it that "suffering is permanent, obscure and dark. And shares the nature of infinity."[9] The suffering of societies is simply a magnified reality of that dealt with by the thousands of individuals in those two towers who faced in some way their deaths and managed to survive or did not. Looked at as a human reality — our inability to master our contradictions as we would like — this is another way of seeing our struggle with the possibility of equilibrium.

The path through this conundrum lies less with constitutions and laws — although they have their essential roles to play — than with the individual's sense of a personal dynamic equilibrium. That is a state of being that we might call responsible individualism. It contains the tools to alter our situations in ways which can allow our societies to function.

Today's dominant rhetoric of power is designed to marginalize this reality of responsible individualism and to replace it with abstract and technological forces beyond our control. I cannot help feeling that it is precisely the opposite which will happen, because it needs to happen.

The rhetoric of global forces, whether economic, technological or military, leaves us as individuals with the demeaning and irrelevant pleasures of self-fulfilment, providing we can afford them. I sense little satisfaction among people with this enforced holiday from the ability to shape their own destinies and the shared destiny of their society. In fact, I sense growing discomfort and anger. They see their lives, their families, their streets, let us say their friendships, as reality. And this reality is the basis from which larger realities must be shaped.

Used in this way, the word *friendship* has myriad implications. It can be to society what the jury is to democracy. These are the relationships we choose. These few people are our personal engagement with the *other*. In the classical sense, friendship has always been a proof of our ability to free ourselves from the exclusivity of love and the narrowing passivity of self-interest.

So this is not friendship as love. And not a relationship of the sort which would corrupt the public good for personal advantage. This is not friendship as a version of the extended family.

Here friendship is the ability to imagine the *other*. It is not easy. It is the beginnings of tolerance. It is, as Conrad said, "more difficult for some than heroism. More difficult than compassion".[10] Friendship is a relationship filled with uncertainty. It is the primary territory upon which we test our dynamic equilibrium — our use of our interwoven qualities.

This assumes a certain honesty within our conscious imagining of ourselves. This is not a romantic or abstract or grandiose proposition. Think over the last years. The upper-middle classes of the West — the literate, informed, influential upper-middle classes — have asserted or passively accepted a theory according to which a rising tide of income for them will raise the little boats and rafts of the poor. Protected by this romantic delusion, they allow themselves to ignore the reality of a good fifth of their fellow-citizens, stagnating or sinking economically, while all numbers show the top fifth enjoying healthy growth.[11] And yet poverty is the one form of suffering over which societies can exercise a great deal of control.

This is the reality of human consciousness or denial. This is the reality of our lives as we open our doors and walk out into our societies. There is a tiny possibility that we may be swept up from our real minutiae into a terrible reality of violence and heightened existential choice. There is also the normal possibility that our actions and choices of the day — however small — may give comfort to a denial of our individual consciousness and the existence of the *other*. We may deny those who are the friends of *others* and live their lives somewhere out of our immediate sight. There is a certain easy comfort in such denial. We may even deny our friends, though with less ease.

I do not sense that we seek that comfort or the false freedom of denial. We understand the truer comfort of a permanent psychic discomfort in which we seek to identify reality. And we deal with reality through the creative tensions with which we attempt to balance our qualities. This is our eternal movement towards equilibrium.

Pond Inlet — Québec City
September 2001

Notes

Chapter 1 — The Shape of Human Genius

1 René de Obaldia, *Exobiographie: Mémoires* (Paris: Bernard Grasset, 1993), 244.
This quote is from an imagined conversation with Louis Jouvet.
"La vie, mon petit père, manque de répétitions. C'est d'ailleurs pourquoi elle
rate si souvent. Au théâtre…"

2 Giambattista Vico, *The New Science* (Third Edition, 1744) (Ithaca: Cornell
University Press, 1968), 3–4.

3 Plato, "Protagoras," *Complete Works* (Indianapolis: Hackett Publishing
Company, 1997), 758.

4 Richard Feynman, *Six Easy Pieces* (Reading, Mass.: Helix Books, 1963), 4.

5 "The Prophets," *The Koran* (London: Penguin, 1956), 299.
Rohinton Mistry, *A Fine Balance* (Toronto: McClelland and Stewart, 1995), 268.
Sōseki Natsume, *I am a Cat* (II) (Tokyo: Charles E. Tuttle Co., 1979), 86. Original
translated by Aiko Ito and Graeme Wilson. Originally published 1904–5.

6 Günter Grass, "To be continued…" Nobel Lecture, 7 December 1999.

7 Leo Tolstoy, "Father Sergius," *Master and Man and Other Stories*
(Harmondsworth: Penguin, 1977), 33. Translated by Paul Foote.

8 Jaan Kaplinski, *Through the Forest* (London: The Harvill Press, 1996), 85.
Translated by Hildi Hawkins.

9 Roger Martin du Gard, *Les Thibault, V* (Paris: Gallimard, 1940), 288.
Sulak Sivaraksa, *Siamese Resurgence* (Bangkok: Asian Cultural Forum on
Development, 1985), 29. From a statement by the Buddha.

Chapter 2 — Common Sense

1 Watkin Tench, *1788, Comprising a Narrative of the Expedition to Botany Bay and
A Complete Account of the Settlement at Port Jackson* (Melbourne: The Text
Publishing Co., 1996), 183. Edited and Introduced by Tim Flannery.

2 Immanuel Kant, *Critique of Judgement* (New York: Hafner, 1951), 139.
Translated by J.H. Bernard.

3 George Berkeley, *Three Dialogues Between Hylas and Philonous*, London, 1713.
G.E. Moore, *Selected Writings* (London: Routledge, 1993), 107. From: "A Defence of Common Sense." Published 1925.
Albert Einstein, "Ideas and Opinions," *Physics and Reality* (New York: Bonanza Books, 1954), 290.

4 Thomas Reid, *Essays on the Intellectual Powers of Man* (London: John Bell, 1785). Essay V1, chapter 4.
See also Keith Lehrer, *Thomas Reid* (London: Routledge, 1989).

5 John Keane, *Tom Paine: A Political Life* (Reading: Bloomsbury Publishing, 1995), 111. See Keane's description of the reception of *Common Sense*, in Chapter 4. This is a remarkable intellectual biography which could be read in tandem with Connor Cruise O'Brien's brilliant biography of Edmund Burke, *The Great Melody*.
Voltaire, *Dictionnaire Philosophique*, Tome VIII (Paris: Librairie Fortic, 1827), 126. *Sens Commun* "état mitoyen entre la stupidité et l'esprit. 'Cet homme n'a pas le sens commun,' est une grosse injure. 'Cet homme a le sens commun' est une injure aussi; cela veut dire qu'il n'est pas tout à fait stupide.... *Sensus communis* signifiait chez les Romains, non seulement sens commun, mais humanité, sensibilité."

6 Hegel, *Phenomenology of Spirit* (Oxford: Oxford University Press, 1977), 42–43. Translated by A.V. Miller.
Merle Miller, *Plain Speaking: an oral biography of Harry S. Truman* (New York: Berkeley Publishing, 1974), 129.

7 Philip Morgan, *Italian Fascism, 1919–1945* (Basingstoke: MacMillan, 1995), 14.

8 Primo Levi, *If This Is a Man — The Truce* (New York: Vintage, 1996), 395–6.

9 Walpola Sri Rahula, *What the Buddha Taught* (New York: Grove Press, 1974), 12.

10 William Duckworth, *Talking Music: Conversations with John Cage, Philip Glass, Laurie Anderson and Five Generations of American Experimental Composers* (New York: Schirmer Books, 1995), 322.
David Summers, *The Judgement of Sense* (London: Cambridge University Press, 1987), 71 and 73. See also the whole of Chapter 5, "The Common Sense."

11 Giambattista Vico, *Vie de Giambattista Vico, Ecrite par Lui-Même, Lettres, La Méthode des Études de notre Temps* (Paris: Grasset, 1981). Traduction par Alain Pons. Quotes from the Introduction, 198 and La Méthode, 225. "Le 'sens commun' n'est pas le 'bon sens' Cartésien, la capacité rationnelle de distinguer le vrai du faux."

12 Aeschylus, *The Oresteia* (London: Faber, 1999). Beginning on page 168. Translated by Ted Hughes.

13 The comments draw on a 1998 analysis of the use of common sense by the then

Supreme Court Justice, now Chief Justice of Canada, Beverley McLachlin. "The Judicial Vision: from partiality to impartiality." The Australian case dates from 1993.

Artisotle, *Nicomachean Ethics* (London: Penguin Classics, 1970), 213–15. See "On Prudence," 1142a, 10–15.

Vico, *The New Science*, 63. Translated by Thomas Goddard Bergin and Max Harold Fish. Third Edition (1744), Book I: Establishment of Principles, xiii–144.

Vico, *Vie de Giambattista Vico*, "tout le contraire de la tabula rasa de Descartes", 199.

14 Xenophon, *Memorabilia* (Cambridge, Mass.: Harvard University Press, 1992), vol. I, II, 23. Translated by O.J. Todd.

Michael Oakeshott, "On Hobbes," *Rationalism in Politics and Other Essays* (Indianapolis. Liberty Fund, 1991), 241.

Connor Cruise O'Brien, *The Great Melody, A Thematic Biography and Commented Anthology of Edmund Burke* (Chicago: University of Chicago Press, 1992), 387.

"Biographical Sketches of Famous Men" — "The Character of George Washington." *The Life and Selected Writings of Thomas Jefferson* (New York: The Modern Library, 1972), 173–5.

Sun Tzu, *The Art of War* (London: Oxford University Press, 1963), 51 and 43. Translated by Samuel B. Griffith. Foreword by B.H. Liddell Hart.

Miller, *Plain Speaking*, 453.

15 Euripides, "The Bacchae," *The Bacchae and Other Plays* (Harmondsworth: Penguin Books, 1954), 204.

16 Immanuel Kant, *Anthropology from a pragmatic point of view* (The Hague: Nijhoff, 1974), 88. Translated by Mary J. Gregor. *"Das einzige allgemeine Merkmal der Verücktheit ist des Verlust des Gemeinsinnes (sensus communis) und des dagegen eintretende logische. Eigensinn (sensus privatus)."*

17 Jean-Jacques Rousseau, *The Social Contract* (Harmondsworth: Penguin Books, 1968), 86. Originally published 1762.

Vico, *Scienza nuova*. Quoted in Pons, 199. "elles dégénèrent dans la 'barbarie de la réflexion.'" "Les peuples [s'habituent] à ce que chacun ne pense qu'à son intérêt particulier...et, au milieu de la foule des corps, [vivent] comme des bêtes féroces, dans une solitude absolue des esprits et des volontés."

18 *The New York Times*, 14 March 1999, page 8. "A Goodbye to the Weight of Leveraging," by Laura Holson.

19 Michael Glanz, speaking at the second conference of the *Grupo de Los Cien*, in Mexico, 10 January 1994.

20 Peter Walthams, of the Scott Polar Research Institute in Cambridge. Quoted in *The Ottawa Citizen*, 20 August 2000, page 1.

21 Miguel Cervantes, *Don Quixote* (Oxford: Oxford University Press, 1999), 206. Part I, Chapter XXIII.

22 *Guardian Weekly*, 17–23 August 2000, page 3.

23 Ghandl of the Qayahl Llaanas, *Nine Visits to the Myth World* (Lincoln: University of Nebraska Press, 2000), 63. From the poem "Spirit Being Living in the Little Finger." Translated from Haida by Robert Bringhurst.
These poems originally made their way into English in 1900, when the oral bard/wiseman/poet Skaay recounted them to a bilingual Haida, Henry Moody, who translated them immediately into English for transcription by John Swanton. This transcription a century ago was until recently treated as anthropology. The poetry of Skaay and of Ghandl is gradually making its way into a world which has ignored it because of the deadening hand of the anthropological label. While it does have a religious, mythological function, this poetry is increasingly seen in the same cultural/poetic context as Homer or Gilgamesh. Today the Haida myths can be found in four versions.
— *Skidegate Haida Myths and Histories* (Queen Charlotte Islands: Museum Press, Skidegate, 1995). Edited and translated by John Enrico. Introduction by Guujaaw.
— A three-volume set edited by Robert Bringhurst
I — Robert Bringhurst, *A Story as Sharp as a Knife* (Vancouver: Douglas and McIntyre, 1999).
II — Ghandl (the volume quoted above).
III — Skaay of the Qquima Qiighawaay, *Being in Being* (Vancouver: Douglas and McIntyre, 2001).
The new distribution of these poems has some of the significance of the discovery of *Gilgamesh* for the European language.

24 Montesquieu, *Lettres Persanes* (Paris: Gallimard, 1973), 76.
Lettre XIV — "Mais ce joug vous paraît trop dur: vous aimez mieux être soumis à un prince et obéir à ses lois moins rigides que vos moeurs."

Chapter 3 — Ethics

1 Adam Smith, *The Theory of Moral Sentiments* (Indianapolis: Liberty Fund, 1984), 235. Based on 6th edition, 1790. Edited by D.D. Raphael and A.L. Macfie.
Plato, "Republic I," *Complete Works* (Indianapolis: Hackett Publishing Company, 1997), 978.

2 Sulak Sivaraksa, *Siamese Resurgence* (Bangkok: Asian Cultural Forum on Development, 1988), 10.
Smith, *The Theory*, 241.

3 Daniel Cordier, *Jean Moulin, l'inconnu du Panthéon* (Paris: J.C. Lattes, 1989), vol. 2, 330. "Quand la résolution est prise, il est simple d'exécuter les gestes nécessaires à l'accomplissement de ce que l'on croit être son devoir...." Moulin's full text is in *Jean Moulin, Premier Combat, écrit en 1941, publié 1945*, Paris, *Editions de Minuit*.
See also Henri Calef, *Jean Moulin* (Paris: Plon, 1983), 162–8.

4 Xenophon, *Memorabilia*, vol. I, II, 21.

5 *The Life and Selected Writings of Thomas Jefferson* (New York: The Modern Library, 1972), 373. Letter to Peter Carr, 19 August 1785.

6 Albert Camus, *Actuelles — Ecrits politiques* (Paris: Gallimard, 1956), 46. From *Combat*, 12 October 1944. "Quand dit-on qu'un homme a mis sa vie en ordre? Il faut pour cela qu'il se soit mis d'accord avec elle et qu'il ait conformé sa conduite à ce qu'il croit vrai. L'insurgé qui, dans le désordre de la passion, meurt pour une idée qu'il a faite sienne, est en réalité un homme d'ordre parce qu'il a ordonné toute sa conduite à un principe qui lui paraît évident."
page 49, "la capacité de dire non..."
page 46, "Mais on ne pourra jamais nous faire considérer comme un homme d'ordre ce privilégié qui fait ses trois repas par jour pendant toute une vie, qui a sa fortune en valeurs sûres, mais qui rentre chez lui quand il y a du bruit dans la rue. Il est seulement un homme de peur et d'épargne."

7 Giambattista Vico, *La Méthode des Études de notre temps* (Paris: Grasset, 1981), 239. Présentation, traduction et notes par Alain Pons. "...étant donné que les chose humaines sont dominées par l'occasion et le choix, qui sont très incertains...."

8 Ken Wiwa, *In the Shadow of a Saint* (Toronto: Alfred Knopf Canada, 2000), 98, 144, 174–6.

9 Plato, *Complete Works*, 575. From "Alcibiades." Some believe this was written by a disciple shortly after Plato's death.
See Thomas de Koninck, *La Nouvelle Ignorance et le problème de la culture* (Paris: Presse Universitaire de France, 2000).

10 *The Essential Jung* (Princeton: Princeton University Press, 1983), 398.

11 Lieutenant-General Roméo Dallaire, interviewed by Michael Enright on "This Morning". CBC Radio.
Published in *The Queen's Quarterly*, Fall, 2000, 107/3.

12 George Steiner, *Errata, an Examined Life* (London: Phoenix, 1997), 135.

13 Tench, *1788, Comprising a Narrative*, 183.

14 Nathan L. Tierney, *Imagination and Ethical Ideals* (Albany: State University of New York Press, 1994), 5.
Jefferson, *The Life*, 431. Letter to Peter Carr, 10 August 1787.

15 Joseph Conrad, *Chance* (Wandsworth: Penguin Books, 1974), 310. Originally published 1913.

16 The Honourable Madame Justice Louise Arbour, Speech: "The Truth to Be Told," Toronto, 15 November 1999.

17 Stuart Hampshire, *Morality and Conflict* (Oxford: Blackwell, 1983), 2. (my italics)

John Rawls, *A Theory of Justice* (London: Oxford University Press, 1973), 433.

See Jürgen Habermas, "Was hasst Universalpragmatic?" in *Vorstudien und Ergänzungen zur Theorie des Kommunikativen Handelus* (Frankfurt: Suhrkamp, 1984), 427–40. And for an analysis of his argument: Charles Larmore, *The Morals of Modernity* (Cambridge: Cambridge University Press, 1996), Chapter 9.

Voltaire, *Dictionaire Philosophique* (Paris: *Librairie de Fortic*, 1827), 307. Tome 48. Definition of "Juste (du) et de l'injuste." "Il me s'agit donc plus que de nous servir de notre raison pour discerner les nuances de l'honnête et du déshonnête. Le bien et le mal sont souvent voisins."

The Essential Jung, Selected and Introduced by Anthony Storr (Princeton: Princeton University Press, 1983), 397.

18 Smith, *The Theory*, 241.

19 Rousseau, *Contract*, 32.

Frederick W. Mote, *Intellectual Foundations of China* (New York: Knopf, 1971), 46.

Albert Camus, *Actuelles*, 22. "Le Temps du Mépris," From *Combat*, 30 août 1944. "Et ceux qui ont fait cela savaient céder leur place dans le métro, tout comme Himmler."

20 Elias Canetti, *Crowds and Power* (London: Penguin, 1984), 347. Translated by Carol Stewart. Original published in German 1960, *Masse und macht*.

Read on the Truth and Reconciliation Commission, the remarkable account by Antjie Krog, *Country of My Skull* (New York: Times Books, 1998), 30–34, 43–51, 74–95. She followed it throughout.

Also, Archbishop Desmond Tutu, *No Future Without Forgiveness* (New York: Doubleday, 1999).

Also Archbishop Tutu's Convocation Address, University of Toronto, 15 February 1999.

21 See Sophocles, *Philoctetes* (Harmondsworth: Penguin, 1933).
and Edmund Wilson, *The Wound and the Bow* (New York: Farrar, Straus & Giroux, 1978).

22 August Strindberg, "The Ghost Sonata," *Plays* (London: Methuen Drama, 1976), 160.

Joe Garvey, interviewed on "Some of the Best Minds of Our Time." CBC Radio, July 2000. See also www.radio.cbc.ca.

23 Thomas Mann, "Goethe and Tolstoy," *Essays of Three Decades* (New York: Knopf, 1968), 101.
Bolton King, *The Life of Mazzini* (London: Dent and Sons, 1902), 252.
Smith, *The Theory*, 231.

24 Sharon Sholzberg-Gray, *The Globe and Mail*, 4 February 2000, A15: U.S. per capita health-care costs are the highest in the world — $4,090 — though 40 million have no coverage;
Recent Australian study — University of Wollongong — Private Health care is 26% more expensive.

25 There are many descriptions of the early-twentieth-century reform movement and its collapse in 1914. Perhaps the most complete and most evocative of the emotional and political drama is Roger Martin du Gard's eight-part novel cycle, *Les Thibault*. It was in large part for this creation that he received the Nobel Prize for Literature in 1937.

26 Aristotle, *Politics*, Book 1, Chapter 11, 1253 a 15.
Rawls, *A Theory*, 243.
Sir Wilfrid Laurier, 29 May 1881. Banquet for Edward Blake in Montreal.
Sri Rahula, *What the Buddha Taught*, 83.
"Worldly Gain," *The Koran* (London: Penguin, 1956), 27.
Euripides, "Electra," vol. 5, 25.
Sophocles, "Antigone," *The Theban Plays*, 144.
Miller, *Plain Speaking*, 177.
Aung San Suu Kyi. Quoted in *The New York Times Magazine*, 7 January 1996.
Aurel Kolnai, Selected Papers of, *Ethics, Value and Reality* (Indianapolis: Hackett Publishing Co., 1973), 98.

27 Plato, "Republic I," 994.
The Dialects of Confucius (New York: Vintage Books, 1938), 102. Translated by Arthur Waley.

28 Margaret Somerville, "Up-sizing Ethics in Corporate Downsizing." Speech, Ottawa, October 1996, 7.

Chapter 4 — Imagination

1 August Strindberg, "Creditors," *Plays III* (London: Methuen, 1991), 150. Originally published 1888.

2 Joseph Roth, *Flight Without End* (London: Dent, 1977), xvii. Translated by David le Vay. Originally published in German 1927.

3 Northrop Frye, *The Great Code, The Bible and Literature* (New York: Harcourt Brace Jovanovich, 1982), xv.

4 Jacob Bronowski, *Science and Human Values* (New York: Perennial Library, 1965), 12, 52. Original edition 1956.

5 Duckworth, *Talking Music*, 19–20.

6 Camus, *Actuelles — Ecrits politiques*, 150. "Réponses à Emmanuel d'Astier de La Vigerie." "[V]ous me demandez pour quelles raisons je me suis placé du côté de la Résistance. C'est un question qui n'a pas de sens.... Je ne m'imaginais pas ailleurs, voilà tout." "J'ai compris alors que je détestais moins la violence, que les institutions de la violence."

7 *The Letters of Marsilio Ficino* (London: Shepheard-Walwyn, 1975), vol. 1, 81. Letter 39.

8 This example taken from *The Edinburgh Review*, January-May 1828, from a review of *The Songs of Scotland*, 186.

9 Steiner, *Errata*, 86.

10 Bronowski, *Science*, 61.
   Albert Camus, *Discours de Suède* (Paris: Gallimard, 1958), 56.
   August Strindberg, "The Ghost Sonata," *Plays*, 189.

11 Krog, *Country*, 43.

12 Smith, *The Theory*, 9.

13 Arthur Schopenhauer, *The World as Will and Idea* (London: Routledge and Kegan Paul, 1964), vol. III, 142. Translated by R.B. Haldane and J. Kemp, 1883. Originally published in German 1818.

14 This is the interpretation of Richard Holmes, in his *Coleridge: Darker Reflections* (London: Harper Collins, 1998), 107–8.

15 Samuel Taylor Coleridge, ed. R.A. Foakes, *Lectures, 1808–1819: On Literature* (Princeton: Princeton University Press and Routledge, 1987). Bollinger Series, vol. I, 81–2.

16 Robert Bringhurst, "Raven Travelling," *A Story as Sharp as a Knife* (Vancouver: Douglas and McIntyre, 1999), 17, 45, 47, 66–7, 225.

17 Dr. T.J. de Boer, *The History of Philosophy in Islam* (New York: Doner Publications, 1967), 2. Translated by Edward R. Jones. Originally published 1903.

18 Vico, *The New Science*, 71. Book I, "Establishment of Principles," xxxix, 189.
   Michael Oakeshott, *Rationalism in Politics and Other Essays* (Indianapolis: Libert Fund, 1992), 497.

19 Elisabeth of Hungary, 1207–1231. Married to the Landgrave Ludwig of Thuringia in 1221. Widowed 1227. Saint 1235. Influenced by Francis of Assisi, 1182–1226. Church begun 1235, finished 1285. Landgrave's chapel: tombs, thirteenth–fifteenth centuries; earliest, that of Conrad, 1240, who would have known Elisabeth.

20 Martin Kemp and Marina Wallace, *Spectacular Bodies; The Art and Science of the Human Body, from Leonardo to Now* (Berkeley: University of California, 2000).

21 Mostyn W. Jones, "Inadequacies in Current Theories of Imagination," *The Southern Journal of Philosophy* (1995), vol. XXXIII, 313–28.

22 Samuel Taylor Coleridge, *Biographia Literaria* (Princeton: Princeton University Press and Routledge, 1983). Billington Scries, vol. 1, 304–50. eds. James Engell and W. Jackson Bates. Two volumes.
Maurice Merleau-Ponty, *Phenomenology of Perception* (New York: Routledge and Kegan Paul, 1962), 12.

23 Daniel-Henry Kahnweiler. *Entretiens avec Picasso au sujet des 'Femmes d'Alger'* (Paris: l'Echoppe, 1991). Original conversations, 1955. "Je lui dirais: Vous, vous pensiez à Rubens et vous faisiez du Delacroix. Ainsi, moi, pensant à vous, je fait autre chose."

24 Angus Wilson, *Emile Zola* (London: Apollo Editions, 1952).

25 David Malouf, *A Spirit of Play* (Sydney: ABC Books, 1998), 38–9.

26 John Ruskin, *St. Mark's Rest* (Leipzig: Bernhard Tauchinitz, 1910), 207–8.

27 Malouf, *A Spirit*, 36.

28 Frye, *The Great Code*, 48–9.

29 Keane, *Tom Paine: A Political Life*, 511.
Wiwa, *In the Shadow of a Saint*, 110.

30 Cited at the Musée Paul Valéry, in Sète. "Une oeuvre d'art devrait toujours vous apprendra que nous avons pas vu ce que nous voyons."

31 Alma Mahler, *Gustav Mahler: Memories and Letters* (London: Cardinal, 1990), 105. Original German 1940.

32 Marsilio Ficino (Marsille Ficin), *Théologie Platonicienne de l'Immortalité des Ames* (Paris: Société d'Edition "Les Belles Lettres"). Tome II, 196, 210, 208. Texte critique établi et traduit par Raymond Marcel. "Les puissances grossières de la sensibilité," "le désir, le plaisir, la crainte et la douleur." "[Q]uand ils sont en délire, ils composent de nombreux chants, souvent admirables, qu'ils ne comprennent plus dès que leur délire s'est calmé, comme s'ils ne les avaient pas exprimés d'eux-mêmes, mais comme si un dieux s'était servi d'eux comme instruments sonores pour les faire entendre."

33 M. Owen Lee, *Wagner — The Terrible Man and His Truthful Art* (Toronto: University of Toronto Press, 1999), 23. An astonishing set of lectures.

34 August Strindberg, "The Father," *The Plays* (London: Secker and Warburg, 1964), 44. Act 1, Sc. 5.

35 Schopenhauer, *The World*, vol. II, 268.

36 Alexis de Tocqueville, *Democracy in America* (New York: Vintage Books, 1945), vol. I, 5. Originally published 1835.

37 *Great Dialogues of Plato* (New York: Mentor, 1956). "The Republic," Book 10 (605C–607B), 407.

38 Learned Hand, *The Bill of Rights* (New York: Atheneum, 1986), 75–6. The Oliver Wendell Holmes Lecture, 1958.

Chapter 5 — Intuition

1 *The Basic Writings of C.G. Jung,* ed. Violet Staub de Laszlo (New York: The Modern Library, 1959), 118.

2 Jung, *The Basic,* 212–13.

3 Henri Bergson, *An Introduction to Metaphysics* (New York: Library of Liberal Arts, 1955), 38. Translated by T.E. Hulme. Originally published in French 1903.

4 See Jean-Paul Kauffman, *The Dark Room at Longwood* (London: The Harvill Press, 1999). Translated by Patricia Clancy. French original: *La chambre noire de Longwood,* 1997. Kauffman meditates at length on Napoleon's other failure, at Eylau, and his obsession with it.

5 Bergson, *An Introduction,* 50.

6 René Descartes, *The Philosophical Writings of Descartes* (Cambridge: Cambridge University Press, 1985), vol. 1, 13, 14. Rule Three from "Rules for the Direction of the Mind."

7 Anthony Giddens, *Durkheim* (London: Fontana Press, 1986), 70.

8 Jung, *The Basic,* 118.

9 *The Epic of Gilgamesh* (Harmondsworth: Penguin Books, 1974), 108, 112, 93. An English version with an introduction by N.K. Sandars. Since this edition new tablets have been found and the texts retranslated. A recent version is that of Andrew George (London: Penguin, 2000). His translation of this passage is, "Demolish the house, and build a boat! / Abandon wealth, and seek survival! / Spurn property, save life!" (page 89).

10 Thomas de Koninck, *De la dignité humaine* (Paris: Presses Universitaires de France, 1995), 73. "Nous ne jouissons pas d'une intuition intellectuelle directe de nous mêmes."

11 Charles Taylor, *The Ethics of Authenticity* (Cambridge, Mass.: Harvard University Press, 1990).

12 David Suzuki, *Time to Change; Essays* (Toronto: Stoddart, 1995).

13 *Gilgamesh,* 106–7.

14 Taylor, *The Ethics,* 72.

15 C.G. Jung, *Memories, Dreams, Reflections* (New York: Vintage Books, 1961), 185.

16 John Stuart Mill, *Autobiography and Literary Essays: Collected Works,* ed. John M. Robson and Jack Stillinger (Toronto: University of Toronto Press, 1981), vol. I, 233.

Rawls, *A Theory*, 41, 44.

17 Steiner, *Errata*, 5.

Jung, *The Basic*, 262.

Jung, *Memories*, 183.

18 Krog, *Country*, 142. See for example Tony Yengeni's cross-examination of Benzien, 92–5.

19 Bertrand Russell, *Mysticism and Logic and Other Essays* (London: Longman, Green and Co., 1918), 8–9.

20 See Ernst Cassirer, *The Philosophy of the Enlightenment* (Princeton: Princeton University Press, 1981), 312–18.

21 Benedict de Spinoza, *The Ethics*, reprinted in *The Rationalists* (Garden City: Anchor Books, 1974), 247. Originally written 1670s.

Erich Fromm, *The Sane Society* (London: Routledge and Kegan Paul Ltd., 1963), 23, 24.

22 Octavio Paz, *The Labyrinth of Solitude* (New York: Grove Press, 1985), 30, 31.

Miguel Angel Asturias, *Men of Maize* (New York: Delacorte Press/S. Lawrence, 1975). Translated from the Spanish by Gerald Martin (*Hombres de maiz*).

J.M.G. Le Clézio, *Le rêve mexicain ou la pensée interrompue* (Paris: Gallimard, 1988), 20. "D'un côté, le monde individualiste et possessif de Hernán Cortes." "De l'autre côté, le monde collectif et magique des Indiens."

Mss Anónimo de Tlatelolco in Mengin (ed.) "Native Chronicles of the Conquest." Corpus Codicum Americanorum, Medii Aevi, I.Fd. 33.

"Todo lo que tene valor desde entonces fue contado como nada."

23 Elias Canetti, *The Tongue Set Free* (London: Picador, 1979), 73.

24 Elisabeth Ayrton, *The Doric Temple* (London: Thames and Hudson, 1961), IX. And her analysis in general.

25 For a description of this period, see François Fejto's masterpiece: *Requiem pour un empire défunt — Histoire de la destruction de l'Autriche-Hongrie* (Paris: Édima/Licu Commun, 1988). Quote from page 23: "Le bruit des congrès et des conférences de paix, d'une ampleur croissante, a recouvert celui, plus discret, des intenses préparatifs de guerre des industries, des états-majors et des diplomates."

See also Roger Martin du Gard's eight-part novel *Les Thibault*, describing the same period.

26 Cassirer, *The Philosophy*, 291. He was commenting on Condillac's eighteenth-century argument.

27 Russell, *Mysticism*, 13.

Bergson, *An Introduction*, 53–4.

E.B. Tylor, *Primitive Cultures* (London: John Murray, 1871), vol. I, 415.

William McDougall, *A History and a Defense of Animism* (London: Methuen, 1911), xi.

John Ralston Saul, *Reflections of a Siamese Twin* (Toronto: Penguin, 1997), 186.

28 Friedrich Reck-Malleczewen, *Diary of a Man in Despair* (London: Duck Editions, 2000), 32. Translated by Paul Rubens.

29 Conrad, *Chance* , 70.

30 See Jean Planchais, *Le Monde*, 3 December 2000, page 13, for a brilliant analysis of what happened. The two officers who expressed regrets were Massu, the commander, and Aussaresses, who was in charge of security. General Bigeard, officer commanding on the ground for much of his period, denied nothing but aggressively rejected any idea of regret.

31 Saul, *Reflections*, 187.

32 James Allen and Hilton Als, *Without Sanctuary — Lynching Photography in America* (Santa Fe: Twin Palm Publishers, 2000), 12.

33 *Gladiators and Caesars; the power of spectacle in ancient Rome*, ed. Eckart Köhne and Cornelia Ewiglelsen (London: British Museum Press, 2000), 11–12 in particular, but the entire catalogue lays out the phenomenon.

34 Bergson, *An Introduction*, 21, 23, 51.

Hegel, *Phenomenology*, 479, 493. Translated by A.V. Miller. Originally published 1807.

Christopher Humphreys, *Buddhism* (Harmondsworth: Penguin Books, 1951), 157.

Joseph Conrad and Madox Ford, *The Nature of a Crime* (New York: Doubleday, Page and Co., 1924), 58

35 Canetti, *The Tongue*, 31–2.

36 Northrop Frye, *The Great Code; The Bible and Literature* (New York: Harcourt Brace Jovanovich, 1982), 61.

37 Werner Aspinstrom, from *Five Swedish Poets* (Norvik: Norvik Press, 1997), 184. The poem is — "If She from Poland Were Here Just Now."
Souren Melikian, "The Enigma of the Old Master Drawings,"
International Herald Tribune, 9–10 December 2000, page 9.
Daniel-Henry Kahnweiler, *Entretiens avec Picasso au sujet des 'Femmes d'Alger'* (Paris: L'Echoppe, 1991). Pamphlet.

38 Thomas Mann, *Essays of Three Decades* (New York: Alfred Knopf, 1968), 98. Translated by H.T. Lowe-Porter.

Chapter 6 — Memory

1 Alasdair MacIntyre, *After Virtue* (Notre Dame, Indiana: University of Notre

Dame Press, 1984), 2.

Aristotle, "Plot: Basic Concepts," *Poetics* (London: Penguin, 1996), 13.

Donald Verene, *Vico's Science of the Imagination* (Ithaca: Cornell University Press, 1981), 98.

Plato, "Theaetetus," *Complete Works*, 212, 191C.

Aristotle, "On Memory," *The Complete Works* (Princeton: Princeton University Press, 1984), 715.

2 Erasmus, *Letter to Martin Dorp* (Harmondsworth: Penguin Books, 1971), 208. Translated by Betty Radice.

3 Keane, *Tom Paine*, 511.

4 Vico, *The New Science*, 67. Book I: Establishment of Principles, xxii–161.

5 *Gilgamesh*, 98.

See Jean-Paul Kauffman, *The Dark Room at Longwood* (London: The Harvill Press, 1999), 133. Translated by Patricia Clancy. French original: *Le chambre noire de Longwood*, 1997. Kauffman puts it "... that the skin covering the past can sometimes tear, that the dead can sometimes be called back to life."

Alessandro Manzoni, *The Betrothed* (London: Penguin Classics, 1972), 19. Translated by Bruce Penman. Original, *I Promessi Sposi*, published 1827.

6 Saint Augustine, "The Confessions," *Basic Writings* (New York: Random House, 1948), vol. I, 153. Book X, chapter VIII.

7 For an interesting argument on this subject, see Pete A. Y. Gunter, "Bergson and Jung," *Journal of the History of Ideas*. Oct-Dec 1982, vol. XLIII, No.4.

Saint Augustine, 157. Book X, chapter X.

8 Paz, *The Labyrinth*, 333.

Kerstin Ekman, "Memories and Dreams," *Swedish Book Review*, 1995, 22. Translated by Sarah Death.

9 For a remarkable anaysis of this phenomenon, see Patrick H. Hutton, "The Role of Memory in the Historiography of the French Revolution," *History and Theory* (Middletown, Conn.: Wesleyan University, 1991), 56–69.

10 Toyofumi Ogura, *Letters from the End of the World: A Firsthand Account of the Bombing of Hiroshima* (Tokyo: Kodansha International, 1997) 163–4.

11 Owen Lee, *Wagner*, 49.

12 Malouf, *A Spirit*, 51.

13 David Cannadine, *G.M. Trevelyan, A Life in History* (London: Penguin, 1992), 7.

14 Russell, *The Analysis*, 159.

Norman Malcolm, Knowledge and Certainty (Englewood Cliffs, N.J: Prentice-Hall, 1963), 201.

Reid, "Of Memory," Essay III, *Essays on the Intellectual*, 304, 307.

15 See a remarkable analysis of Descartes and memory in Timothy J. Reis,

"Denying the Body? Memory and the Dilemmas of History in Descartes," *Journal of the History of Ideas* (Baltimore: Johns Hopkins University Press, 1996), October, 587–607.

16 Quote from Gottfried Wilhelm Leibniz, *Discourse on Metaphysics (1686)* (Manchester: 1788), 34. Translated by R.N.D. Martin and Stuart Brown.

17 Krog, *Country*, 32.
Jung, *Memories*, 205.

18 Isaiah Berlin, *The Crooked Timber of Humanity* (London: Fontana, 1991), 63.

19 MacIntyre, *After Virtue*, 2.
Jacques Ellul, *The Technological Society* (New York: Knopf, 1964), 74. Originally published 1954.

20 T.S. Eliot, "Burnt Nation," *Four Quartets* (London: Faber, 1959), 13.

21 First quote from Harold Innis; second quote from Dr. James Carey, summarizing Harold Innis's argument; both quoted in *The Innis Research Bulletin*. No.3, December 1995.

22 J.M. Le Clézio. From a talk given at Harbourfront, Toronto, 1993.
Saul Bellow. Quoted by Bryan Appleyard, *Sunday Times of London Magazine*, March 1995.

23 Report in the *New England Journal of Medicine*, from *The National Post*, 28 December 2000, A1.

24 Thomas Bernhard, *Wittgenstein's Nephew, a Friendship* (Chicago: University of Chicago Press, 1990), 99. Originally published 1982.
Reck-Malleczewen, *Diary*, 34.

25 Natsume, *I Am a Cat (II)*
Russell, *The Analysis*, 161, 163, 165.

26 Frye, *Great Code*, 43.

27 The definitive history, description and analysis of Auschwitz is Robert Jan van Pett and Debórah Dwork, *Reclaiming Auschwitz* (New York: W.W. Norton and Co., 1996), 225, 362 and all of the Epilogue.
Caryl Phillips, "The High Anxiety of Belonging," *BRICK*, issue 67, Spring 2001.
Tutu, *No Future*, 54.
As explained by The Honourable Madame Justice Louise Arbour in a speech in Toronto, 15 November 1999.

28 Paul Ricoeur, "La conférence Marc-Bloch", *Les Annales*, No.4, juillet-août, 2000. See also Paul Ricoeur, *La Mémoire, l'histoire, l'oubli* (Paris: Le Seuil, 2000). "Je veux dire combien il importe de ne pas tomber dans le piège du devoir de mémoire." "[O]n ne met pas au futur une entreprise de remémoration…" "[L]e devoir du mémoire est aujourd'hui volontiers convoqué dans le dessein de court-circuiter le travail critique de l'histoire."

29 See, for example, Ernest Renan, "Qu'est-ce qu'une Nation?", conférence fait en Sorbonne, le 11 mars, 1882.

30 Le Clézio, *Le rêve mexicain*, 4. "C'est l'extermination d'un rêve ancien par la fureur d'un rêve moderne, la destruction des mythes par un désir de puissance. L'or, les armes modernes et la pensée rationnelle contre la magie et les dieux."

31 Reid, *Essays*, 303

32 Homer, *The Odyssey* (New York: Penguin, 1996), 194. Book VIII, lines 100–3. Translated by Robert Fagles.
   Steiner, *Errata*, 17.
   See Patrick Hutton, "The Art of Memory Reconceived: From Rhetoric to Psychoanalysis," *Journal of the History of Ideas*, July-September 1983, vol. XLVIII, No.3. For an interesting discussion of oral myth as purpose.

33 John Locke, "Of Retention," ed. Peter H. Nidditch *An Essay Concerning Human Understanding* (Oxford: Clarendon Press, 1975), 149. chapter IX.
   Tutu, *No Future*, 31.
   Verene, "Memory," *Vico's Science*, 102.

34 Tutu, *No Future*, 28.

Chapter 7 — Reason

1 Fyodor Dostoevski, "Underground," *Notes from Underground: Part I* (New York: Vintage Classics, 1993), 28. Translated by Richard Pevear and Larissa Volokhonsky.

2 Blaise Pascal, "The Apology and Translations," *Pensées* ed. and translated by H.F. Stewart (New York: Pantheon Books, 1950), 356–57, 661. "Deux excès: exclure la raison, n'admettre que la raison."
   From Wilhelm Müller's poem cycle, set to music by Franz Schubert (1827). Die Winterreise, "*Mut*" or "Courage".

3 Quoted in Robert Bringhurst, *A Story as Sharp as a Knife* (Vancouver: Douglas and McIntyre, 1999), 225. The poet is Skaay.

4 Aristotle, *Nicomachean Ethics* (New York: Macmillan, 1986), 30–1102a. Translation and notes by Martin Ostwald.
   Aristotle, *Poetics* (London: Penguin, 1996), 11, 45. Translated by Malcolm Heath.
   Aristotle, *The Politics* (Chicago: Chicago University Press, 1984), 27.
   Re: Aquinas see: Erwin Panofsky, *Gothic Architecture and Scholasticism* (New York: Meridian Books, 1957), 28.

5 Sri Rahula, *What the Buddha Taught*, 39.

6 See Fritz Stern, *Einstein's German World* (Princeton: Princeton University Press, 1999), 6. And Theodor Heuss, *Robert Bosch* (Stuttgart and Tübingen, 1948).

7 *Guardian Weekly*, 26 April 2001, page 23.

8 Samuel Beckett, *Waiting for Godot* (New York: Grove Press, 1954). First staged 1952, in French.

9 Camus, *Actuelles — Ecrits politiques*, 95, 98.

"...l'exercise raisonné de cette haine. Des hommes comme vous et moi, qui le matin caressaient des enfants dans le métro, se transformaient le soir en bourreaux méticuleux. Ils devenaient les fonctionnaires de la haine et de la torture."

"Et il n'y a pas de liberté sans intelligence et sans compréhension réciproques."

10 Michael Oakeshott, *Rationalism in Politics and Other Essays* (London: Methuen, 1962), 6.

And in another edition, "The New Bentham," *Rationalism in Politics and Other Essays* (Indianapolis: Liberty Fund, 1991), 138–9.

11 Sophocles, "Oedipus the King," *The Theban Plays* (London: Methuen, 1986), 54.

12 Beckett, *Godot*, 29. Again from Lucky's speech on 'thought'.

Plato, "Phaedo". Phaedo is from Plato's middle period, when he was beginning to deform the ideas of Socrates. See also Gregory Vlastos, *Socrates: Ironist and Moral Philosopher* (Cambridge: Cambridge University Press, 1991), 68.

Euripides, *The Bacchae*, 204.

Cervantes, *Don Quixote*, Part II, Chapter XLII.

13 David Malouf, *12 Edmondstone Street* (Ringwood, Victoria: Penguin, 1985), 8, 132.

14 René Descartes, *Discourse*, vol. VI, 57.

15 Oakeshott, *Rationalism*, 18, 16.

Grass, "To be continued...".

Jung, *The Basic*, 208.

Paz, *The Labyrinth* , 283.

16 Pascal, *Pensées*, 30. "La dernière démarche de la raison est de reconnaître qu'il y a une infinité de choses qui la surpassent."

Hegel, *Philosophy of Right* (London: Oxford University Press, 1967), 11. Translated by T.M. Knox.

Hegel, *Reason Is History* (New York: Library of Liberal Arts, 1953), 11. Translated by Robert S. Hartman.

17 This evolution is neatly put in the Introduction of Jonathan Barnes, *Early Greek Philosophy* (London: Penguin Books, 1987)

Morgan, *Fascism*, 79–81.

18 August Strindberg, *Thunder in the Air* (Bath: Absolute Classics, 1989), 50. Scene 3.

M.G. Smith, *Corporations and Society* (London: Duckworth, 1974), 117.

Duckworth, *Talking Music*, 326.

Joseph Stiglitz, "The Insider," *The New Republic*, 17 April 2000.

19 Frye, *Great Code*, 48.
Bronowski, *Science*, 12.

20 See Edwin Black, *IBM and the Holocaust, the Strategic Alliance Between Nazi Germany and America's Most Powerful Corporation* (New York: Crown, 2001).

21 Blaise Pascal, *Pensées* (Paris: Editions du Seuil, 1962), 264. "Quand la malignité a la raison de son côté elle devient fière et étale la raison en tout son lustre." Bronowski, *Science*, 60, 32.

22 Owen Lee, *Wagner*, 23–4.

23 Ayrton, *Doric Temple*, ix.

24 George Grant, *Philosophy in the Mass Age* (Toronto: University of Toronto Press, 1995), 10, 11.
Peter Dews, "Morality, Ethics and Post-Metaphysical Thinking. New Books by Jürgen Habermas." *International Journal of Philosophical Studies*, vol. 3, No.1, March 1995.

25 Taylor, *The Ethics*, 4–11. The following three paragraphs lean heavily on Charles Taylor's work.

26 *International Herald Tribune*, 11 September 1997, page 7.

27 *Le Journal du Dimanche*, 26 November 2000, page 9. "Ce qui vient de se passer, même si c'est terrible à dire, c'est la faillite de l'expertise et le triomphe du politique. Car au fond, les documents préparatoires sont si complexes qu'il est nécessaire d'aller au-delà. Depuis trois ans, les experts se battent, sans résultat, autour de virgules et de parenthèses. Nous n'avons donc plus le droit, aussi performants soient-ils de nous abriter derrière leurs prudences. C'est aux politiques de prendre des décisions."

28 Plato, *The Republic* (Indianapolis: Hackett, 1992), 115. Book IV. Translated by G.M.A. Grudes and C.A.C. Reeve.

29 Rousseau, *Contract*, 140. Opening of Chapter 15.
Tony Blair quoted in a profile by John Cassidy in *The New Yorker*, 6 December 1999. "If the New Labour leader has one 'big idea', it is that the key to future prosperity is 'human capital', the skills and learning embodied in people."

30 Benito Mussolini, *The Corporate State* (Firenze: Vallecchi Editore, 1936), 46. "Before the Assembly of the Councils of Corporation," 10 November 1934.

31 Sénèque (Seneca), *Consolations* (Paris: Rivages poche, 1992). Traduit du latin par Colette Lazam. Original between AD 37–45.
Ernest Hemingway, *Winner Takes Nothing* (New York: Charles Scribner and Sons, 1933), 98, 100.
Miller, *Plain Speaking*, 153.

32 Friedrich Nietzsche, "Twilight of the Idols," *The Portable Nietzsche* (New York: Penguin, 1976), 478.

33 Natsume, *I Am a Cat* (II), 141.

Chapter 8 — Normal Behaviour

1 W.H. Auden, "Musée des Beaux Arts," *The Collected Poetry* (New York: Random House, 1945), 3. "About suffering they were never wrong, the Old Masters: how well they understood its human position; how it takes place while someone else is eating or opening a window or just walking dully along;..."

2 Thomas Homer-Dixon's comments the day after the attacks were the most relevant and least reactive I came across. *The Globe and Mail*, 12 September 2001, A17.

3 Vico, *The New Science*, Book II: VI , 62.

4 Edgar Rice Burroughs, *Tarzan of the Apes* (New York: Penguin Classics, 1990), 166. Originally published 1914.
   Wagner, "Tristan und Isolde," 1858. Wagner wrote the libretto.

5 Emir Abd El-Kader, *Écrits Spirituel* (Paris: Éditions du Seuil, 1982), 50. Chapter 3: "Du pur amour." "Prétends-tu M'aimer. Si tel est le cas, sache que ton amour pour Moi est seulement une conséquence de Mon amour pour toi."
   The New Testament, John 4, 7–12.
   Beckett, *Godot*, 39. "Nous sommes contents. Qu'est-ce qu'on fait, maintenant qu'on est content?"
   En attendant Godot (Paris: Les Éditions de Minuit, 1952), 84.
   Bolton King, *The Life of Mazzini* (London: Dent and Sons, 1902), 253.

6 Vico, *Vie de Giambattista Vico*, 279. "Dans toute ma vie, en effet, je n'ai vraiment craint qu'une chose, être le seul à savoir, situation qui m'a toujours paru la plus périlleuse, puis qu'elle expose à être soit un dieu, soit un insensé."

7 Northrop Frye, 17 October 1970. "Address to the Social Sciences and Humanities Research Council of Canada," in Toronto.
   Paz, *The Labyrinth* , 216.

8 Donald Kagan, *Pericles of Athens and the Birth of Democracy* (London: Secker and Warburg, 1990), 284–5, 10, 153.

9 Learned Hand, *Bill of Rights*, vi.

10 Conrad, *Chance*, 160.

11 There are endless statistics. This is one example. *National Post*, 25 January 2000, A15.

U.S.A. 1988–98:	Poorest fifth	— 1% increase in income
	Middle "	— 2% increase
	Wealthiest "	— 15% increase

The statistics in most industrialized democracies are comparable to these.

ACKNOWLEDGEMENTS

I owe particular thanks to Penguin Canada and Penguin Australia for their patience and understanding; and especially to Cynthia Good for her help and friendship.

Andrew Cunningham's wonderful lateral research methods were very important to thinking through this book. My thanks to Donya Peroff for making the manuscript possible in exhausting conditions. And to Mary Adachi for her exacting calm and clarity.

With thanks to the many people in Pond Inlet who welcomed me, in particular Mayor Paul Haulli, as well as Norman Simonie and Simon Kautak for an indefinable moment out on the land. With thanks also for their help to Brigitte Emond, Reg Russell, Bob Neibert, Denis Thibault and Isabel Rodrigues Alonso in San José, Bob Jickling in Whitehorse, Hjalmar Hannesson and the boys on the Bay.

To Adrienne, as always, and to Philip Coulter, for their comments, suggestions and ideas.

INDEX